Castle &
THE STORY

[From Page 142]

The guardian of the Royal virtue was none other than her tutor and companion, one Constance, a comely beauty herself, only four years senior, who possessed the unabashed charm, clarity and acumen of natural thought to keep her young and exceptionally beautiful charge one step ahead of the hordes of excited male libidos in hot pursuit.

And it wasn't easy. How to prepare for marriage and divulge to one so curious the infinite pleasures that can be wrought between two consenting bodies, and at the same time warn away the very same indulgence that could lead to so much disaster.

And not that there wasn't an abundance of guilt eating away at the double standard she imposed. Constance saw in Isabella's eyes her own hypocrisy.

On more than a few mornings, had Isabella not burst into her bedroom only to surprise her either asleep in the arms of, or grappling in the moment of ecstasy with one or other of the eligible, and from time to time, not-so-eligible, young men at Court? Some of the same who also, unabashedly, demonstrated their smoldering lust for Isabella.

Getting her married was coming not a moment too soon. She was the number one prize in the world, and yearning to be won. Every eligible titled Heir and feudal Lord of any consequence sought her hand. Never mind that she was betrothed. Never mind that marriage was imminent, and never mind that it was to the King of England; some believed that the race wasn't over until it was over and even there could still be a chance. There was no question of what it would do for one's station in life, not to mention the accolades at home. But just to bed this exquisite beauty would be worth all the risks on earth.

THE TRUE STORY OF ISABELLA

There comes a tale that defies imagination, that no writer/creator of fiction could estimably create without entering the realm of fantasy and yet this tale of intrigue, treachery, infidelity and murder, is all true. I am going to take you into the dark past of the medieval age into the dangerous life of the little known, beautiful French Princess who saved the British Empire from extinction.

The world today would be a very different place if it weren't for her.

After the death of the Scottish freedom fighter William Wallace (Braveheart), things got even more dangerous on the tiny island. And at the center of it all was the beautiful Princess Isabella of France, the unwanted wife of the evil English King Edward II.

For ten years the Empire had reeled under the blows of its enemies until it faced collapse. The damage caused by Wallace and later, Robert The Bruce, was devastating. And it didn't help that her King Edward was a weakling, indifferent to the plight of his country, indolent, narcissistic and obsessive about a fantasy Court where reality played no part. In the short time he had been on the throne, the nation was reduced to a land of beggars cowering within its borders, its armies corrupt and bankrupt, while he delighted in confiscating valuable lands and titles and doling them out to whomever pleased him most.

Then in the year 1308 Isabella arrived and the unexpected happened. The country went crazy for her. This made Edward very unhappy, so unhappy that he wanted her dead.

CASTLE RISING

Is located in Norfolk, England; a small castle, high atop a lonely, desolate, wind swept promontory jutting well out into the North Sea. It is the cold, damp, eerie place where Isabella, the Queen Mother was forced to spend the remaining thirty years of her life, exiled by her son Edward III on the inconclusive charge that she was responsible for the murder of her evil husband, Edward II.

It became the inspiration for the title because of two things. It was her thankless reward for having saved the Empire; and, some believe, in her respite, it was from here, unobserved, that she engineered the events that triggered the one hundred years war for the domination of Europe. A war that laid the groundwork for the rest of history.

Library of Congress Cataloguing-in-Publication Data
July 18, 2003 – TXu 1 – 119 – 544
United States Copyright Office Official Seal

ISBN 0-615-12448-8
Stone, Albert,
Book design, photo and Cover owned
by Albert Stone Enterprises, Inc.
Designed by David Sloan, Sloan Creative,
Celebration, Florida
& Albert Stone
www.castlerising.us

ISABELLA

In favor of presenting my readers with an image of the exquisite Isabella, I cannot resist the likeness of Sophie Marceau, the delightful actress who portrayed Isabella in the movie Braveheart.

Casting her in the role was a poignant depiction. Isabella (like Princess Diana in many ways) was an outstanding beauty who won the hearts and minds of a nation, an age, and a world.

"**Who was she, this beautiful Queen of ours?**" Asked the BBC interviewer, who surprised me by admitting his ignorance. "There is not a whole lot known about her." The question attracted one Royal to join our conversation.

"Her enemies called her The Harlot Queen", I replied, "and The She-Wolf of France, and The Frenchman's Daughter, but those who loved her, believed her to be saint."

"You write about those years with the Bruce, her illegitimate children, and the strange and violent deaths of so many of Edward's friends? Not to mention when she herself, in front of thousands of troops, suddenly sliced off the head of the King's number two man, Lord DesPenser. How did she not meet the same end?"

To which the Royal who had joined us responded with "a phenomenon to be sure, perhaps it was because she did it all with such style!"

And that word 'style' framed my answer. "She was a thrill to write about. From the moment I discovered her, I needed to know everything about her; and the more I discovered, the more she was willing to tell me."

DEDICATION

To Abby
without whose determination it was
to keep me at my desk,
this book may have never
been written.

CONTENTS

Histories

CASTLE RISING

THE STORY OF ISABELLA

ALBERT STONE

ABOUT CASTLE RISING

In 1998 a film entitled Braveheart broke box office records around the globe with a story that captured the hearts and minds of people of all ages.

It was a great story, told in magnificent style about a Scottish highlander and warrior who won freedom not only for a nation but for a people. A people who to this day revere his memory, and in that memory still cry freedom.

And yet I believe that the movie told only half the story. And I think that it's fans would agree. In its wake it left audiences wanting more; there are millions still, who loved or hated the characters, eager to know "what happened next?"

At the close of the film we are left to believe that the

Queen Of England is pregnant with William Wallace's child; that The King Of England has gone mad; and that the British Empire is about to go up in flames.

So luring was the story, and so alluring was she, that I dutifully followed the credits, and I hope so will you, into the pages of this book as I continue on with the tale. It picks up where all of this real-life adventure left off, and I assure you that things were just as exciting.

Castle Rising, like Braveheart, is history told in glorious style, in the story of its most dynamic person of the time.

Mel Gibson introduced us to William Wallace and his life and death struggle to gain independence for Scotland.

The rest of the story is about Queen Isabella and her life and death struggle to save the British Empire.

How the tables turned after Wallace was executed.

PREFACE

The characters tell their own stories.

When putting together the material for a book like Castle Rising one is dependent upon information that isn't entirely reliable. Not that reported information necessarily makes up the true story (take a look at some media), only the people involved can do that.

So I looked to my characters first. Not to over simplify my process, but it boiled down to a primary question asked of each, "who" are you? And by that I don't mean name, rank and serial number; I mean the whole being of the person. And when I focused on them they were more than willing to reveal their personalities. People love attention, past or present, and that's when they came to life. They led me through the story they wanted to tell.

Unto itself the medieval period tends to dish up conflicting bits and pieces and generally, depending upon whose point of view one relies, stories differ as to what characters did, where they did it and even if they did it.

I believe my characters to have been thorough, but I also recognize that they were at the forefront of things, glamorous, egotistical and eager to be in print. I was on my own when it came to some of the material handed me for background research which often turned out to be limited, divergent and inconsistent.

You see, most medieval history got here by word of mouth, and events were not necessarily written down for many years after they happened, and rarely by eyewitnesses. Very few people back then could read or write, even the wealthy, and so any of what was written was usually second or third hand information, and largely influenced by interpretation and exaggeration.

So individual's histories even varied. Their stories were told differently from one community to the next, and from one generation to the next.

Castle Rising is our interpretation, that of mine and my characters, of the events that took place in British history, or should I say their history, through their years 1297 to 1327.

At the center of it all stood an alluring little girl, a Princess from France, who, at the age of 14, became the Queen of England. Her name was Isabella. From there, her story sizzles. Using her information, I put together what I believe to be the best pieces of her life.

The same is true with all of my characters.

I am sure many, especially those that can't accept or deal with the fact that life is actually played out on a day to day, one on one basis, by the big and the small alike, will disagree with my treatment. And yet I believe that I came to know her (and those around her) and am closer to the truth than anybody.

CASTLE RISING

THE WARRIOR POET

Chapter 1
1295 AD

1

"Wil...Wil, wake up ya bastard — get your sorry arse out here — now!"

The sharp command was barely audible over the noise of the storm, but the voice behind it was unmistakable. It stopped the charging William Wallace cold in his tracks.

He was already awake and waiting – to kill.

Even in the pitch black and driving rain he knew his own ground well so that just by the sound of an intruder's steps he could place the spot precisely. Those steps would be their last.

Billy, his horse, had given him the advantage.

Hamish knew that riding in. There was no need for quiet on his part, it wouldn't work anyway; there was no amount of quiet that Billy couldn't hear.

Hamish would say to William, "there are only two things in life a man needs, a good woman and a great horse. We know what ya got ta interest Marin, only Lord knows what else she sees in ya; but that horse is too fuckin' good fer ya on yer best day."

Everybody called him Billy, ever since he was a foal. He had been a pretty little fellow, Andalusian, jet black, long mane and tail; who, as William boasted, "had grown into a right handsome young lad," and who along with Marin, he loved more than anything else, "on this or t'other side of heaven."

Billy attracted attention everywhere they went, and always immediately. He was even especially clever at tricks that William had taught him and which he seemed to relish practicing at every opportunity, especially when his master was up to no good and he could play a role. Some of his best performances were his diversion tactics, like the one he and Wil had perfected so well and which never failed to thrill the locals – his famous sudden dead horse masterpiece. That always caused pandemonium, especially at times when Wil and his friends didn't want or need any attention, of any kind, coming their way, particularly from the constabulary.

The trick went this way. William would send Billy trotting, riderless, into the very center of some village square where more than likely most of the redcoats hung out as the best place to feast hungry eyes on the comings and goings of the local female population. Billy, without further queing, would literally stagger into the square, let out a long, loud snort and drop straight down, like a stone, ostensibly dead.

Women and children would scream in horror at the sight of the poor animal in a heap of unmoving flesh, saddle and stirrups akimbo; the men and the soldiers would come running, as if they knew what had to be done. And in the time it took some official to come forward and propose a plan to remove the carcass, Wil would have done what he needed to do, and Billy somehow sensing it, would suddenly raise his magnificent head, snigger contemptuously at everyone gathered around, virtually pop to his feet, and trot merrily off in the direction whence he came.

Those who knew Wil, and knew him well, were more than aware of the clever guise; but it never ceased to amuse or distract, and young and old alike gleefully joined in the act.

On the other hand, those people seeing the splendid young equine specimen for the first time, could not resist a comment and a compliment, and there was nothing William liked more.

Hamish would warn any newcomers to their circle, especially when drinking together, "do yerself and all of us a favor, don't be drawin' any attention to Billy, unless you want to spend the next few hours hearin' the minute by minute account of the bugger's life from the day William found him."

Billy would have died if William hadn't found him.

He had come across the tiny foal about eight years earlier, badly cut up, the victim of a wildcat, high in the hills above his father's property. He wasn't more than ten years old himself when he discovered the injured little fellow laying in deep grass a few yards from his dead mother and a dying mountain lion.

It had obviously been one hell of a fight. There was blood everywhere.

William had been hunting, was on foot and had just come over a rise in a small meadow about to head down into a wooded copse that led to a ravine, which would take him along the complicated trail back to his valley when he saw the prone body of the mare. She lay only a few dozen yards ahead of him and the clearly bloodstained grass all about her made it obvious that something terrible had happened.

He broke into a run, the sound of which also startled the dying lion, which he hadn't seen. Its chilling scream coming from so close, scared him beyond any fear he had ever felt, so much so that his legs stopped working and he went tumbling part way down the hill.

He stopped rolling and lay frozen, not daring to move. Where was it? It was so close; it would have had him by now.

Slowly he raised his head and peered above the grass, looking wildly in every direction; but all he could see was the body of the mare.

Then the baby squealed and that brought him to his senses. It was all the courage he needed. Lion or no friggin' lion he had a good sharp knife and his bow and arrows. He was on his feet.

Cocking the bow, he made his way more cautiously towards the scene. There was the lion, but it too was laid out on its side. For a moment he watched its futile struggle to raise itself, but it could not. It was dying, its side kicked in and split open.

As for the mare, she had bled to death, her neck ripped from her jaw to her shoulder.

The relief he felt at seeing the big helpless cat didn't overshadow his sadness at what had to be done. Highlanders, young and old, saw the life and death struggle for animals almost every day of their lives; it didn't make it any less painful to have to help one across.

William drew back the sharp arrow, stood inches from the big cat's neck, and fired. It was a good and true shot, the poor thing was out of its misery.

That's when he spotted Billy.

Some nasty cuts, some bleeding, would need attention, but more frightened than anything else. So the young William Wallace half carried and otherwise held safe this very young, very wobbly little creature for all the miles all the way back to his home.

"You save him, you can have him," said his father. William had never loved anything more than he loved that horse. "And that's why we called him Billy," Hamish would say. "They're never wi'out each other, Willy and Billy, get it!"

~

Long before William had heard anything but the rain, the animal had sensed that someone was approaching from a ways off. He knew never to doubt the warning signs. His friends often joked that 'William could sleep like a baby because Billy could hear a British soldier breathing all the way across Scotland.'

Six inches of fieldstone wall separated them, but the first gentle snort might as well have been a scream in his ear.

Warm and dry, with a full stomach, the beast was all too glad to be settled in his own soft straw; his stall attached to his master's croft, grateful for sleep after a long and somewhat uncomfortable night of waiting for his master with only an eave for protection from the rain, followed by an even longer wet ride home. And even though William was not on his list of things to like right now, nothing was going to come by that wasn't invited.

By what intelligence man can never measure, Billy knew the split second he was not alone in his valley. And in the next second he knew to share that knowledge.

William was on his feet with the first snort.

It didn't take long before he too detected the low rumble. Galloping horses, no question - still a long way off, but getting closer.

Normally intuition served him well, never mind the din and confusion of the wild outbursts of thunder and lightening, never mind the dead of night, he could usually tell friend or foe. But this night was different. As the sound of the rapidly approaching riders grew louder it penetrated the storm in a way that he felt threatened. It meant that there were many, and they seemed to be coming from all sides.

This did not frighten him; nothing ever frightened him; it was simply the Wallace mechanism that prepared him for what he must do. And never would he be taken without killing as many as possible. The time had come, as he knew it one day would, that he was no longer safe anywhere, not even in this valley, and he could not afford to gamble that his visitors were friendly.

~

Wallace had restored the little three-room fieldstone croft several months earlier on this bit of land once secretly owned by his long dead father. Since then it had been his secret - up to now.

At one time in the service of the Crown, his father had been a Knight of the Earldom of Carrick, for the most powerful Lord in all of Scotland, and a man steadfastly loyal to the King of England. For this service, William's father was often rewarded with bits of choice land. Never with tenants because that would mean his Lordship would be parting with income as well, but then he didn't care because the lands were often fertile or provided abundant grazing, affording his family a comfortable living.

And he served his Lordship faithfully. That was until he was ordered to betray his own clansmen.

As many as there were Scots who favored the alliance with England, there were more and more joining ranks all the time that opposed it. Those who were once considered nothing more than annoying troublemakers, were becoming numerous enough and forming armies that could be dangerous to England.

The then newly crowned King of England, Edward the First, was of a mind that his father Henry had been too lenient and too generous with Scotland and that the real strength of a leader of the Empire would come to better stead by putting an end to the illiterate savages that opposed his authority, on or off his beloved island.

Edward put forth a challenge to all of his Scottish nobility and their clansmen - if they weren't part of the solution, they were part of the problem. All were called upon to pay homage and allegiance, and those who refused were deemed traitors to be routed out and destroyed.

That kind of ultimatum just made matters worse. Henry had often tried to warn his headstrong, warrior son, "the Scots are not like the English, they don't worship their nobility." But Edward didn't care. He believed 'so goes the power, goes the country.' Scotland was the knife at his throat throughout all of his reign.

Although, as Edward demanded, many of the Scottish nobles were willing to comply, it didn't mean that the men who served in their armies, knighted or not, would go along with it – and most would not.

He had hugely underestimated these people and had created no small problem for himself. Were it just a handful of upstarts, he could have ignored them, but it affected most of the population.

Thanks to Edward's ill-fated notion of occupancy - Scotland was now officially England's closest enemy.

And William's father was one of them. And for that, and for his high profile amongst the commoners, along with so many others, he was labeled a traitor and stripped of his lands and title. And for having been a Knight of high caliber, a death warrant was issued by no less than Edward himself.

Most warrants went unheeded, for very few Scots, even the Nobles, had any stomach for killing their own.

But the edict did drive the rebels underground. It didn't take Edward long to realize that his strategy of divide and conquer had turned a tenuous ally, into a strong enemy and if not checked could become a most powerful enemy, without an ocean to protect him.

Reversing the process was out of the question. Seldom daunted, the generally impressive King could be driven by the darker side of his prodigious legacy, especially when thwarted. He called it, "turning adversity into opportunity," when in fact it amounted to beating the crap out of anyone who pissed you off.

Proud of his ancestry of legendary crusaders and conquerors, and eager to keep company in their fold, he readily turned up the heat. Even as the Scottish nobles were tripping over themselves desperately seeking ways of pleasing him, he unceremoniously informed them that he was going to ravage Scotland and "clean up" every last stinking rat hole from Dumfries to John O'Groats, and if that meant that they all had to die, then so be it.

If that couldn't shake up the long suckling nobility then nothing could. And perhaps they all did deserve to die. They certainly afforded Scotland no leadership.

At any rate it had the right effect. Many went begging for mercy, like children promising to do better. And in fairness to most, it was they who believed it would be unconscionable that Edward would make war on them. The majority were second-generation half-breeds, of English mothers with offspring of their own that lived in London, in the bosom of their English families, and were schooled in London and Exeter.

They thought of themselves not as Scots but as Brits and only knew loyalty to Edward.

Edward listened to all of their pleadings like he might listen to a troupe of vaudevillians. "Then keep out of my way," he replied, "and make sure there is plenty of wholesome food and fresh horses for my men."

~

That left the clans to defend themselves.

And they mounted an impressive defense. So much so that Edward's plan to run roughshod over the country was foiled and he found himself contained at Edinburgh and facing a pitched battle. One way was a good as another. It was still his edge, for there was nothing that the British army was more adept at, and there were none other that met their match.

William's father along with most of the outlawed clansmen rallied to Scotland's defense. It cost him his life, along with tens of thousands of others at what the Scots came to call the massacre at Edinburgh.

For now England owned Scotland. Edward's closing comment to his English Lords after the battle, "I should have done this in the first place."

II

At the time, William was just a small boy and although the death of his father had an effect on him, like any youngster he didn't fully understand its implications. Not until he became a young man and came to understand what the great loss had meant for his country.

Now here, in this violent storm, under attack, he was about to defend with his life the one piece of his father that England had forgotten to take. And it had been an ideal oversight. Close enough to Dumfries, and for him about 20 miles from the passionate arms of his beloved Marin; yet far enough from the prying eyes of the British constabulary.

It was the perfect spot at the end of a remote river valley nestled in the Ochills Mountains. Provident and yet notably difficult to find because of a winding maze of steep ravines, all which seemed to go nowhere and which had to be carefully negotiated to even access the valley.

The valley itself was perhaps a mile wide and three long. A gently rolling, quilted meadow, patched by lush shades of green and purple, and streaked by all the colors of highland wild flowers. Windbreaks, naturally formed hedgerows and copses of mountain ash and silver birch trees guarded its upland slopes before giving way to steep rocky cliffs on all sides.

Marin and he had spent many a soft day and night, locked in each other's embrace, safe from the world in this little valley. Even the rugged croft had become a thing of intimate beauty. Warm, dry, sweet smelling; comforted by her hand and a far cry from anything he could have done. Now it was all about to disappear. The secret was obviously no longer a secret.

He could imagine that the pig of a Sheriff was more than a sick enough bastard to believe that this would be the perfect night to put an end to him.

Wallace could ignore the odds. He possessed a certain characteristic that most people did not. People said that his old uncle Argyle had taught him this, along with the rest of his 'European' education; but Hamish said not – no one could be taught to think that way.

And although he was one against who knows how many, he still had the advantage. They could make all the noise they liked; it didn't intimidate him and certainly would not roust him out. It remained for them to find him, and as difficult as it would be on foot, it would be impossible from horseback. They were on his turf, and he knew every treacherous inch of it.

The ground approaching his croft was uneven, rocky, pitted and dangerous to a galloping horse. Especially on this sightless night, in the heavy rain it would be sodden and slippery.

And in the last few minutes the lightening had become more frequent and the light more intense. The irregular jagged effect of the eerie blue flashes would only blind and confuse men and horses. If they didn't slow their pace, and soon, this foolish charge was certain to end in a catastrophe of fallen horses and crushed soldiers. He may not have to raise a hand.

Then as if they read his mind, all at once the pounding of hooves stopped. It took him a moment to catch it, leaning into the storm straining to discern the sounds. Yes, they had definitely stopped. For the next several minutes he heard nothing through the storm but he knew the ploy. They're closing in on foot. Now they were playing his game.

He waited for it. An advance mob would creep as closely as they could and then suddenly burst out shouting and at the same time charge the cottage. The more to come at him at once, the merrier. Frenzied assailants were also frightened assailants, survival their only stake in the fight, safety of numbers their only courage.

Regardless of all the training and all the bullying from their superior Officers, the intrinsic goal of any soldier is to get the job done with as little pain to himself as possible. At best attacking an armed, unknown opponent is a thoughtless act, which only serves to bring about their own death more easily.

Consumed by fear, with no room to battle, their weapons flail. And as more and more crowd in, they get in one another's way, and more often than not their own errant blows fall deadly on one another.

Mentally and physically he was superior in battle. In hand to hand combat there was no more perfect, natural killing machine. Overwhelmingly powerful and possessing imperceptible speed and agility his sword had more than once cut down hordes of attackers without his receiving so much as a scratch. And now, here, he had only to strike like a cat on ground only he knew. The dead of night gave him control and regardless of their number they were not going to find him.

He was ready and waiting. Now, sword poised, as the first rider came at his doorway, he lunged into the pitch black wet night, intent on making the kill. His friend Hamish Campbell had spoken none too soon.

~

This night William Wallace and Hamish Campbell had been officially declared the most wanted and dangerous outlaws in all of the British Empire.

The King of England offered huge rewards for their capture, dead or alive. It would be welcome news to their enemies. To their friends and followers, it would add fuel to a fire already out of control. Their fearless exploits were the source of pride and legendary gossip that thrilled and delighted all of Scotland, and angered and frustrated British authorities. Their bloodthirsty assaults on the English establishment gave hope to a suffering nation and terrified a despicable Monarchy, and as was expected, they had incurred the wrath of the highest office in the land.

To the Scots, Edward I, King of England, was a hated despot whom they called Longshanks, as an insult to his height. He had this very day declared them murderers and ordered that the two were to be stopped at any cost.

Confident that greed would do the job, he put a huge price on their heads, certain that at least one of their own would turn them in. He was wrong. None came forward. The message was clear; William Wallace was no ordinary foe. The young Scot had become the champion to his people. He and his growing army of ragtag highlanders represented freedom to the Scottish people, and no ambitious English King and his fat purse could compensate for the cruelty of British rule.

Enraged that no one, no single man or woman sought the reward; anger clouded his judgment and Longshanks, who rarely made tactical errors, except where Scotland was concerned, made the worst mistake of his long and fruitful reign. He resorted to maniacal attempts to capture the two and devised a brutal plan that he was sure would rout them out.

"I have offered to make rich any peasant vermin who would give me Wallace. And still they shield these bastards. They spit on me! So be it. They will learn what it means to spit at their King. Let it be known that the offer is repealed. Now the ungrateful scum will co-operate because I say they will. These ignorant mutants will regret their choice."

Without warning English troops attacked a peasant village where Wallace and Campbell were known to have friends. A family was chosen at random and every member, including the infants, were hacked to death in front of the entire community, with the message that it would continue to happen until someone turned on Wallace. If it meant slaughtering every village in Scotland, then so be it.

It also wasn't to be. This time he was dealing with a different kind of Wallace.

The King's method of certain persuasion backfired with such swiftness and excess, that Longshanks for once feared for his own life. The news of the brutal slayings reached Wallace within hours. His response was swift and terrifyingly gruesome. He delivered a message to the Commander of the garrison at Dumfries telling him that the same would be revisited on the British – only tenfold. If the message itself didn't frighten, the way in which it was delivered certainly did. It had been carved into the back of a Platoon Commander who was alive as it was being read.

The Scottish people had long been passionate in their hatred of the English, and these murders of an innocent family gave them the best excuse of all. Retaliation came in the specter of a grisly and deadly game for any British soldier stupid enough to venture outside the walls of his stockade. Wallace had a penchant for effective messages.

The very next platoon sent to raid a village, was returned to a man, each with the skin pealed from his body, arms folded cradling his intestines, and strapped naked to his horse – alive.

~

So it was on a stormy, wild September night, in the year 1296, that Hamish Campbell, the youngest son of the rebel Chieftain of the vast Campbell Clan; along with outlawed cohorts, narrowly escaped a fiery death, at the hands of the Sheriff at Dumfries.

It had been that at one moment Hamish and the others were sitting in their favorite pub, drinking and waiting out the storm, and at the next they were shattering doors and windows, hurling themselves from the tiny, ale and whisky soaked, wooden structure, as it quickly became engulfed in flames. The cowardly Sheriff had somehow learned of their whereabouts, and pleased with his good fortune had gladly chosen to forego combat in favor of burning them all alive.

Under the noisy cover of the thunder and lightening, no one inside the pub heard the Sheriff's men as they went about dousing the exterior of the building with lamp oil so that it would burn in spite of the rain. It caught fire easily and the flames spread rapidly, made the more deadly by the fact that the wooden structure was so old, and the floor planks so saturated in years of spilt alcohol, that the wet of the rain had no effect. Hamish and his friends had little time or chance, and simply charged in all directions from the burning mass.

The unexpected suddenness and ferocity of the inferno also forced the soldiers to retreat from the soaring flames and intense heat, and so they were unprepared as these wild-eyed, roaring Celts, came bursting out of the conflagration in all directions. Hamish and his men ran full flight into the frightened soldiers. Sudden and unexpected fights were second nature to the highlanders, so they were able to react swiftly and were on the soldiers in an instant. The Sergeant commanding the unit never knew what hit him.

With his sword still in its scabbard, the body of the young Officer remained standing only yards from the doorway, continuing to clutch his torch even as his head with its laughing face tumbled over and over across ground to come to rest at the Sheriff's feet. It become the fate of most of his terrified soldiers as they scrambled in a vain, futile, comic attempt to escape sudden, violent death.

In minutes the slain troops, many dismembered or decapitated, lay strewn around the pyre, and a horrified Sheriff, trailed by a handful of survivors, rode off panic stricken into the crackling night, screaming for reinforcements.

His bravery only returned after he was safe behind stockade walls. Vowing to get all the rebels, he ordered out the entire garrison.

Hamish and his friends knew they would not be so lucky against those odds.

~

Through the hours past midnight they had ridden hard through the driving wind and rain. The soaked darkness was a blessing and bought them time. Any immediate pursuit by the enraged Sheriff would be stalled.

Still they had no choice but to hurry. On they blindly rode defying the swollen angry rivers and slick, pitted roadways, pushing their horses and themselves in a desperate need to get to Wallace, and still make it across the Ochills ahead of the huge army that would follow.

William Wallace, the now undisputed Warlord of all of Scotland, was unaware of any of the night's events. He had spent a blissful evening of love-making in the arms of his woman Marin and not even the storm or thoughts of the next day's journey to Doon could keep him awake. He had no idea of the plot that the Sheriff had hatched that very night to kill him, Hamish and any other Scot that got in the way.

Part of that plan had been to wait until Hamish and William were separated and first take out Hamish. The Sheriff got his opportunity sooner than he thought. With him out of the way Wallace would not be so well protected. So he had no idea that an entire battalion was in pursuit of a fleeing Hamish and about to descend upon all of them. Alone, unconcerned, at peace with the pattering of the rain, he had fallen into an easy sleep.

William heard the riders only after his horse had given warning. He reckoned that at this hour, under these conditions, with there being many, it was unlikely a friendly visit. He did not guess at it being Hamish even though few others would attempt to go there at night, and especially on a night like this. His cottage was a difficult place to get to at the best of times, the route being dangerous and complicated, even in the daylight.

The way was confined to a long and precipitous mountain trail that eventually led through a confusing network of heavily forested ravines each of which seemed to dead end against towering rock. An intruder would have to know every trick and turn along those deceptive paths.

However, once through, the trail opened to reveal the long narrow lake, abruptly guarded on one side by soaring granite walls, and softly bordered on the other by rolling meadows. All in all the gentle lake and it's low fertile plain made up the five mile valley which had been the pride of and safe haven to various members of his family for over two hundred years. Now it would be confiscated by the King of England, and declared the new property of the Sheriff, if he could capture it.

///

Wallace lit a torch from the smoldering fireplace and anchored it by the doorway. Seeing his friend's reddened and agitated face in the soft light, he couldn't resist teasing in spite of the fact that it was he who had made their wild ride a necessity. "So, Hamish, where the hell you been? What kept ya?" William had no idea of what had taken place, or why Hamish was so excited. He knew that he was supposed to have been at the pub, but that night had given in to another temptation.

Marin Broadfute, William's young mistress, had begged him to stay with her, which meant that he had stayed at her parent's cottage long after it was safe to venture into the village and the pub. So shortly after midnight he headed for home unaware of the pending attack. Blissfully satisfied from his visit with Marin, his thoughts were on the plan to travel to meet with the council of Campbell elders, which was scheduled to get underway the next day. Hamish's arrival was not unexpected, just earlier than he thought necessary.

Hamish ignored the ribbing. "Wil, yer goin' to have to go wi' us lad — now. There's nay time to tell you why, but trust me, the whole fuckin' garrison's after us as I'm speakin." Hamish paused and suddenly changed the subject. "You were supposed to be wi' us, what the hell were you doin'?"

"I'm comin', I'm comin," William hissed back. He trusted his friend absolutely. It was obvious something big was wrong. He would learn the reason later. "I'll get me things, you get me horse." William laid his sword across a large rock near the doorway and went back into the dark cottage. Emerging moments later he carried a small satchel and wore his heavy woolen over-blanket.

Hamish returned just as quickly leading William's horse and held out the reins to him. "Here lad, mount up, let's go."

William took the reins, slung the pack over the saddle and turned to pick up his sword. It was gone. "Hamish I canna' find me sword." The same sword that only moments before had almost killed his friend was nowhere to be found. "And what do ya mean the whole fuckin' garrison? What'd you do this time?" he was trying to mount his horse and spot the sword at the same time. Now with one foot in the stirrup and the other on the ground, the jittery animal began to dance quickly forward and he was forced to hop along on one leg.

"Damn! Hamish this is fuckin' impossible…!"

Hamish spurred his horse up to William, who was now bouncing comically along on one foot, being dragged through a bush, "Wil, what in Christ's name you doin' now lad. We gotta be goin — now! The others are leavin' and you're playin' games wi' yer fuckin' horse."

"Hamish," William snapped back, "you can see I'm kinda havin' a wee fuckin' problem here." He was now barely able to hang on as the horse became more and more excited at the tension in Hamish' voice.

"Yer havin' a problem," Hamish yelped. "If I had even a second more tu spare right now, you'd have a problem al'right. Now get on that fuckin' horse…"

"I can't you dumb sod, my foots caught and I'm bein' dragged tu death, and on top o' that, I canna' find me bleedin' sword. It was just here a minute ago."

Hamish was close enough to grab William's reins and jerk the horse to a stop. "Then you best be mar careful with your things, shouldn't you."

With the help William got his balance and swung onto the saddle, "fuck you."

"Same to you. Now listen, it's not your best one anyway. So stay up or I'll pick ya up. We'll get another for ya. Besides, me Da' has got your Claymore. That thing you've lost is just a pig sticker; and there's lots where that come from. Buggar, we'll just kill us another Englishman."

"Fuck Hamish, I don't like ridin' unarmed — you know that." If there was one thing William could no longer be without, it was a sword.

"It'll be full light soon, and sure as shite them fuckin' Brits are comin' here first."

"And just why is the whole fuckin' garrison comin' here?"

Hamish was off. The answer would have to wait. William gave up arguing. He got the message. The delay was putting them all in danger. Tragically Hamish had revealed that the location had become known to the constable. The daylight would only make his getting there easier. A faint glow of sunrise had tipped the horizon behind the mountains to the east giving just enough light to make their ride visible.

The house sat at one end of the valley, at the foot of a low meadow that ran down to the shore of the lake. To the east lay the rugged Tweedsmuir Mountains. At both ends the valley was guarded by narrow canyons; not easily traversed at night, but they could have counted on the darkness for some protection.

Now with the dawn, the English were coming from the south. It was to the north they had to ride and into the mystery of these ancient mountains that they would seek refuge. It would be a race to get there.

While on open ground, the group kept their horses at a gallop. Once out of the valley and in the hills, the trail narrowed and was often steep, slowing their pace to a walk. The storm had ended and there was a calm about the foothills. There was no wind, a rare occurrence, and the unusual stillness made it possible for them to hear sounds from a way off, particularly those that would mean they were being followed. Their horses especially seemed to know what was expected of them. There was none of the normal whinnying and snorting at every little sound and smell.

IV

Wallace and the others strained to hear for sounds other than the soft plod of their own animal's hooves. No one talked, nor even whispered. On they rode in silence, exposed and vulnerable out on the open hillsides, the shelter and protection of the Doon forest still miles away.

Then it was visible in the distance. A long way off, but unmistakable; the massive granite wall marking the first plateau and secret entrance to the vast and densely forested Campbell highlands which stretch over most of central Scotland.

~

William and Hamish each were just eighteen years old. Prime specimens of highland youth, lean, strong and handsome, they had earned the respect and loyalty of almost every commoner and clansman in Scotland. Unfortunately this same respect had not spread through most of the nobility, whose allegiance to the King of England had, over the years, been bought with lands and marriages.

Born and raised in Dumfries County, on the southern edge of the central highlands, a handful of miles north of the border with England; neither was of noble blood, but no one would have guessed it from their brashness and sophistication. They were of a new breed of educated Scot that didn't fear their English rulers, and were passionately intent on driving them out of Scotland — even if it meant killing them all.

Their fathers had been the last of the Scottish Knights. Hamish's father, Struan, had survived Edinburgh and because of it had turned against his Lord Carrick, and now rode with his son and William. He too had a price on his head.

Struan Campbell was a man filled up with hatred. He had watched in horror as Carrick and the other nobles had deserted the battlefield, leaving thousands of his countrymen to be surrounded and slaughtered, and then helplessly watched while those same Lords made a grand spectacle of gentlemanly defeat, bowing their backs and surrendering the last of Scotland's meager independence.

The people had been betrayed, as the nobility yielded to save their lands and titles. It had been the final straw to almost one hundred years of English cruelty and domination; of lurid promises of a peaceful co-existence, which only came in the form of brutal oppression.

Edinburgh and the brave coming together of the clansmen to take on the formidable English had actually inspired some of the more passionate nobles to rally for a shot at independence. More than a defense it was supposed to be the battle to drive the English out. It was in reality just a staging for Edward to teach the Scottish people one more lesson in English supremacy.

Since the death of William's father, Struan and the two boys had become the newest champions of freedom. To the English they were wanted outlaws.

~

The worst of it came late one soft gray May afternoon, two weeks earlier. William, Hamish, Struan, and three others were returning from hunting wild boar, along the Nith River. A light rain fell, which felt good on their shirtless bodies. Passing near the Duncan McDougal farm, they decided to make a gift of one of the pigs, and hopefully relieve Duncan of some of his fine homemade whiskey.

The acrid smell of smoldering ashes hit them before they actually reached the farm. Struan, knowing that smell of death all too well, spurred his horse into a gallop.

Duncan's life was very close to an end with a gaping wound across his head that only Struan's quick thinking and careful stitching saved.

Duncan's wife, Elizabeth, and their two daughters — the twelve year and the eight year old — had been raped and sodomized repeatedly, especially the twelve year old whose mouth looked like someone had driven a post into it; and their ten year old son — named Struan, after his Godfather — lay dead with his young neck broken.

The livestock was gone.

Elizabeth, her pretty face smashed beyond recognition, bravely fighting back hysteria, managed to tell William and the others that it had been a band of English soldiers and one who said he was a tax collector.

Leaving Robbie Karn, the youngest of their party, to take the McDougals to his family farm, William, Hamish, Struan, Peter Taylor and Dale Barnes rode off after the English.

They tracked them for several hours, along the forested road that followed the Nith River back to Dumfries, until coming from ahead of them they heard the unmistakable sound of drunken laughter and smelled wood smoke.

Tethering their horses, the five crept on foot through the thick forest and brush that bordered the trail, until they were only twenty few feet or so from the camp. They counted seven men; six in red military coats; all were sprawled about on the ground around a small fire. All were drunk and passing a jug of whiskey, evidently pleased with their day's work.

Struan had to control himself from charging the camp right then. He recognized and hated them all. Motioning for his lads to huddle close, he whispered, "Look here," and he pointed to an area beyond the scene, to where the soldiers' horses were tied to a line between two trees, "why do you suppose they've also got three goats and a cow wi' them?" It was not a question that needed an answer.

For several minutes the group crouched in the bushes, trying to hear what the soldiers were saying, but nothing was clear. It was also obvious the drunken group was here for the night.

Struan signaled for the boys to follow him as he led away, back to their own horses. When he knew they were out of earshot to any quiet conversation, he stopped. "All right lads, get everythin' ya need. We'll spread out around them. When ya hear my signal, don't leave anyone alive."

The following morning, the dead bodies of the Dumfries tax agent, and six English soldiers were found outside the gates of the garrison stockade. All had been decapitated and their heads were tucked under their lifeless arms, and each carried his penis protruding from his gaping mouth.

This brought to thirty the number of officials and British soldiers missing or killed, in and around the counties of Dumfries and Galloway, over the past six months; and all since Wallace and the Campbells had made it known that the English weren't welcome in their territory.

Reining up only a few times and only momentarily to let the animals rest, they knew they had lost their pursuers. Still none of the group spoke. All were bundled in their kilts and cowls against the crisp morning air. The tightly woven, proudly worn tartan of the clan was designed to protect the wearer in any weather, and serve a multitude of uses — from a sleeping blanket to a shroud. Now they used their tartan wraps over their sheepskin tunics, which kept them dry and warm.

Finally they moved on up to more open terrain and were able to once again ride along beside one another. Continuing to keep their horses at a walk because of the rocky and unfamiliar footing, it gave them a chance to talk. Here they were safe. The English wouldn't venture into this country. No matter how many or how they outnumbered the group, it would be suicide to try and take them.

William used the opportunity to ride alongside his friend. Something wasn't right about the group. "Hamish you said a while ago that four had gone ahead?"

"Ya, that's right, Wil."

"Well then, that should have left you, me, Duncan, Shawn, and Robert. That would have made five of us. So who's the sixth? The one still wearin' the cowl; I didn't notice earlier."

"Uh, ya, Wil...uh listen I dinna' have time to talk wi' ye' just now, I've got to talk wi' Robert."

"Fine, talk wi' whoever you want; but tell me who that is."

Hamish pretended not to hear and rode away.

William looked strangely after Hamish, and was about to shout at him, but thought better of it. "What the fuck!" he muttered, and spurred his horse up to the newcomer. He couldn't help notice how slim the build compared to the others. Most of the lads he knew were broad shouldered, and heavily muscled. "Hello, stranger, me name's William Wallace — who might you be?"

No answer.

Thinking he hadn't been heard, William inched his horse up so that he was almost directly along side, and said louder, "stranger, who might ye be? I'm Wil..." Then he saw the small boots in the stirrups, the slender legs turned to the hunt position in the saddle, the fine-gloved hands on the reins, and the coil of auburn hair against the incredible profile, as the beautiful face peeked around the cowl.

"Jesus Marin, wha' in the name of Christ are you doin' here." he was stunned.

He had not expected to see her for months, confident that she was at home and safe in the village with her parents. Just the night before he had asked her to marry him. Now, in flight with Hamish and the others he was certain that any thought of marriage was remote at best. Even though her father was a good man, and one of them, he would never risk his daughter to the cause. And William wouldn't either. But his only refuge now was the Doons.

"Marin, you can't." he stammered. "You shouldn't ... what are you doin'..."

She had flipped back the cowl to expose her mane of gleaming hair, burning red in the early sunlight; and had turned in the saddle to look directly into his eyes. The answer was obvious.

He could look at her forever, he wanted her with him forever, but he couldn't risk her being hurt or killed. "Marin, you're goin' to have to go back home...you canna be here."

"Why not," she cooed, "it's where you are!"

"Clever, very clever...you know what I'm talkin' about. You canna' go wi' me...and that's all there is to it!"

"So you say."

"Jesus girl...listen to me. This is impossible. I don't know what we're goin' to do right this moment, but ya canna' stay wi' me. Now somehow I've got to figure a way to get you back, and right away." He ached to have her with him, but knew her father would rather turn him in than lose her. He didn't blame him.

"William, look at me!" Her tone suddenly leveled and the coy smile disappeared. "Wil, I'm goin' with you, and that's all there is to it." He knew by the look, it was not a request.

"Please Marin, you can't. It's not the way. Besides I'll only be gone for a little while, please?"

"No Wil, where you go, I go, and that's final."

"Look, I know you think that this is the best thing, but believe me it's not. For one thing, your Da will have me balls for his slingshot, and for another..."

"Not if he knows what's good for him, he won't. Don't worry about me Da. If he ever wants back in me Ma's bed again, he'll go wi' the deal."

"What do you mean?"

"I told me ma, — if ever you're goin' then I'm goin' too...and she's wi' me on it. Now, what's the other thing?"

"It's not safe and it's not seemly!"

"Not safe! For who? For you maybe! By the way, where's your sword William?" Her expression mocked him.

"I don't know...I've lost... How do you know about me sword?"

"Because I have it, ya feeble bastard! " In a flash she was waving the tip under his throat. She was as good with a light saber, as he was with a Claymore. "Don't be tellin' me I need lookin' after. It's you who needs lookin' after. I took this right behind your sorry back — I could'a been the enemy Wil — I coulda' killed ya.

Besides, I can kick the shite out of you any day. And as for seemly, what's seemly William Wallace? How many more ways do you want me to drain that pecker of yours before it comes seemly? I've been lookin' after that little thing ever since the first day it got stiff. I knew what it needed before you did! And me only a babe of thirteen then! Maybe that's what we should be tellin' me Da?" With that, she whipped open her tunic to reveal her splendid breasts. "You'd like to be forgettin' about these, eh Wil, would ya?"

"Jesus Marin, lower your voice, and for Christ's sake cover your whorin' self up. Do you want everybody to know about us?"

"Fuck, Wil Wallace, you're dumb as a post. Everybody's watched us, never mind knowin' about us."

"Jesus Marin..."

"Jesus, nothin. Are you goin' to ride along prayin' or are we goin' to get on wi' this fuckin' escape?"

He thought about the prospects of trying to get her off her horse, putting her up with Robert, and sending her home; but that would not be easy. First of all, it would be like trying to pull a wildcat out of a tree, and secondly, it would only put her and Robert in mortal danger. He had no choice; they had to ride on to the Doons. He would decide what to do with her when they got there.

~

Again the trail changed. It began to get narrower, and steeper as they entered a heavily forested area at the base of the Doons. They had started their climb and were all forced to string out in single file to negotiate the heavily wooded ravines. Only Hamish knew the way.

William reined in behind her, and for the next few miles no one talked, as the horses plodded carefully along. He was overjoyed at having her with him; but it may have put a price on her head too.

He had known her all his life. And even before he understood what it was he was feeling, he had been in love with her.

By evening, they had reached the legendary Doon Castle. William had never been there before. Hamish had, a few times — his lover Andrea was a Doon.

As they approached from out of a forest, in the half-light of sunset, William was awestruck by the brilliance and regal achievement that welcomed him. It was nothing in the way of a traditional castle; and as they drew closer, he was captivated by the graceful lines and ornate details of the elevation he could see.

Bordered by a low stone wall, which seemed more to enhance the landscape rather than for defense; the architectural mastery of its gothic design, triumphed by fluted columns and wide, sweeping arches, rivaled the artistry of Westminster. He had envisioned a massive, austere, battle-ready, walled fortress; instead he gazed upon a monument to elegance, grace and sophistication, safely hidden in these impenetrable hills.

$$V$$

Life at Doon with Marin was idyllic. Summer came to the highlands.

He had the woman he loved at his side always: caring for her, talking and sharing, and filling his bed with endless pleasure. He knew it was selfish to hold her, but she was his other half: the completion of his life.

The gentle wilderness of these swept hills and bowered glens was the fuel for their passion. Rustling trees and hidden forest creatures were the only witnesses to the lovers' appetite.

At home, unmarried lovers, if brave enough, could only steal moments of intimacy in the overcrowded woods, fearing the prying eyes and perverted interference of soldiers and thieves. But here they found their secret and secluded spot. It was in a tiny glen by a riverbank, hidden from the world, where they could lay free with each other for hours in the warm sun, holding on tightly to a life they couldn't have back at home.

Doon offered a freedom and a safety that William and Marin had never known before. Wallace's resolve to send her back to Dumfries soon gave out. This was their place. This is where they would live.

The castle and its miles and miles of lands, including most of the mountain range, had been home and refuge to generations of Doon and Campbell families. They wanted for nothing and their foreboding territory had proven to be too much for England's grasping hands. It was the perfect place to live and from which to plan and prepare for war.

And the Campbells were ready to make war, spreading the word and encouraging dedicated Scots, who came by the thousands, to rally behind Wallace. There came the McGregors, and Stuarts, and MacDonalds and more Campbells — all the clans came. Then to Wallace's surprise there came the half wild nameless Celtish bands from the far north. Never before had they supported any cause for Scotland. It was even thought by most Scots, that the Celts were not human. They were to be feared and best left to themselves.

Then came the biggest surprise of all, the arrival of the Irish and the Welsh.

He knew they were sympathetic but they were not expected. For both it was a long journey.

But then there was no second-guessing of what was going on in the world those days. There on the Campbell fiefdom of the central highlands, in the year 1297, grew the largest army ever raised to the cause of Scotland's freedom. Stretching from valley to valley, as far as the eye could see from the battlements of Doon Castle sprang up camps the size of cities.

And with the droves of fighting men came their families, wives and children, parents and grandparents. This was not just a gathering of lusty warriors hungering for a day's bloodletting and pillaging, this was the will of a people; everyone of every age driven and eager, committed to do whatever they could to support William Wallace. Everything William and Hamish dreamed of seemed about to come true.

~

Then one day in August, a message came for Marin. Her mother was ill. There was no call for her to come home, but that made no difference.

William could not stop her, so he was prepared to go with her. Hamish talked him out of it. The other clan leaders insisted. It was too dangerous, and if he were spotted, and captured, it would bring down and erase years of horrendous struggle and render meaningless the loss of countless thousands of lives never mind everything they were accomplishing now.

It would be difficult enough to spirit Marin in and out of the village, never mind the two of them.

Hamish commandeered his cousins Robert and Duncan, two young, up and coming Campbells as yet unknown to the law, who wanted more than anything to serve with Wallace and himself, and who he knew could be trusted implicitly to take her to Dumfries. "Wait until dark before ya go into the village," he told them. Marin was to slip away to her mother for a while; you lads lay low — and stay out of the pub — and get your arses back to Doon before mornin'. Be oot of the village before sun up," he warned, his huge fist in their faces, "if they're gonna' do a search they'll do it then, and sure as shite, catch one of you asleep wi'some doxie under a hay pile."

No one counted on a green-eyed enemy.

Marin's secreted arrival at her parents' cottage did not go unobserved. A neighbor woman, awake late, saw her arrive, which under normal circumstances would have been of no concern for either, but in this case it was one particular woman who was fiercely jealous of her and Wallace, and so in her spite, sneaked off into the night and reported her to the authorities.

Were it any other person, even of some notoriety, most constables wouldn't have cared less about the hissing of two cats over some stud, but this one was different.

As Marin sat by her mother's bedside, the Sheriff, William DeHeselrig himself, got into the act and he and several of his more brutish soldiers kicked down her parent's door, struck her father unconscious, and carried her off.

This is so much easier, and much more civilized, thought DeHeselrig. Now he had the bait to lure Wallace. And better than that, with the right kind of persuasion, this lovely piece of bait could be worth even more than Wallace; she must know everything that's going on at Doon.

So many of the other young girls in the villages had surrendered their lover's secrets very easily. One didn't need to attack the whole village and kill children; besides it never worked; they never got any information that way, they just got a lot of their own men killed in return.

There was another way, and it was so much simpler and quieter. Most of the women in these villages were lovers or wives of men who served with Wallace, and they knew more secrets about the Highlanders than any of these peasant farmers would ever know, and they were much easier to capture.

Torturing them was effective and entertaining. The men loved to watch, and afterwards he had the most exciting sex he ever thought possible. He could already feel this rare beauty, flat on her back, naked, legs tied apart, without doubt this one would be exceptional and this one he would keep for himself; there would be no sharing.

First he would take his knife and slide the tip just a little way inside that wonderful place that can be so welcoming to some and so forbidden to others. Then he would just threaten to push and twist it – they always believed him.

He would have her taken to his quarters, she was special, there would be no show. He had heard the men talk about Marin Broadfute, but none of their accolades came even close to describing the real thing.

Marin had not gone easily. She fought wildly to escape, and in the struggle, much of her dress had been torn away on one side, revealing her long slender leg and thigh; and the entire bodice had been ripped in half, forcing her to clutch the separated material over her breasts.

Most of these peasant hill women, while pretty and desirable, their bodies were usually over developed from all the hard work, had, as a result, thick muscular legs and thighs which he did not find particularly appealing.

This one was altogether different. DeHesilrig couldn't control himself. And he was being treated to it all. Here she was exposed and vulnerable; it was driving him mad.

The torture could wait. First he would have her in every way possible.

He tore his clothes from his body, to let her see his need. "And now it's yor turn little lady, let's see wot yor hidin' behind then shreds."

Her defiance made it even more thrilling and was all the excuse he wanted. When she spit at him, he struck her with the back of his hand across her face. As she reacted by grabbing her cheek, she dropped the folds of her bodice.

He grabbed the loose material and ripped it completely away.

The sight hypnotized him. He had never had an experience so erotic as this nor anything remotely like her. She was incredible, this beautiful young savage, naked, defenseless - his victim.

The need for release was overwhelming. A powerful surge in his groin told him he would soon spill his seed. He began stroking himself with one hand, and striking out at her with the other, again and again. The surge through his body caused him to flail wildly, and soon down she went.

Forgetting himself he tried to cradle her heaving breasts in his hands, to squeeze her nipples. She jerked herself away, and tried to kick at him. Again he slammed the back of his hand across her face, harder this time, knocking her flat to the floor. She lay for a moment, gasping, stunned. He shoved his hardened penis to her mouth, and slowly massaging it he reached down, grabbed her by the hair, and hauled her face into his groin.

She turned her head just in time. At the feel of her cheek against him, he began to lose control. Gripping her by the hair, he hit her again and again across the face, demanding she open her mouth.

The pain was unbearable but all fear had gone. She clenched her teeth, and kept pulling away from him. Harder and harder came the blows, two, three, four times, full force, crazed blows with his large, meaty fist; and with each the excitement brought him closer to release.

When exactly DeHesilrig realized the fight had gone out of her, he didn't know. He let her head slump to the floor. The face beneath him had become a bloody, unrecognizable mess. He was in ecstasy and throbbing to the point of explosion. He now could have his way.

~

When Marin didn't return to Robert and Duncan by dawn, they went to look for her. It was then they learned of her capture, and headed for Doon Castle. They had barely got the words out before Wallace was in the saddle. Hamish and his other friends followed. It wasn't until he met with Marin's parents, that he learned of her death; that her beaten and raped body had been deposited naked in the gutter outside the fortress walls.

It was said that the fate of a nation changed that day. Certainly it did for Scotland and certainly everything did for William Wallace. He vowed at her mother's knee then to spill every ounce of English blood found in Scotland. The war he sought and envisioned and the war he would now start would have two entirely different meanings. And while one would eventually end, the other would never be over.

The gates of hell had been opened.

VI

He began with DeHeselrig.

The plan - to kill every Englishman in sight. He and Hamish and the McCaulaghs decided that the only way for it was to charge the Sheriff's stockade and see what happened.

It was reputed to be well defended so Wallace thought, "let's see how well."

Witnesses told the tale the way they wanted to remember it; they said that all of a sudden on that one day the heavens opened and they were held frozen to the sight; that like monsters called back from death Wallace and his men hurled themselves at every redcoat in their path.

The stories that were told over and over again kept many a bonfire roaring through the night and held rich and poor, young and old from Edinburgh to Paris, spellbound. How lightening bolts flew from his mighty Claymore, how it took on a life of its own how the hilt sprouted horns and the blade shattered armor.

All of London rattled in terror as they were told that English heads flew from English bodies as it cleaved and hacked it's opponents into pieces. Wallace himself, so the stories went, battered his way through a surge of dozens of guards, as if he were clearing a path through tall grass.

As the ones stationed inside the walls watched their comrades falling like skittles, they were overcome with terror. None of the Scots seemed touchable. On they came, relentlessly, hurling lassos and pulling down the wooden gates as if nothing held them. No inside guard fired a single arrow. Instead, they threw down their weapons and tried to flee. If it was DeHeselrig that Wallace wanted; it was Heselrig he could have.

And when he entered the compound, and slid from his horse, he didn't have to ask. The frightened soldiers eagerly showed him the hiding place. He found the Sheriff cowering in an underground bunker, built beneath his quarters, which were in the center of the compound.

Wallace himself dragged the constable, begging for mercy, from his hole and strapped him to a makeshift Gurney. He then raised and tilted it so that the man was clearly on display.

DeHeselrig was now screaming in terror. Wallace announced that they were hearing the sound of one about to enter hell, and he wanted every Englishman within earshot to learn it.

Stripping him of his clothing, Wallace took his knife and made a perfect incision across DeHeselrig's abdomen. It opened like a purse, and with a rush of blood and entrails, his insides spilled to the ground. Wallace then, very precisely and carefully, using the manner of a surgeon, sliced around Heselrig's scrotum and removed his penis and testicles.

Tipping the Gurney flat, Wallace scooped up the mess of organs and intestines, and then as a mid-wife might place a newborn at its mother's breast, he deposited the entire contents on DeHeselrig's chest. Next he stuffed the penis and testicles into the man's mouth. He was still alive.

For a few moments he looked at his work, and then at Hamish. "Take him to the Broadfutes — it's their turn — let them finish him the way they see fit. And kill the rest of these pigs."

No one from the garrison at Dumfries survived. Wallace returned to Doon to prepare to make good his promise.

THE FALL OF THE EMPIRE

Chapter 2

1296 AD

/

Meanwhile in August of the same year, in London, the King of England was acting on misleading and grossly over-estimated news.

He had been told that the Scottish rebels were finally on the run. That the Constable at Irvine, near Dundee, on the Scottish east coast, had uncovered a plot to burn his garrison, and that he had further discovered that the McGregors were behind it.

The King had been delighted to hear that, and that the response had demonstrated such initiative. Without warning, the Constable had retaliated by burning to ashes the entire village, including farm houses for miles around, and captured and hanged, on the spot, every McGregor — man, woman and child — that he could find.

And as most of his advisors believed that the McGregor's were the last inspiration of the Scottish people, the news satisfied Edward that - "this was the end of the matter" - and he became confident that without the McGregor family to lead and inspire the rabble, he had nothing more to worry about. Now he could return to France with a clear mind and focus on his problems there.

His complacency was short lived. After weeks of arduous and painstakingly detailed preparations to transport thousands of men and horses across the Channel, and tens of thousands of pounds invested, all but depleting the Royal treasury, just two days prior to his departure, he received a dispatch with a most disturbing message from Lord John de Warenne, the Governor of Scotland, telling him that the Scots were preparing for more war.

"My Lord King," he wrote. "I am not sure what to make of it yet, but this young rebel, Wallace, has the Scottish people worked up, and we hear widespread talk of revenge for Irvine. He has already decimated the garrison at Dumfries. While it may amount to nothing more than an isolated event, it is my recommendation that we take every precaution and prepare for more disturbances.

Herewith you will find my budget and requirements for necessary upgrade and refurbishment.

- Earl de Warenne, Governor, Scottish Territories."

At first the request was irritating – 'make the goddamn soldiers pay for their own equipment and then we'd see how much refurbishment was needed.'

"Warenne cries wolf, Sire!"

"Warenne is great warrior, Hugo!" It was all Edward could do to stop from smashing this bloated coward in the face. "If there is a real need, and I suspect there is, I can't overlook it." He had called in his Treasurer, Hugo DeCressingham, to investigate what was left of the budget. Edward did not have the time or the patience to do it himself, and besides the request involved only money, so his money man could handle the job. Besides, DeCressingham had ways of wringing it out of unwilling or unprepared "donors" that he preferred no part of.

Warenne had itemized replacement weapons, stores and food. Edward showed the report to Cressingham. "I don't know Hugo. There's a lot of detail here, perhaps too much. It's going to be a great deal of money that may be better spent elsewhere."

Regardless of the circumstances Cressingham never disagreed with the King. He was too cleverly obsequious to open his mouth until he was sure of the right thing to say. "My Lord, I too am skeptical. The Governor is getting old, and, I suspect, tired of war. Perhaps he thinks that refurbishment will make it easier for him — if there is to be any trouble from the Scots?"

Edward listened, and watched, with contempt; and bit his tongue as the fat little man postured and gestured expansively, strutting about the Throne Room convinced that his actions bore him as a man of superior rank and intelligence. He wanted to shout, 'of course there's going to be trouble from the Scots, you fool', but he merely grunted his distaste.

~

The King could barely hide his loathing for this unmanly Treasurer, but kept silent his thoughts, 'what an overbearing, self-righteous, pontificating blob of suet the man is, but he is good with numbers, and he is afraid of me.'

And like the man or not, Edward had seen a tremendous advantage in hiring him, and had turned it to opportunity.

Cressingham was an Abbot and overly prideful of it. Pride was a mortal sin for a priest, a sin with which Edward had been delighted. Better to make use of it, than to condemn it.

He promoted Cressingham to a Lord of the Realm, and to Controller of his treasury. The advancement had bloated the little man's ego quite out of proportion. The priest was more afraid of losing his title and prestige, than how he appeared in the sight of God. Would he steal from the King? Never. So even though Edward disliked the horrible creature; he was one of the few who could be trusted.

However, the Treasurer had a different opinion of himself. He rationalized that his rise within state and church as clear sign that he was in God's favor. And like most other powerful churchmen who, as a result, regard themselves as chosen, he was no less avaricious and greedy.

But in his position, stealing would be foolhardy and unnecessary. By guarding the royal purse, discretion was on his side. He could use it, within reason, as if it were his own — his commissions were unquestioned. And even if he were questioned, errors in judgment were forgiven, blatant theft was fatal.

Together, they picked away at Warenne's lists.

~

As a high priest and England's Treasurer and Chief Tax Collector, Hugo DeCressingham had enormous political and social power. He also had many enemies, especially amongst the lesser nobility and the common people. Particularly every man and woman in Scotland despised him.

He believed that in order for England to maintain tight control over its provinces, his office would best serve by divesting the average Scot of any opportunity to accumulate wealth or assets. That meant collecting taxes often and taking everything — every penny; every living asset. If the people were kept poor, weak and begging, they would have no energy and certainly no resources for war.

Cressingham cared not at all who died from illness and starvation. Often, to make his point, in the winter months he would have whole families dragged from their crude little huts, stripped of their clothing, of every last possession, of every living thing on their tiny farm, even of the food on their plates.

Then he would have their pathetic thatched hovels burned to the ground, and the grain in their fields torched; leaving them naked, exposed, freezing and destitute; and then have put to death any who tried to help them. He enjoyed playing God to Scotland.

~

Edward was so anxious to be on his way to France, that he was more than content to delegate the problem. "Hugo, perhaps you are right. I don't think the Scots have anything to give us trouble with, but I want you to go to Carlisle, meet with Warenne, and see what kind of condition the northern army is in. If they need refurbishment, within reason, approve it. Otherwise, if it is something more, send a message to my son and he will see that it gets to the right hands."

A few days later, Cressingham with an entourage of his equally distasteful minions regally ensconced themselves at Warenne's estate in Carlisle. The Treasurer wasn't with the very annoyed General for long when he too accepted the undeniable fact that William Wallace was promoting all-out war.

In the short time it had taken the Treasurer to get to Carlisle, Wallace had already plucked at the Crown by marching into England where he sacked a castle and fortress near York, on the northeast coast, and sent Warenne a gift of the head of the King's nephew.

Then just days later, with Cressingham and Warenne still reeling from the news of York, came the grisly evidence of more disaster.

Wallace had stormed and liberated the cities of Dundee, Irvine, and Dunbarton, three former strategic English strongholds in Scotland, and not one soldier or Officer had survived. The dispatch was pointedly marked by the delivery of three more heads and a terse message that he was marching to take back Stirling.

Warenne's earlier pleas for more money, arms and support were not hollow after all. Even the arrogant Treasurer joined the plight, dispatching several desperate messages to London; but there came no replies. With Edward in France; both men knew that The Earl of Lancaster was normally always regent in the King's absence; and further knew that he was a capable substitute. Why was he not responding?

What neither Warenne or Cressingham were aware of was that the King had had a last minute change of Royal plans; that of leaving his thirteen year old son, Edward, to act as regent. The King had been utterly convinced that his domestic problems were well in hand, and that this would be a good easy time to test the mettle of his son. It was a decision that Edward I would regret for the rest of his days.

Prince Edward had little time for official Royal duties.

And he knew nothing of war, and even less of the Scots.

His favorite pastimes were far from the battlefield, and not even remotely King-like; and he held no interest in acting as Royal steward.

The dispatches lay unopened in his chambers; unbeknownst to Lancaster or to any member of England's Privy Council. There were no reinforcements, and no extra supplies. The containment of the northern army was in it's own hands.

//

"Never treat anything you hear about Wallace as casual rumor," cautioned Warenne to his lieutenants. Wallace's plans were clear, and every commander of every post along the border dreaded that he was next. Wallace's messages were graphic statements of who were his intended victims, and so far he hadn't missed.

His intentions were clearly marked by the series of events, which started three weeks earlier.

The devastation of each of England's primary strongholds was a major step on the way to reclaiming Scotland. Upon taking the ports of Dunbarton and Dundee, he made his point of expelling the English from the country, and he did it with a terrifying flair. Every English soldier alive or dead, was taken from the battle and thrown from the sea-cliffs into the frigid waters of the north Atlantic.

Then to close each victory, he observed a ritual, which became his trademark.

It involved slicing off, wrapping in burlap and sending the head of the ranking Commander, along to the Commander of his next objective.

Warenne had received his gift from Dundee, Wallace's last stop. Prophesying Warenne's head in the burlap, Wallace promised it would be sent to London.

~

The night of the attack on Dundee, Wallace took an arrow in the leg, and had been tended by Struan McCaulagh. The old warrior had himself taken, and pulled, many arrows in his day.

As William lay recovering from the violent intrusion to his body, he asked Struan why more help didn't come from some of the Scottish nobility. "Aren't there at least a few who want this country back?"

"Lad. The English King gives 'em more than they could ever get on their own. And, besides, half of them don't know who or what they are anymore. This war has always been fought by us, the commoners, but up until now it's always amounted to the same thing; wee bands of lads pickin' fights, and endin' up dead. It were useless and t' no avail. We had no way to fight as a country. We had no way of gettin' the clans together. Christ, even hold a family weddin', and the bloody English are all over us for illegal gatherin', and then his God almighty Lardship demandin' to be the first to fuck the bride.

That border," said Struan, "which is supposed to divide the two countries, crosses only a wee strip of land, and seems easy to defend. Christ, it was lost so long ago, that no one even hardly remembers its there.

There was a time, but not any more," continued Struan, shaking his old head, "even our own nobility are all fuckin' half English now. And even when they were true Scots, they weren't willin'. Too afraid of the English takin' it all away from them. Our own had titles, land, even a King, as long as they kissed English arse. They called themselves our Lords, and called themselves Scots, but they didn't give a shite about the people. And all them bleedin' fat Lords and Ladies from London, shovin' their milky white daughters up here with their soft big tits and easy pussies. They all started breedin', and now we got a bunch of half-breed Earls and Lords runnin' things, who don't have clue in hell who or what they are, and would rather spend all their time sunnin' and whorin' in France, and leave the job of Scotland up to the fuckin' constables."

III

The next quarry was Stirling Castle.

Formidable, impregnable, it was the cornerstone of England's control over Scotland. Wallace was convinced that taking back Stirling would mean freedom.

And this time William had a masterful plan.

He ordered his men to camp in the low mountains, several miles north of where he ultimately planned to fight. Here his army would wait and rest. It also would give him a chance to scout the enemy, up close and without being detected.

At the same time, he knew the British would never venture into these hills after him. It would be suicide. Their heavy warhorses would be to no advantage, except as pack animals, and would be unable to maneuver the steep, rugged slopes, and rocky terrain.

The foot soldiers, as burdened with gear and weaponry as they always were, would find it impossible to negotiate the deep ravines and craggy outcrops, all of which were second nature to his wild Scots. He half hoped the English would try, because they would be easy sport.

During the ride into the hills to establish a camp, he and Hamish had been asked by one of the younger cousins, "if we're hidin' up here in the hills, how're you goin' to know what the British are plannin'?"

They both looked at each other as if the answer was obvious, and replied in unison, "we'll go ask them."

Two days later, dressed as poor farmers, and riding wagon horses, they rode boldly through the gates of Stirling Castle, daring some slow-witted guard to challenge their presence. The guards took no more than a casual look at them. They took it as a sign. But the irony of the ease of their performance made them even bolder and more daring.

"William, we're never goin' t' take Stirlin' the way we took them other three — you know that lad." They were huddled over mugs of ale, in a toffers' public house, across the narrow stone walled street from the garrison offices, surrounded by English soldiers. "It would take us a hundred years to send every lad in here two by two." Hamish chuckled. He liked his own jokes; especially the one they were playing now. Looking over to the table next, he smiled and mugged a cheer to four senior Officers. They tipped back.

"I know that, Hamish, and you know that, but they don't." Wallace whispered through clenched teeth, as he too grinned at the four uniforms. " Listen to these assholes, they think we're comin', and they're laughin' at us. They think we're just goin' to charge this fuckin' rock like a bunch of wild dogs, and they'll just pick us off like dinner. Well that's what we want them to think, for now." He knew he could not win against the well-armed English in an all out open fight.

He and Hamish had had a good long look at the situation outside the castle, and even he had to admit it was daunting.

They were outnumbered almost five to one, by the best equipped, best trained army in the world. The most effective weaponry his brave lads carried were old, captured, battered swords, and sharpened wooden pikes. Their protective armor consisted of wadded sheep's wool to hopefully soften the blows.

"We're goin' ta' have ta' out-smart these arrogant bastards, and then we're goin' ta' kick the shite out of them. But we're not goin' to show ourselves just yet. Let's leave them stay bottled up here for awhile thinkin' they've got to defend this place."

"Aye, and then when they see we're not comin' they'll think we're layin' siege, and that'll force them to make the first move." Even though he didn't like the odds, Hamish loved the way William's mind worked. It was the only way under these circumstances — hide and divide.

All the way to Stirling, they had ridden along the bank of the north shore of the River Forth in order to reconnoiter. On the south side the English camp protecting the castle stretched for miles. There were tens of thousands of combat troops, and archers, and at least a thousand heavy horse. Any initial thoughts of storming the castle, as he had with the others, were quickly ruled out. Stirling was the exception.

As he and Hamish sat on two old inconspicuous horses chosen especially for this little venture, they pondered the sanity of their act.

The only thing that might work in their favor was the single bridge that crossed the river.

Fascinated by the enormity of the scene around them, they realized that it would be impossible to take the city by traditional methods. Towering hundreds of feet above them high atop its vertical rock cliffs, it sat massive and well fortified. From there the British could rain arrows and balls of fire down on them all day and he and his men would never even inflict so much as a bruise.

It only remained, that to take Stirling Castle, he would have to draw the British out of it — out onto ground where he had the advantage.

For three days and nights he and Hamish donned the work-worn attire, and riding the old horses, they were able to plod the network of roads which crisscrossed around the mountain fortress and idly explore both banks of the River, right under the noses of the English. They rode in and out of the camp with impunity. None of the English rank and file knew their looks, only their reputations.

His plan began to take shape. Although there were thousands of British assembling almost daily, all were stationed along the south shore, with none occupying the north. It was obvious that they saw the bridge as a defence.

The second evening, as they rode through the rows of tents, they spotted a group of Officers, under a large canopy, drinking ale. They stopped, dismounted, went in and asked for "a wee draught."

"'Ere, " said a steward, " wot the bleedin' 'ell you doin? You can't be in 'ere; this is for Officers only. Get the 'ell outa 'ere!"

"Aw lad, don't be throwin' a fit. We've just got a thirst, is all. We been loadin' cattle for you lot all day; we're just lookin' to down a pint."

Before the steward could speak again, a fresh-faced young Officer stepped forward. "It's all right steward, give them a drink."

"T'anks mate," said Wallace, removing his cap, and grinning at him like a country clod. "T'ank the capt'n, Hamish," he said, smacking him on the arm with the cap. The steward handed each of them a large mug. "Cheers yr' lawdship, and 'tanks ever so."

"Not a problem — cheers." The Officer seemed a little fuzzy.

Wallace sensed an opening. After a long pull, he said, "So how goes the battle capt'n?" It would not be customary for a poor farmer to be familiar with an English Officer, and certainly not cheeky, but Wallace sensed that this one had let them stay for ulterior reasons; why not seem willing to talk.

"What battle is that sir?" The response was stiff but pleasant.

"Just an expression capt'n, sir — just an expression." Humility was still expected.

"Well, your expression has a ring of truth to it. I'm afraid we may be in for one any day now."

"Yeah, it sort of looks that way capt'n. Either that, or you've got a lot of people comin' over." Hamish and his jokes. The Officer laughed.

After a pause, the Officer asked, "what part of the country are you two from?"

"To the north, sir. A cattle farm to the north." Wallace loved playing the part.

"How far?"

"About ten mile, capt'n." Wallace drained his mug. "You'll have to come see the farm. Best beef in Scotland." He turned to Hamish. "Drink up lad, we best be goin'. It's gettin' late." Back to the Officer, "thank you, sir. Maybe we can do this again some time." Again, the clodhopper grins.

Hamish choked as he swallowed, and spit beer down his front.

"Take your time, lads. No hurry. Did you come down here today?" He motioned for the steward to give them each another.

"Yes sir, we did. T'ank you, sir. Brought about a hundred head down."

Other ears had turned their way. "Did you happen to see any large numbers of men in your travels, or camped thereabout?" The noise level under the tent suddenly dropped.

Wallace scratched his stubbled chin. "No, nothin' unusual...except maybe...'ere Hamish, what was it you was tellin me about those lads you seen yesterday?" He turned and winked at his cousin.

"Yeah, shite Wil, t'anks for remindin' me." Put on the spot, he tried to look thick.

"Yes, uh Hamish, tell us, what did you see?" The Officer tried to sound casual.

"Right, right. Well, you see, I'd lost a few cows and went lookin' for them." For a moment he thought it best to fake the choking, and stumble out of the situation. But then a story came to him and he chuckled at the fun he could have with these toffeye-nosed farts... "And, and I come to the top of a ridge, where, as I was lookin' down into a valley, I seen these lads. They was leadin' off me cows. Well I'm no shrinkin' violet, as you can see, and me temper got the best o' me, so I went chargin' down to bust some heads. But as I got closer, I seen they was big lads — bigger n' me; and there was maybe ten of 'em.

That's when I started thinkin' better of it, when they spotted me. One of them called after me, but I was makin' tracks when a huge rock, the size of a pig, went flyin' by me ear. Fuck, I says to myself, what in 'ell threw that. So I stopped, and now I'm near shittin' m'self as these lads come ridin' up.

'What the fuck you doin', says one. 'I think he's after stealin' the cattle', says another. 'Let's kill 'im'.

I'm thinkin', jesus, their after accusin' me of stealin' me own cows, and now their wantin' to kill me. Ain't this fuckin' nice.

Then one, who seemed to be the leader, told the others to shut up. He said that they were takin' the cows. It weren't for discussion. They needed the food. He says that if I liked livin', I should fuck off, and forget I ever seen 'em. I got me arse outa there."

"What happened then? Did you see where they went?" The Officer looked worried.

"Nope. But I headed north, and they wasn't goin' in my direction."

"How many cows did you say?"

"Ten."

"Ten cows. That's a lot of meat, sir." It was another Officer who spoke.

"Yes, yes, I know. What did they look like — uh — Hamish?" said the Captain.

"Yes sir. Well, they was big lads, strong — 'ell, one of 'em threw that boulder at least fifty feet," Hamish stared up at the roof, pretending to be thinking. "And one other thing — Wil I forgot to tell you this — I thought I heard one lad say, 'if William finds out we didn't kill him — he'll kill us — sure as shite'. I don't know who they were talkin' about, but I guessed this William was the boss."

"Fuck me, he's here'" said another voice. And they all looked from one to the other.

"Who's here," asked Wallace innocently.

Most every voice answered in unison, "William Wallace."

IV

To anyone, standing in the valley beneath the towering cliffs, Stirling Castle is an impressive sight.

Sitting high atop a tableaux it appears that the peak of a mountain has been severed off, and the castle built to occupy the leveled surface. It needed no more than a few archers up in the battlements to repel any kind or size of attack. The only way in and out is along a narrow sloped causeway leading to the castle's only gate, at the base of the south wall. No charge could be mounted there either.

Below the cliffs, stretched a level plain, dotted by thickets of tall brush, through the center of which cut the River Forth, a tide river and the principal inland commercial waterway of Scotland.

William stationed a man to study the times of the tide flow, and he reported that first high tide was at approximately eleven o'clock in the morning. By that time the river became at least a quarter of a mile wide, and the current so strong, no man could swim against it. Even at low tide, he reported, the river was still too wide and deep to ford, other than by boat.

The only crossing, for miles, in either direction, was by a single bridge, which joined the main highway from the south.

As William studied his options, he realized that this bridge would set the trap. The course was clear; lay seige, and draw the English out. "It is the key to Scotland," he told his men. "He who occupies Stirling, occupies the country."

Situated in the very center of southern Scotland, on the River Forth not ten miles from the North Sea inlet of the Firth of Forth, twenty-five miles from Dunbarton on the Atlantic, and eighty miles north of the border, it meant control.

Stirling would be the gateway to international trade and that meant independence. Moreover, as a military base and stronghold, Stirling was second to none. The geography was perfect to house, feed and train every able-bodied man in Scotland. And the impregnable fortress would make the perfect seat of government. This was the objective that now sat so stolidly before William Wallace and his followers.

And it seemed that the English generals took him seriously. Fifty thousand troops had been assembled to defend it.

For three days and nights he and his men hid in the hills, and for three days the two, dressed as farmers, slipped in and out of the English camp, listening and watching. It seemed that none of the rank and file soldiers were aware of any orders or battle plans; and that many were beginning to doubt that Wallace was even in the vicinity.

Then on the third day, the English camp was buzzing.

As William and Hamish made their rounds, the talk was all about the seige.

Warenne had known that the Scots weren't actually going to attack the castle. He also reasoned that they were not intimidated by the massive presence of troops. It was a simple deduction; Wallace was going to remain out there, invisible, and wait until the English army ran out of food.

Acting on the growing paranoia of the English troops, on the fourth day, Wallace quietly moved his men into the wooded hills and valleys on the north side of the river, directly opposite the English and the castle on the south.

"They'll cross the river, Hamish, mark my words. Sittin' out a siege is not their style. All we have to do is wait — it won't be long. That many men will gobble up supplies very quickly, and just as quickly they'll be needin' more."

Hamish grinned with smug satisfaction at his own efficiency. Although Warenne had caught on to their intentions, Hamish had been one step ahead. He had already cut off shipping coming up the Forth, and had evacuated the farms for miles in all directions. This prevented food and stores from reaching the massive army. When the next round of river barges failed to arrive, the English would have to make their move.

Although he couldn't see them, Warenne knew the Scots were in those hills on the other side, and he was afraid.

The news of Dunbarton, brought as it had been with the burlap sack and its hideous, putrid contents had arrived from Dundee. Warenne saw his own fate.

However, British military strategy dictated that he send a dispatch back to Wallace through Dundee with a message demanding that if Wallace surrender, no harm would come to him or his men.

It was a lie. He knew that Wallace knew it was a lie, and yet before every encounter, offensive or defensive, all over the world, the British observed that ritual. Against some, in the past, it had worked, but it was futile to think that it would work with this man.

Wallace responded by sending the courier back with his own. It contained no terms or conditions. It was a simple farewell. "I intend to see that every single Englishman, now on Scottish soil, dies in one way or another. You are all trapped and dare not venture away from Stirling. Sooner or later you will all become starved and desperate, and easy to kill. I will wait."

It was now up to the English. Warenne had known from the very beginning that their numbers meant very little in this incredible battle of wits.

He reckoned he had about another day without fresh supplies, and his troops would be without food. Weak men cannot fight.

A meeting was called with his senior Officers and advisors; chief among them was DeCressingham.

"Gentlemen, let me begin by saying that whatever we decide here, now, please do not underestimate this fellow Wallace. We know he is out there, and that in itself is dangerous enough. Believe, he is not sitting idly, he knows everything, whatever we do. Mark me, he has a plan, and he has anticipated every move we can make..."

DeCressingham, scoffing at Warenne, rudely interrupted, "so what if he can anticipate our next move?. A child could do that. We only have one. That is to cross that bridge and teach the barbarian a lesson. There should be nothing to that.

First of all, never mind what he knows of us, what do we know about him. He is outnumbered, at least two to one; he has no weapons to speak of; no armor; a couple of hundred horse; and most of his men are still recovering from his last two battles. I say we are in control, and we certainly have the advantage." DeCressingham wanted it to be said later to the King that he took charge, that he was empowered to override the cowardly Warenne.

"A typical observation from one who has never been in combat," thought Warenne. "Lord Cressingham, your eminence, with all due respect, those are exactly the sentiments which will lull us into a false security with this man. It wouldn't matter if he had only feathers with which to fight, we would be well advised to take every precaution." All others in the room nodded assent.

"For God's sake man, we are British, and ours are the finest fighting men in the world. All right, we don't walk into a trap, I agree, but what is to stop us from sending a well mounted, well armed battalion to lift his embargo on the river? What then is his strategy? There is an end to this seige, and he, most certainly, is not going to attack this castle. There you have it, he might as well go home. We can continue to import troops until doomsday." DeCressingham thought, "touche, you cowardly old man."

"My Lord," said Warenne, still feigning respect, "that is exactly one of the moves he would like us to make. It is called Scottish strategy."

"And what, pray tell, is Scottish strategy — hurl sacks of haggus at us?" DeCressingham began to laugh at his own joke — no one else did.

"No sire, it is a battle strategy which has stung all of us more than once. It is their way of divide and conquer. Only it is more unique and more deadly than any textbook describes. He would like nothing more than for me to send some troops to try and lift the embargo – we'd never see them again."

"Lord Warenne, excuse me sire, permission to speak?" one of his senior Officers had stepped forward.

"Of course Lieutenant."

"Sire, there is another way to resolve the problem."

"Explain."

"Just a few miles up river is a place we can cross. The river is shallow, and without all the tide mud we have here. We may have to build a small dam, but it shouldn't take long, and then we can take the entire force around behind Wallace, and we truly will have the advantage, sire."

Warenne was impressed. "How do you come to know this, lieutenant?"

"There are some half breed Scots here, sire, who want money more than independence. They say we can buy all the food we need, fresh horses and supplies..."

"What do you mean buy?" DeCressingham demanded. "The supplies which we are now denied, have already been paid for Lieutenant, we shall not be 'buying' more!"

"Well, your eminence, the only supplies available to us right now are from pirates. They are the only one's who don't care about Wallace..."

"Pirates," the fat man roared, "we are to do business with men we normally hang?"

"Lord Cressingham," Warenne cut in, "I realize that the situation is outrageous, but the fact remains, we need food, and if this is the only way to get it, then we have little choice. And in the doing we can turn the tables and perhaps also defeat Wallace, I say we do it."

"How much money, lieutenant, are we talking about?" DeCressingham appeared to ignore Warenne's reason.

"One pound per man sire."

"One pound per man — never." DeCressingham began blustering. "My God, sir, one pound would take care of a soldier for a year, never, never," DeCressingham looked ready to explode. "What has this army come to, Warenne, that you are all afraid of this illiterate, ignorant little Scot? You have fifty thousand men sitting in your lap. If they are hungry, and want food, all the more reason to fight. I say, cross that bridge and kill that bastard Wallace, and put an end to this. As for more men, I know we sent dispatches to London for re-inforcements. I don't know why we haven't heard anything, but really who cares? How many more men do you need anyhow? No, forget more money, more anything. You don't need more, and I will not authorize it."

~

Word came to Wallace at nine o'clock in the morning that British cavalry had begun crossing the Forth at, of all places, Stirling Bridge.

Somewhat amazed at the suddenness, and the danger of this move, Wallace quickly left his camp, and took up a position high on a ridge above the north meadow, which flanked the river basin. Here he could see the activity clearly, and marveled at the stupidity of choice.

Considering that several miles further upstream, there were better opportunities where virtually all could get over in a matter of about a half an hour.

The bridge could only accommodate a double file and would take several hours at best to cross them all.

In terms of an attack on the castle, Wallace could see then that the bridge had its advantages; it would certainly slow an army down; but in terms of this particular offence, it was suicidal. He sent orders across the hills to his waiting men. They would attack the advancing soldiers, before all could cross, and the signal would be his arrival on the field.

He then stripped to just his kilt and had his entire upper body, and the body of his magnificent black stallion, coated in the blood colored war paint he had reserved for this occasion.

He encouraged Hamish and the others to douse themselves as well. In the sunlight they appeared to be ablaze, engulfed by iridescent flames. As they prepared to take the field, one of his men said that they looked as if they had emerged from the gates of hell.

Wallace watched and waited until he reckoned about one half of the British army were on his side of the river. It was eleven o'clock in the morning; time to make his move.

With Warenne's army split on two sides of the impassable river, and in disarray, Wallace suddenly appeared, as if by magic, on a low rise above the disorganized British troops.

At the incredible sight, every one of them fell silent. The breeze flicked at and tossed about his long gleaming red hair; it seemed a halo of flames leaping and dancing; an aurora around his head.

Just his name terrorized most of these poor miserable illiterate sods, none had ever seen him. Then out of the glare of the dazzling sunlight came a blazing, giant, mythical creature; engulfed in fire and brandishing a huge sword from which it seemed lightening bolts slashed the sky.

And then for several moments it remained, poised upon the hilltop. Thousands of soldiers fell to their knees, begging the Lord's mercy.

The field was his. Wallace stood in his stirrups, held his massive Claymore high for all to see, and roared to the frightened English, the battlecry — "Freedom." And at that second all the hell that so many feared, broke loose.

The clash was enormous and furious. But William knew his fanatical highlanders. They ignored sword and pike, and came like a swarm of bees from all sides at those who had made it to the north side of the bridge. The English were overwhelmed so suddenly and could not structure themselves into their normally effective battle formations. Only a small number of heavy horse chargers had crossed, but Hamish's deadly javelin throwers quickly speared them from their saddles, and ran the horses off to safety behind Scottish lines.

None of the English archers had crossed, and their attempts to lob arrows across the river had little effect. The battle was up to the foot soldiers, and sensing they didn't have the numbers or the advantage, many panicked. Some tried to retreat back over the bridge, only to cause a disastrous bottleneck for the continuing flow of advancing troops.

Others, desperate to escape, leapt into the churning water and tried to swim for it and were swept away by the high tide current.

William never left the battlefield. Leading his Scots as they hacked and slashed and stabbed their way through the remainder of the English force; driving some to choose the river as an alternative death. The more experienced Scottish fighters stole weapons and armor as they went, making them even more formidable in their relentless slaughter.

Within an hour William controlled the bridge, and his men were pouring over it onto the south side, where the demoralized British were in wild retreat. The unprotected archers had exhausted most of their arrows, and were running in desperation. They were of no value to protect what remained of the cavalry; and the will to fight had gone out of the foot soldiers.

Wallace's first order upon taking the bridge, had been to seize all the horses and use them against the retreating soldiers — "every Englishman is to die" — no one to his knowledge would be allowed to escape.

~

It was a sound no one wanted to remember. The noise of horrific death; not the clashing of swords, metal on metal; not the cannons roar. It was the unimaginable sound of the human price of war. The mayhem, the panic and the bloodshed had been more than even some of the young Scots could stomach.

Many of the devout, no longer thought it a joke – they had crossed into hell.

Within another hour, close to eighty thousand warriors had clashed on one square mile of meadowland, and in two short hours, every English soldier, who could be found, lay slain. Even for those who tried to retreat, it was in vain. They were relentlessly pursued, and hacked to pieces. Only four thousand Scots lost their lives.

~

The attack had come so suddenly, and there were so many Scots, everywhere and all at once, that DeCressingham had panicked, and in trying to flee, had spurred his horse so furiously that it bolted and reared in fright. The priest, being so fat and ungainly, lost his seat and was easily thrown. Under the crush of his own weight the fall broke both his legs, and he was left to flail and scream helplessly on the ground, while all the others with him, equally panic-stricken, sought whatever means of escape they could find.

He had tried to pull himself to safety, away from the fighting; certain that if he could get to the castle, he would be rescued. Unfortunately he crawled in the wrong direction.

As the battle raged on, just a few yards from his hiding place, he managed to lie still for the two hours, feigning dead. He might as well have been; his fear was so great that he had expelled his own excrement repeatedly, thereby smelling and appearing to be dead.

Eventually the fighting wore down, and for a time he believed he had been spared. Until he realized that the flailing Scottish swords and axes were not being wielded in defense; but were desecrating what was left of the English. The victorious Scots were ravaging the battlefield, and those approaching him, were searching the river's edge, stealing from, and hacking every English body to bits. Cressingham began to scream hysterically, and his bowels completely gave way.

It was William who heard and found the crippled, and terrified Priest cowering and sobbing hysterically in some blood splattered bushes by the river. William had been foraging for his own wounded, and recognized the hated face immediately: the ugly, round ball with its tiny oval mouth and pee-hole eyes.

So eager was he, to see this man dead, that he leapt from his horse and raising his gore-stained sword, was about to decapitate him. DeCressingham's screams for mercy were not the deterrent. A sudden voice within stopped William. This was too great a spoil to be snuffed right then and there. Others, who had suffered more than he at this man's hands, were the rightful one's to decide his fate.

Listening to him beg and plead, made winning all the more sweet. This day's battle was providence. It could mean separation for Scotland, if everything was handled right. Freedom from one hundred years of tyranny under the English bastards.

There was no way Wallace could carry this huge bulk by himself, nor did he wish the filthy, stinking burden on any man or horse. He called for his men to rope Cressingham by his ankles, even though it was obvious both his legs were broken, and drag him to the battlements and there to suspend him in a post frame, until he, Wallace, could arrive.

Cressingham was a coward, but had always had his clerical office and robes to hide behind.

This would not be the case now. He was very clever at waving his role as a churchman, to claim immunity and justification for the consequences of his earthly endeavors. He excused his cruelty and avariciousness by preaching that the condition of the life of every man was either a reward for his godliness, or atonement for his sins.

He reasoned that all of these lowly Scots, therefore were sinners. Why else would God have delivered his servant, himself, into their midst. He saw himself as their redeemer; and their redemption was fealty to their rightful lord and master, the First Edward, King of England, Scotland, Wales and Northern Ireland.

"Well," thought Wallace, "maybe Cressingham was right about atonement, God had delivered this scum to him."

By four o'clock the same evening, William Wallace stood triumphant on the battlements of Stirling Castle, his Claymore held high.

Twenty-five thousand delirious, exhausted Scotsmen, standing knee deep in the now infested carrion of English bodies, which spread to every corner of the battlefield and beyond, wildly cheered and loudly paid homage to their valiant leader.

The fat priest hung in a frame, high on a parapet, skinned alive.

Every inch of flesh, from his neck to his ankles, had been expertly peeled away. There remained, suspended between the posts, only the hideous resemblance of a man. A grotesquely distorted face atop mutilated sinew, bleeding muscle and snow-white bone. Large slabs of yellow fat and cellulite, which accounted for his enormous bulk, dangled from the grisly sight, mixing with dripping blood and excrement.

Every slice of skin symbolized the peeling away of a hundred years that his people had suffered oppression. The victims were now the victors. His army: commoners; farmers and peasants. No woman in Scotland had been safe from rape or sexual servitude; no man or woman was safe from murder; and none were spared from slavery. Now it was over.

William Wallace and his cousin, Hamish McCaulagh Campbell, sat in special chairs, and watched in unperturbed silence, as the execution took place. When the abattoir had finished carefully slicing away the last strip of skin, Wallace stood, picked up his sword, and prodded the dangling figure. The screaming had stopped.

"'Tis too bad, Hamish, I think it's dead." Wallace sounded disappointed. "I'd hoped we could 'ave kept him alive 'til the end."

"The butcher was good, but not that good, Wil." Hamish hurled his dagger at the hanging meat. It stuck. "I'll take the strips to the tanner. You'll be writin' love letters on 'em by tomorrow. " Hamish hated the priest. His family had been burnt out by this churchman. "The fuckin' bastard," he snarled, as he plunged the protruding knife clean to its hilt into the torso.

"There's one more gift to send to that fuckin' little faggot in London." With that, Wallace raised his heavy Claymore, and with one mighty stroke he severed the head and a piece of the shoulder clean off. The roar from the battlefield below was deafening.

V

The following day, Wallace, his cousins, several Scottish nobles, and all the clan leaders met, for the first time, in the Great Hall of Stirling. Here, they learned the outcome of the battle.

"How many?" asked Wallace.

"Every last fuckin' one of 'em," said Hamish. "You seen any red coats walkin' around this place in the last twenty four hours!" He was pleased with himself.

"Hamish, was there not at least fifty thousand of them." Asked one of the clan's leaders. "How could it be? Are you sure?," Everyone looked incredulous.

"All ... fifty ... thousand ... of ... them." Hamish slowly enunciated each word. Cheers went up from the room.

"What about our lads?" asked another.

"From the consensus taken with all the leaders, about four thousand." The room went silent. The odds were amazing, but it was still a lot of brave men to have lost.

Wallace spoke next. "Even one Scot dyin' is too many. Now a lot of brave lads died here, and it sure as fuck won't be for nothin'." His expressionless eyes went from noble to noble, who had taken the prominent positions around the meeting table.

In his gaze there was no effort to mask his distrust and dislike for some. The King of England had bought most of them in the past; he could do so again. His faith extended to one only, the young Earl of Carrick, the one they called Robert the Bruce. "Our lads won, gentlemen. With no armor, no heavy horse; with rusted old swords and sharp sticks — and they won. We've been given somethin' here, and we're not givin' it back. The English are out. We've given you lot back your country. It's yours to govern, but we'll be watchin'."

Now it was time to instill fear. Upon each strip of Cressingham's flesh was written a message to the King of England, telling of the total annihilation of the English forces at Stirling Bridge. Also written was his warning to the English King to never set foot on Scottish soil again, lest the same fate befall him.

Warenne had predicted all of this. He had argued the futility in trying to fight Wallace on that plain.

It had been the parsimony of DeCressingham, which had handicapped the English forces. The ugly priest had left them no choice other than to cross that bridge. It was a vain hope that they could get enough troops to the other side before Wallace could come at them. It was well known that the Scots were hiding in those surrounding hills, and he knew that it was just a matter of time and British arrogance, and they would be drawn into Wallace's trap.

His troops hadn't survived two hours and for them he wept bitterly. It wasn't until later when he heard of DeCressingham's fate, that he felt some relief and a sense of payback.

VI

The King of England was in Flanders, on route to the coastal town of Port De Panne on the North Sea, when he got the news of Stirling.

It was not the only bad news he had to deal with. The campaign in Europe had been of near equal disaster.

Daily, heavy cold rains had turned fields into quagmires, gentle streams into raging torrents and hoof sucking bogs where roads once existed. Moving large numbers of cavalry became impossible, and no amount of planning made battle a reality. His efforts to reinforce his hold on Flanders had been futile, and even more, any hope of sustaining a force on the continent through the winter was dashed. And now, this news marked the end of any more time he could spend in Europe.

The first in the village to react were the dogs. Some barked and growled frantically, and others winged, cowered and wet continuously. At first the sound was barely detectable, away off in the distance. People's ears prickled, trying to define it, this slight vibration in the air, the ground, in everything. Then it grew louder and louder until it was like the sound of roaring water, descending upon the town of Port de Panne.

The specter of Edward and his one hundred men-at-arms, mounted upon their massive war horses, fully clad in heavy protective armor, charging at full gallop, would have, in other places, caused pandemonium.

Fortunately for the busy, seafaring town, the King and his men chose to ride the shipping road that, for practical reasons, circled the town and avoided the residential and commercial streets.

There was no way they could have maneuvered the narrow streets without trampling to death anyone or thing caught in their way.

The town's livelihood was wholly dependent on the sea, and so it was the necessity of this highway that spared the town and its inhabitants. This too made it ideal for the comings and goings of a King's army.

Bordering the docks and facing the harbor was the heart and soul of the port; a raucous, brawling collection of brightly lit, brightly colored taverns, cheap hotels and whore houses; it was life to its endless stream of playboys, hustlers, sailors, soldiers, drunks and prostitutes.

The sight presented a continuous semi-circle of three-story, timber frame buildings. The businesses of innkeepers, publicans, pimps, money-lenders, shipping brokers, lawyers, chandlers and weapons dealers.

The same style of construction continued up-town; only to serve a more discreet level of commerce and housing: bakers, butchers, up-scale inns and public houses, doctors, accountants,

more lawyers, dry goods retailers, the cathedral, and the courtesans of the working trade.

Further on, as one climbed away from the sea, these same streets gave way to larger residences; thence to the suburbs and landed estates; and finally to the local Lord's castle.

Moored in the bay were the hundreds of small vessels, which plied the daily trade of the town. Tied dockside were three large merchant vessels along with his Majesty's Royal Frigate, The Dover.

It was not a gentle evening. Most people were indoors. Some businesses were closing for the day; for others bad weather signaled gearing up. As usual a hard rain began falling, and the wind, which had played havoc with the moorings all day, was now blowing with such force that it threatened to wreck most of the smaller boats tethered in the bay.

The scene on the pier had become a melee of muddied, sweating, swearing men, and muddied, sweating, high-strung horses. Rank clouds of steam rose from the huge beasts; their rich, equine blood still fired, still wanting to run. They danced and skittered and occasionally reared at the end of tightly held reins.

Edward turned his great white over to its personal groom with instructions to rub the animal down, bathe and wrap his legs, and bed him on fresh straw. It was the same for all these prize stallions — their welfare came before that of their devoted masters.

The King was soaked through and chilled to the bone, but he refused to take shelter.

It was his punishment, and this his penance. Just as others swore fealty to him, his fealty was to God, and he knew that if he hid from Him, things would only get worse.

Longshanks devoutly believed in his Divine connection. As he looked to the heavens and the coming storm, he felt God's hand as if about to strike him. The heavy, blackened, churning clouds began to spit fire and roar in anger, bemoaning his folly, and the tragedy he faced at home.

Wallace had not only spilled a great deal of English blood, he had rocked the Throne of England. It worried him that this could be the deciding factor in the on-going see-saw for power which teetered between the King's forces and those of the Barons who opposed his absolute power. Edward ruled now because the balance was currently in his favor, but that could change in a heartbeat if he was seen weak or ineffective.

These European conflicts were no longer applauded as the first priority of his Monarchy, and most of his nobles were openly critical of his constant absence. How he governed at home was now the major issue; the growing unrest of the people, and the urgent need for change was not lost on him.

His first act would be to give England back her pride. He would show these ignorant Celts what it meant to prick the Lion. He was Edward the First, King of England, Scotland, Wales, Ireland, Gascony, Aquitaine; Lord of Normandy, Guienne, and Protector of Flanders; and his mighty hand was the account for it all. "The only part of Wallace that will ever come near my Throne," he promised, "will be his head, stuck on the end of my sword."

His worlds had collided. And although striking back at Scotland might be a solution to part of the problem, he had more than Wallace to blame for it. Time was running out for him, and therefore for England.

~

His Parliament, his own creation, was already divided on the issue, and the boy was just thirteen years old. It was no secret that the cousins hated the youngster, and looked for every excuse to demand a regent, until an acceptable Heir was found or born.

The Throne was safe for now, but Gloucester and Lancaster, individually, were powerful enough to seize control, given enough provocation. Imagine what they could be capable of together.

How could these loins have produced such a foundling wretch?

He ordered that they sail as soon as possible. He was not in the mood for conversation, and remained by himself on the upper cockpit, aft of the pilot. This gave him a remarkably high vantage point, not only to serve as watch and observe the loading of horses, men and supplies, but so that all could clearly see him.

He was well aware of his impressive physical stature. Even at his age younger women and no trouble finding his bed.

Both of his wives, the first and exquisite, passionate Eleanor, now passed, and now the delicate, sweet Marguerite, each admitted to finding the sight of his naked muscular body tantalizing.

He hadn't yet removed any of his heavy chain battle gear, save his protective helmet, even though the metal added to his chill. He shut that out of his mind. As long as those serving him were made too busy to seek shelter, so he would remain.

There wasn't the usual boistering that accompanied the loading of a ship. All went about their tasks subdued by the pain and the helplessness they felt over the tragic news from home. Every one had heard the details. For some it meant great personal loss, and out of respect, none talked.

As he watched the loading, he searched for answers. How could it have happened? British troops are the best armed, best trained in the world; never mind they outnumbered the Scots; and Warenne may be old, but he is a military genius ... "Let your enemies see your hands," he always told his soldiers. "They carry the message of your intentions. If your hands are seen as ready, your enemy will know you are ready."

Edward looked down at his own chain mail and leather gloves, blood stained and battle scarred. Were they not testimony to his brave command?

"I should have been there," he chastised himself. "I should have led them? Why was there not a battle plan? How could Warenne have left himself so open? And if he didn't have enough men — why didn't he wait for more?"

Then there was this damn problem. This fighting with the French was blatant stupidity. Nothing was ever resolved and he always ended up losing good men and horses.

The rivalry between the King of France and himself was not healthy for either empire. There were other, greedy, prying eyes, lusting for the rich lands on either side of this narrow channel — eager, hungry and waiting for us to weaken each other. "And besides," he mused, thinking especially of not only his late wife, but of his current one as well, "French aristocrats both, and French nobility provide a great source of English Royal brides. Their women are beautiful, generous lovers, and cleaner."

~

An enormous bolt of lightening struck in the hills behind the town, shaking the valley. It reminded him of those treacherous, Prussian cousins of his, and Philippe's — "always wanting more territory, always coveting, and always ready to strike. And right along behind them, is that filthy Russian fellow, Romanoff. They say his barbaric hordes could outnumber Philippe and I put together — if he ever got them organized.

Even Philippe! Never mind he's my brother-in-law, he's still Capetian — God curse the old pirate. He would spring on us in the blink of an eye if he thought our belly had softened. Never mind that his youngest sister is now my new wife, I sometimes believe that he is the worst of his blood-thirsty lot."

He could visualize his enemies coming at him from all sides — within and without. "The French would love the opportunity to take England, especially now, if they thought Scotland would hold the door open for them."

Whenever Longshanks thought of his kingdom, which was now frequently, he thought of his young son Edward, his namesake, and his blood rose.

Now, with this disaster, he was forced to make an unimaginable decision. If it were anyone else, the solution would have been simple.

There was no doubt his son wanted the title of King, and the power; he just didn't want to be a King. This absence had been a test, and the Prince had failed it miserably. The disaster would only make the case against the boy, even stronger.

Against his better judgment, he had taken the bold step of nominating the young Edward as Regent in his absence. The decision had outraged the entire House of Lords and incurred violent opposition from the King's two powerful cousins, the Earls of Gloucester and Lancaster.

Lancaster was the high steward of England, and the chair was rightfully his.

Both had demanded that he fill the post, citing the fragile nature of the problems with Scotland and Wales, pointing out that this was no time to let the younger play at being King. But the senior Edward felt certain he was doing the right thing. He had been convinced that this was the very best time for his son to show his mettle and earn respect. He had been explicit with the boy, and assured Lancaster that nothing would escape the elder statesman's attention, no matter how trivial.

Nevertheless, the cousin had become so angry at the King's stubbornness, that he virtually threatened a mutiny of the House. Edward knew, in his heart, that Lancaster would never perpetrate such a thing; but as he departed for Flanders, tempers were hot, and had remained so. This mess would only make things worse, and could be the breaking point for his son. He had failed in the most shameful and humiliating of ways possible.

~

His thoughts were interrupted by the insistent urgency in his captain's voice. "Sire, excuse me sire, I beg your pardon."

"Yes Captain, it's quite all right — you're not disturbing me." He was relieved to be distracted. Longshanks very much liked this highly capable young Captain, and clasped his shoulder. "What is it my friend, what can I do for you?"

"Sire, Lieutenant DeGaveston hasn't shown yet, and we cannot remain docked for too much longer, lest the ship rest aground. With the storm, the tide is going out much faster, Sire, and unless we ...!"

"Yes, yes, I understand. How much longer, at best?"

"Twenty minutes, Sire, no more. With this wind, and rough seas, we'll have to depart on an upwind tack, and that will make our going slower."

"Carry on, Captain."

"Thank you Sire," and with that preparations to set sail were underway. The young Commander never uttered a word of the danger that lay ahead. He trusted himself, he trusted this ship. It would be a rough go, but he would make it.

From where the King stood, he could observe and feel the strength of this excellent warship. Her length to the bowsprit was one hundred and sixty feet, and her beam at midships, sixty feet. Efficient, and fast, she carried four masts and twenty cannons; and for this voyage comfortably ferried one hundred prized fighting men and horses.

From the aft deck and above the pilot's quarters he could better command, share in the duty watch, and aide his helmsman in the event of a bad storm or attack, while keeping a constant presence on deck — fair or foul. He saw what it did for morale.

The captain and crew admired this King, so did most of his military. His soldiers were loyal, and he could count on them to serve him, no matter the cost. Would they do so for his son? It was at this moment that he realized he had not yet seen DeGaveston arrive. "Arnold, where in the name of hell are you," he said under his breath. Obviously something was wrong. DeGaveston had only been a mile or two behind, as was planned. He should be here by now.

Then he felt the ship move. The gangway had been raised and the ports battened. He watched as the lines were tossed, and the Dover slipped away from the docks, and across the harbor. His valuable friend was on his own.

VII

All of the Prince's friends and playmates of choice were either boys or young men.

Normally this would not be a worrisome thing, but the youngster's so-called friends were not exactly what Edward called the flower of England's manhood. Most boys loved to play games of war; play at sports; and at thirteen should be eager to learn to what part of a female's anatomy, their anatomy should attach. Not so for the Prince and his friends who preferred games of dress-up, and philandering about with London society absorbed in dashing about trying to outdo one another with the most outrageous piece of gossip.

He had come to see his own son as dissolute, and this was a terrible way for a father to think. This creature would one day assume the much-feared Throne of a great empire, and the signs were already there, he was not fit to rule. Without a strong hand to guide him, the King could visualize it all crumbling into a wastrel's junket, and falling prey to the ever-present European jackals. Just as these scavenging, low creatures were dependant on the lion for their survival; so they would devour the lion when he was down.

Yet for young Edward's weakness, he blamed himself.

The boy was spoiled, and molly-coddled. Regrettably all of his children were. Nothing had been too good for his family. He had put their comfort above protocol, even going so far as to move the official Royal household sixty miles outside of London. A move, which greatly and adversely affected communication with the Court.

Ever since he could remember, he had always wondered why The Tower was considered the official Royal palace, when there was so much better around. It was a cold, ugly building; half palace, half prison, in the worst part of London.

It was originally designed as a barracks, and the interior offered no luxuries whatsoever. The Royal Bedchamber was nothing more than a cubbyhole in the wall, and all of their tiny apartments gave them a wonderful view of the prisoner's yard.

He had changed all that. It was his reign, it would be his call. The official palace had to be the best that King and kingdom could offer, and there was only one — Windsor Castle. It would be his Camelot.

Those days were his favorite memories.

The serendipitous life at Windsor better suited his beautiful family. There they were surrounded by thousands of acres of rolling meadows and dense forests, filled with game, and perfect for every kind of Royal sport and adventure.

Better than the squalor of London streets. Here he had kept the finest stables in all of the British Isles, horses being his late wife Eleanor's passion. There they would ride, sometimes all day, when the sun was warm and the air sweet, alone, talking — those were the days when he hadn't been so feared, so hated.

Stopping by wherever their fancy took them, with a picnic lunch, and those fine French wines; they would make love, slowly and tenderly. Her fine, eager body filled him with a hunger. She would lead and he would follow, to depths of joy and passion that he had not felt before or since.

All he needed to do was close his eyes and think of her, and he could actually feel the heat of their locked bodies; and after, bathing each other in a cold, fresh stream.

He could lose himself in those memories, and often did, dreaming he was back there. Sometimes he wished he could sleep, and never waken. So often now did his dreams take him to her.

~

The young Edward was the only one of the children for whom Windsor may have not provided an ideal upbringing.

The youngest and preceded by five girls, he became their charge; like a new doll, to play with, amuse and practice at being little mothers.

Protected by distance and walls, the young royals were not exposed to any of the vagaries of life that they may have experienced in London.

They invented their own games, conjuring heroes and villains, and settling matters in their own secret Court.

Childhood friends were judged according to rules established by the sisters and those deemed unsuitable were ceremoniously and figuratively executed — banished from any association whatsoever. Of the male children brought as playmates, the ones not willing to participate at his sisters' games were cruelly rejected.

How wrong he, the father, had been to ignore this, but he had believed that it was better for children to sort out their own friendships.

It came to be that, in addition to the youngster being indulged in the most feline of ways, he was tutored mainly to see life only from a female perspective. He had no understanding in the ways of a man's world.

As he grew into boyhood and young manhood, he then preferred only the company of females or those who acted like females. As a result his mannerisms and temperament were markedly female. And he languished in the protected, soft, uninvolved world of the Royal women.

They were pampered, and waited upon hand and foot. It was not just for custom, nor done for effect; it was doctrine.

By them were carried the seeds of Royal children; hence they were special; women of a divine destiny. Edward expected to be treated the same way. As he was still not much older than an infant, much of this was ignored, until the King made a surprising and unprecedented move.

Young Edward's uncle, the Earl of Gloucester, "hated the intolerable little wretch." He told his wife, the Heir's aunt by blood, "there's not an endearing bone in his repulsive body, and if he ever becomes King, I'll kill the horrible little bastard." Gloucester was not the only one who felt this way.

Edward had seen none of it. Yet it had become the cause of a rift between his cousin and himself.

How clever he had thought he had been, creating the House of the Prince of Wales; and how angry his cousin had been when it was voted into law.

When the Prince turned five, Edward made him Regent of a newly created principality. He became the first Prince of Wales, without having to earn it, defend it or fight for one foot of it.

In retrospect, later Royals came to be grateful, as it was a clever and farsighted move on the part of his father.

The Household and Principality had been created, in perpetuity, to be thence assumed by every Heir to the Throne of England.

The title would virtually guarantee the ascendancy, not only as a divine right, but as the will of the people.

The seat had been proposed by the King, but voted into existence by both the Houses of Commons and Lords. A clever manipulation indeed.

Only minutes after the vote was taken, Edward was in the Throne Room, when Gloucester burst through the door, ranting. "Very clever Edward, very bloody clever indeed!"

"Excuse me cousin, is it not customary to at least knock before you enter the King's office?" Edward was mildly offended, but Gloucester held higher sway than most.

"Excuse me, cousin," came the angry reply. "I am just as royal as you, and have as much right in this room as you. You will not tell me to knock!"

"What's up his ass?" thought Edward, becoming annoyed. "Fine! Don't knock then." The two glared at each other. "So, what do you want? You obviously have some kind of problem?"

"This won't work!"

"What won't?"

"This new principality. Making your son Prince of Wales, It won't work!"

"What the hell are you talking about?" Edward was getting mad. What kind of stupid talk was this? "What's your problem? The idea is brilliant. It's the best damn thing that could ever happen to this whole family."

"How so?" Gloucester didn't see it.

"Don't you get it? It guarantees the Throne, and by guaranteeing the Throne, it guarantees the future of the family. What's so wrong with that?"

"No, no. What you've done will see all our heads chopped off. You can't force your son on the empire — you're asking for civil war." Gloucester was shaking his head, and pacing erratically about the room.

"What do you mean — force my son? My son is the natural Heir, like it or not, and by God he will be your King. The nobles don't go about choosing, no matter how liberal we've become." Edward could feel his temper rising.

"Edward, you're wrong. Up to now, the nobles have chosen. You, your father, our grandfather were each kings because the nobility and the rest of the family, were in favor of each, at the time. The birthright is sanctioned, cousin — not absolute."

"Well, my so clever cousin, that also left the Royal Family up to the vote; and now that's taken care of, isn't it. How far out of line would you and your royal wife be, if I hadn't been sanctioned? Think about that. You are now the first cousin of the King — by sanction. Which means you have lands and titles you might otherwise not. How would you like it if you had been passed over, just because somebody else had been sanctioned?"

"Edward, what you say is all too clear, and I would never dispute legislation to protect the family, but what you've done could backfire. Your son is very unpopular, and most are adamantly opposed to his succession." Gloucester expected an explosion.

Instead calm. "Why? There is no reason. He is only a child."

"Only to you, cousin. To others he's intolerable. He's an obnoxious child, and no one is ready to hear that he is the absolute Heir. Not yet. Not now." Gloucester knew he could be truthful with the King, to a point. But there was nothing to be gained by pushing it. "He's got to be older, earn respect. Show the Baronage he's deserving. Right now, Edward, he's anything but."

It was a good point. He didn't like hearing it, but it made sense. However, he couldn't let Gloucester think that he could be persuaded that easily. "Cousin, I will think about it."

Gloucester was right. He couldn't afford to alienate the Baronage. They were his primary source of income and military support.

So he had compromised, but again he had been clever. He kept the newly created principality, but would hold off nominating his son as its head for another eight years.

Now he realized he had bought time, but nothing else.

Over the years Edward sought every way imaginable to turn his son into a man, and one deserving of the Throne.

Miraculously he had managed to keep the Heir's questionable proclivities from public view, but once on his own, the boy quickly proved to be the disappointment expected.

~

Edward had gone to Flanders believing that the problems there were more urgent. The situation in Scotland appeared to be well in hand.

He had not known that the boy ignored Warenne's and Cressingham's urgent dispatches, being otherwise preoccupied.

The Prince got the message when Wallace had Cressingham's severed head delivered in a sack, to be dumped at his table. He had screamed himself into apoplexy.

Meanwhile the entire northern army had been wiped out.

VIII

The Forth River ran crimson for days, carrying the sludge and decay of human remains. The battlefield became so putrid with rotting carrion, and so thickly infested with vermin, that the fields for miles around Stirling had to be fired, and kept burning for days.

Meanwhile, the young Edward had been completely absorbed by his main interest.

Because of his money and power, he could snap his fingers and receive anything he wished. This impressed his friends, and he loved to play the part. Now with his father away, he could show London how a real King should act. Maybe his father would be killed this time!

He let it be known that there would be a party each week, and that each party would be to honor the friend who had pleased him most during that week.

And to make things even more exciting, he had all the latest fashions imported from southern Europe, and rewarded anyone who attracted his attention with their pick.

He and his growing coterie were soon up to Westminster's rafters parading the latest ensembles around London. This excitement always meant that the parties and games and delicious new pretty boys, never ended.

As the favorites streamed to his bed, the gifts became even more lavish. He loved how they fawned and worshiped and easily did his bidding, as he conferred minor titles, and awarded Royal properties to those who gave him the greatest pleasure. This was power, and he loved it.

Given the boy was just thirteen years old, Edward blamed himself, and raged inwardly at his own stupidity for underestimating the Scots. But he still wanted some answers.

He was also furious with Lancaster, first cousin by birth, and Edward knew that Lancaster considered them equals. The powerful Earl never hid his opinion that he could do the job just as well — if not better. Edward tolerated this. That way his cousin took his responsibilities seriously, and so Edward trusted him implicitly. So why was he not on top of the situation?

Lancaster was there to meet the King when he arrived at Westminster. Both wanted a piece of the other.

Edward jumped first, and tore into the waiting Earl, the minute he entered the Throne Room. "Why in God's name did you not help Warenne? Why? Just because you objected to my son as regent, you wouldn't help him, you wouldn't advise him, why, why?" he was shouting.

In this ornate and elegant room of white, red and gold, a room reserved for ceremony, where decorum and quiet dissertation was the rule, the King exploded. He kicked chairs and hurled articles at the walls and windows. He tore his chain mail toque from his head and lashed it across the surface of the huge, oak table, which dominated the room. Like a harrow, it slid most of the length, carving in its wake a long, jagged, white scar.

Lancaster was not afraid of the King, and the insult set him instantly to the boil. He leapt from his seat, hurling it backwards, "Edward," he bellowed, deliberately side stepping the title, " shut up or I'll knock you down, and you know I will," his clenched fist was raised to strike. He had no weapon.

The King's hand went for his sword, but he didn't draw it. "Cousin, be careful." The tone of his voice was low and flat. His anger and frustration had pushed him to the breaking point. The cousin was infuriated by the gesture, and stepped menacingly closer. "Edward, your son is a complete and utter moron." Lancaster's eyes were blazing and his face, a mask of fury. He was not about to spare feelings. "I did not know Warenne was calling for help — none of us did! The dispatches came directly to your son, where they lay, unopened, while he hugged the cabin boy. The stupid little queer was too busy parading his pretty little troop around London to pay any attention to business. I am not sure if he was even aware of Warenne's predicament.

The news didn't reach me until it was all over, and then only because Wallace wanted me to know." As the words spilled out, he calmed down. So did the King.

For several seconds, Edward stood motionless, his hand gripping the hilt of his sword, desperately wanting to rail against something, somebody. The torment of his mis-trust, confusion and utter disappointment, breaking his old heart. A moment ago, he had been ready to kill his trusted and loyal cousin, now Edward was completely deflated. He slumped to his chair, utterly despondent.

"I'm sorry, your Majesty, none of us knew." Lancaster said quietly, again using his title, feeling now more sympathy than anger.

"Where is my boy now," it was almost a whisper.

"I think he is at Langley, dear cousin, but I am not sure." Lancaster was guessing to try and be helpful. It turned out he was right.

~

The King rode through the early morning and reached Langley at about dawn. The small palace was quiet; it seemed deserted; not even a guard to acknowledge his arrival. If the ride had calmed him in any way, the effect had been erased. What more could this boy do to inflame a father's ire?

He stormed into the house and and went straight to his son's room. There he found him more passed out than asleep, sprawled across his bed, with two others, whom he'd never seen before. He was relieved, and thanked God they were clothed, but the sight was the last straw.

It was the first of only two times that he was ever to strike the boy, but his anger was too great, the boy's ignorance too appalling, and the loss too painful, for him to go unpunished.

Edward grabbed his son by the hair, as he slept, and violently hauled him from his bed. The boy screamed, which in turn, caused the other two to suddenly awake and start screaming. Without speaking, he dragged him, stumbling and tripping, through the building and out to a waiting carriage.

Hurling him inside, he ordered the driver back to London, to Westminster, and to keep the boy imprisoned in the carriage until he arrived. Under no circumstances was he to be let out.

It took until the following evening, before Edward could convene a session of the House of Lords. It was only then that he released the Heir from his confinement. He had been kept in the carriage, without food or water or a toilet break, for the entire day. It was October.

Once the House had assembled, Edward went to the carriage, and in the same fashion as he had placed him there, grabbed the boy and hauled him bodily into the assembly.

The room exploded into an uproar of shock and surprise at the scene before them, of the King standing center floor, gripping his blubbering, frightened son by the hair. It took some time for the speaker to restore order. All the while the King stood silent and waited for calm, maintaining the cruel grip on the boy.

When there was silence, he immediately spoke right to the point. "My dear gentlemen and valued Lords of the realm. You all know what happened at Stirling. It remains painful for all of us. But please know, I do not blame any of you. I know that none of you were made aware of Lord Warenne's predicament. For that, only one alone can take responsibility.

For the crime of ignorance, for not attending to those duties assigned him, and for disrespect to this House, withholding vital information, whether he understood it or not, I place the burden of fault solely upon my son and it is he who shall pay." He angrily jerked his youngster's head back so that all could see his reddened, tear stained, terrified face.

"Look at him. This is a pathetic excuse for a human being, and he wants to one day be your King, your ruler. He will want you to respect him, to follow him. Are you prepared to accept him, to accept his leadership?"

He let the question hang for a few moments. Then he continued, " If he is ever to earn your respect, then he must learn at your hands," and with that he hurled him to the floor.

"Gentlemen," his voice intensified to the deep powerful roar for which he was famous, "He was assigned to represent this Crown, to act like a King, and to respect your office. He let you down, he let England down — you decide his fate!" And with a dismissive wave, the King of England turned, and without a glance at his groveling son, strode out of the House of Lords, not once looking back. The life of the Prince, and hence the question of his succession, was in their hands.

As the massive oak doors closed behind him Edward could barely contain his pleasure. His performance had just saved both of them.

Too few of those men were cold hearted enough to do what he would have done. He truly wanted his son punished, but not at the cost of the crown. He knew that his display of a King caught between bias and the despair of a broken hearted father, would appease his chief executives, and when word spread, would appease most of England as well.

As he expected, none were prepared to take up the offer. Many came to him later agreeing that the boy had been too young to understand the gravity of the role, even at that terrible cost. Only Lancaster remained steadfast in his hatred and openly accused the King of grandstanding.

For some time afterward, Edward thought he might have won his son over. The Prince appeared to be contrite and eager to learn from his lesson; to become a worthy Heir— it wasn't to last. However, it no longer mattered. It gave the King time to work out the perfect plan to save his kingdom.

FALKIRK

Chapter 3

1297 - 1305 AD

/

Wallace was sensing that the very people who should benefit most from his victory at Stirling, did not seem very grateful.

Those whom he had expected would rally around him, were instead avoiding his company, and openly bemoaning the injury to England. He had handed Scotland back to its nobility on a platter, and they wanted no part of it.

The people's victory seemed now a hollow one.

In the days that followed the battle, village prefects, elders and clan leaders from all over southern Scotland, decked out in their finest, flocked to his new headquarters at Stirling Castle, to pay their respects. He was moved by the unconditional, and often emotional demonstrations of loyalty from these, the common people, but it was the smallest part of what he needed, and it saddened him.

Even as he smiled gratefully into the stream of devoted, worshiping old eyes that paid homage to him on a daily basis, he was tortured by a growing despondency at how many more young and old Scots would have to die; and maybe to no avail.

Deceptively the first nobles had gone so far as to bestow a knighthood on him – not as a reward, as he originally believed – but ironically as an inducement to join their club.

Even as John DeBalliol, the country's self-anointed King, performed the ceremony, they were squabbling over how they would make amends to England.

Balliol, ever the politician, was using him as an opportunity to feather his own nest by appearing staunchly on the side of the people. Otherwise none of the Scottish Barons, including Balliol, were prepared to support any further campaigns against England. Even though some had been with him at Stirling, as the contemplation of Edward's wrath became paranoia some were openly voicing the opinion that perhaps Wallace should be turned over.

William heard rumors that Balliol was plotting to discredit him and cautioning some clan leaders that their support of him could backfire. He accused William of being a sadist, a monster who had found the perfect excuse for his brutal killings and warned leaders that he was nothing more than a low-minded rebel whose popularity with the bloodthirsty masses was dangerous.

Most knew Wallace to be clever, instinctive and anything but low minded, but Balliol was persuasive in gathering support.

By decrying the feudal way of life, and blaming England for all of their troubles, William had performed a miracle with the people. In the past the best attempts at rebellion, which had kept Edward busy from time to time, were comprised of localized unruly mobs whose dissatisfaction flared every now and then, resulting in ineffective skirmishes with British garrisons.

Wallace had changed all of that. He had turned the unruly mobs into a vast, organized militia, an army of one mind whose numbers were linked throughout the length and breadth of Scotland, and who to a man had become skilled at banding together at a moment's notice.

Now, with Stirling as horrific proof, not only was the baronial feudal system at stake, so was England's hold over Scotland. None of Scotland's feudal lords had any great desire to see an independent country. This could mean the total loss of their titles and estates.

Many of them were of mixed blood, English and Scottish, and French, and a few were even married into or related in some fashion to the British Royal Family. What would happen to them if Wallace succeeded?

The privileged way of life was all that mattered, all that they knew. The freedom of peasants held no significance over their own fate, and their loyalties were to whatever or whomever supported it. Wallace, and the common people, did not.

The popular warrior's strength now threatened the fate of the Empire. His once rag-tag armies were rag-tag no more. The series of quick and decisive victories over all of the well-garrisoned British strongholds had brought great rewards. His armies now possessed an enormous hoard of state-of-the-art weaponry, horses, armor and money, which enabled them to fight on even greater terms than the English. They possessed the ultimate weapon, passion and commitment.

Edward knew only too well how close to his throat was this Wallace. The man would not be stopped by war. The only way to defeat a purpose is with another. For everyone who has something to gain, there are those with something to lose. And so he called upon those highborn Scots, desperate to hold onto their status and their lives, and offered to make things even better in return for their absence from the battlefield.

The easiest purchase was John of Comyn, called by Wallace, Comyn the Red. Comyn had been with Wallace at Stirling, boasted of his love for him, and although born into nobility, had sworn loyalty and fealty to the cause. He was the one Baron who swore to put ten thousand cavalry into the field with Wallace, who loudly demanded the loyalty of all the others — all the way.

Edward saw otherwise. Comyn was on the Wallace bandwagon because it was the way to ultimate power in Scotland.

With Balloil openly declaring his enmity with Wallace, what better way to the top than to be his friend. He may be the hero, but he was not a noble. He could only be the man behind the Throne, which, with his support, would make John of Comyn the logical alternate choice to be King of Scotland.

So Edward would just make it easier and safer for Comyn and promised him the Throne of Scotland, if he would do just the opposite; stay away from Wallace. Within weeks of his return from Flanders, Edward had all the support he wanted and declared war on William Wallace.

When William heard that Edward himself was on the march he knew it would be more than a skirmish. This meeting would require every defense he could muster. Waiting for the right moment would not work. Somehow he had to weaken the English advance.

Along the border on the English side were several towns, which he knew would be vital to any hope of success for the British. Here they would already be provisioning food and supplies. To take these towns and destroy them would give him a great advantage. He deployed clan armies in such a way that all the towns were attacked at the same time giving him the element of surprise. The plan worked. They burned the fields and the storehouses, stole all the livestock and killed every soldier who opposed them.

He concluded his bold offence with the city of Carlisle, intended to be Edward's headquarters

The devastation seemed to have stopped the advance. When word reached Edward, he halted his troops for three days. It was rumored that the English might even turn back, having no way to sustain themselves.

What Wallace didn't know was that the hold up was so the Scottish Barons, whose lands and supplies were promised safe, had time to raise their own stockpiles in preparation for the British army. On the fourth morning they were on the march again.

~

The two sides met near a small town just over the Scottish border known as Falkirk. With one exception, none of the Scottish Earls, who had once been vociferous in support of the cause, showed up to support Wallace. And then, the one who did, John of Comyn, at the last moment, withdrew his cavalry and rode away, exposing Wallace's troops to annihilation. All the Barons had made secret deals with Edward.

Wallace promised that they would all pay for their cowardice.

He survived the battle, but not without injury. Some of his friends and comrades fell, others he was able to save.

Edward won the battle but failed to exact the price he had wanted. Wallace foiled any opportunity for that to happen.

Upon recognizing the inevitable, Wallace sounded retreat, and because his people knew the terrain so well, most were able to escape a bloody aftermath. That was the only good fortune for them.

For Edward, it counted as a resounding victory. The double-edged sword pointed at Scotland, with Edward's boot on her throat. The Baronage, John de Balliol and John of Comyn came to realize their folly in trusting his promises, but it was too late.

//

Arnold DeGaveston, the father of Piers Gaveston was an entirely different matter.

A loyal soldier and personal man-at-arms of the King, he had made it his life's work protecting this First Edward, and it made for a lasting friendship. The man was dangerous, levelheaded, instinctive in battle, a clever campaign strategist, and lethal in hand-to-hand combat, with or without a weapon. The only man Edward ever completely trusted.

DeGaveston had been unable to make it to the Dover. The only comfort the King could take at having to abandon his friend, was knowing that he was too clever to get himself killed. The game would be ransom, and Edward would pay it to get him back.

As it turned out, he had been captured on the road, covering the Royal party's return to the port. Just before crossing into Flemish territory, he and his troops were surrounded and every man taken without a shot fired.

He and a small crew were the rear defense for the King's party as they made their way to the coast, and the awaiting ship. Riding some distance behind, in the customary manner, he was set upon by French soldiers, largely outnumbering his own, and every one was captured.

DeGaveston knew this was no accident. The French contingency was extremely large and for so many troops to have appeared so suddenly and be so well organized, it had to be planned. Their bows were armed, and fully cocked as they emerged from the undergrowth. And while the bow was the most effective weapon known, it was not a weapon that a marching soldier could manage while loaded. To put up any fight would have been suicide.

The French had to have known that the King's party was just ahead, but obviously the plan was to let him pass. Capturing Edward would have only caused immeasurable grief and unnecessary work for Philippe.

It was not so easy, or cheap, to house, feed and protect another Monarch, especially one so important as this English King. Forget a ransom. The matter of how much would be almost impossible to determine; never mind the method and location of exchange, and the amount for Edward would have to be unreasonably large. Then, in order to prevent the financial loss, and retrieve their ruler, it would most certainly invite an attempt to rescue him, and without doubt during the trade. More embarrassment.

Moreover, Philippe would incur the wrath of his sister, Marguerite, and that was an experience he wished to avoid at all costs.

Hence the King of England was allowed to pass. DeGaveston and his band of elite troops were, however, another profitable matter. They could be ransomed for an acceptable price, which would be good business for the French coffers, it would not incur the wrath of a nation, and Philippe's sister would curb her remonstrations.

There was nothing Edward could do. By the time he was aware there was a problem, the time for DeGaveston's arrival had passed. Although his life and the lives of those attending him were put in jeopardy, Edward waited as long as the tide would permit, running the risk of the ship grounding and being vulnerable to capture. And although he would be allowed to walk, or row as the case may be, away, the Dover would be a prize Philippe could not resist.

It was within a week of his return to England, that he learned the details of the capture. Much of it was routine, except for one disturbing detail. All had been ransomed except DeGaveston. Philippe had been forced to change his plan. An accident of birth determined DeGaveston's fate.

Once in custody the Court had quickly determined that he was to be held as a traitor to France. His birthright was French, even though his family had emigrated to England, his mother's homeland, when he was a child. The only thing French about him was his name, but it made all the difference to Philippe's ministers. Treason was unforgivable, by any standard and could not be ignored or forgiven by the Monarch, and the reasons were justifiable.

This would be a strategic opportunity to make an example to all those of French nationality living abroad. DeGaveston was easily found guilty, and sentenced to be hanged, drawn, quartered, and lastly guillotined, in keeping with the order and letter of the law pertaining to punishment for traitors — a punishment accepted and practiced throughout Europe and England. As much as Edward would have liked to attempt a rescue, he could do nothing for him. This was the right of French law, and after all DeGaveston was born a Frenchman.

The punishment was carried out by first hanging the victim, but not so that he would die from it, but rather choke and suffocate by slow, painful strangulation. Then just as he or she passed out, they would be cut down, revived, stripped naked, and stretched on their back across the rack. Next, it was the executioner's role, using a large, hooked knife, to slit the offender open from chest plate to groin permitting their intestines to spill from the body cavity, whilst they were still alive and able to witness their own disembowelment.

In the case of males, an extra insult was made part of the gruesome display. The genitals were ritually sliced off and tossed to the inevitable pack of homeless dogs that the event attracted.

The traitor's four limbs would then each be tied to an individual horse, and the four horses set charging in different directions. The body would be instantly torn into pieces. If the victim were lucky, sometimes the body itself would be cleaved, and death would be instant.

Philippe didn't count on DeGaveston being as tough and formidable as he was, and didn't count on the fact that DeGaveston had no intention of dying, certainly not on French soil, if he could at all help it. And DeGaveston made his point during the last moments before he was to be transported to the gallows.

During his weeks in prison, he had been treated rather carefully. But then, it would not have been in the French King's best interest to parade a starving and near dead prisoner, to the gallows, lest it generate sympathy from the crowd, possibly martyr the man, and defeat the purpose.

Too many of those accused of treason were, by virtue of it, champions of the people. To drag him from prison emaciated and half dead, would only invoke sympathy. It was important that he appear fat and pampered, as one would look if he were well rewarded for his treachery. That would infer that he was an enemy of France — not a messiah to the downtrodden.

So his quarters were those reserved for a more noble captive, and his fare was such to support the good health of a man about to be exchanged for a fat ransom. Thus he was better fed and more fit and rested than when he was taken.

~

The day for his execution arrived. The route from his cell to the prison courtyard, where he was to be carted, was through a long, narrow and darkened corridor where any number of men walking would have to troop in single file. The purpose of this type of construction was to render impossible any attempt to rescue a prisoner, and make equally impossible any means of escape.

The prison keep was early Norman architecture. A style of building which dictated massive, straight, connected towers of layered stone blocks; the lower courses supporting walls some ten feet thick, with narrow slots which passed for windows, no more than six inches wide and three feet high. These windows, as they were called, were foremost a defense measure. The inside portion being a cubicle large enough to house a crouching man with a cross bow; and the outer opening tapered to allow a bowman to shoot out, but make a virtually impenetrable target for any shot coming at any distance from the outside.

The doorways were not much bigger; just enough to allow a man to crouch and pass. They connected low, narrow, tubular, ten-foot tunnels, which also provided an excellent defense. The interior corridors were nothing more than honeycombs, some with barely room enough for one man to walk.

Therefore DeGaveston's jailers were confident that only two guards were needed as an escort to the yard.

It was in just such a narrow corridor, that one marched ahead and one behind. As they moved along the dingy tube, the one ahead quickly moved on to the outside, to wait at the cart, just in case he tried to bolt at the entranceway. For the next few seconds this left himself and a single guard behind him, alone in the tight space. This would be his best, and probably only chance. He feigned a collapse.

Pretending to break in fear and despair, he dropped to his knees moaning and begging for mercy.

For those few seconds, the two were unseen and alone. The guard, a large bellied, reeking, pig of a man, urged by a life-long perversity to inflict pain on the helpless, reacted to the cowardly act with glee. Driven by his lust to hurt, especially one who he believed couldn't fight back, he came in too close and reached down to grab DeGaveston by the hair, a most painful way to haul anyone to their feet.

The mistake cost him his life.

DeGaveston, whose instincts at times like this made him lethal, sprang instantly snaring the short length of wrist chain neatly around the surprised guard's neck, and with one mighty jerk of his powerful arms, simultaneously crushed the guard's wind pipe, and his larynx.

Terrified, suffocating, any hope for air an impossibility, the man tumbled to the cobblestones, unable to cry for help, gasping and thrashing about on the slimy stones, in the throes of an agonizing death.

DeGaveston didn't hesitate. The man's life meant nothing to him. The chain had done its job. Releasing his murderous hold, he grabbed for the guard's short sword and leapt through the open doorway.

Now outside, he saw two more guards, one close, standing with his back to him attending the horse, the other standing at the rear of the cart waiting to assist in loading him if necessary. The one by the horse never had a chance. DeGaveston flew at him and plunged the short heavy blade down and through his upper back, which slid from top to bottom between his ribs, slicing his heart in two, inside his chest.

The sword jammed. But long experienced in hand-to-hand killing, he was ready for this. Immediately he released it, and grabbed this second, unfortunate victim's weapon, and readied to do battle with his next opponent. The third man however, seeing his companion die so suddenly and by such an expert hand, suspected the same was true for him, and ran squealing like a pig.

These were simple prison guards, not trained soldiers. They were mostly recruited from cowardly bullies who roamed country roads and city streets looking to mug, rob, rape and even kill anyone who looked like they couldn't fight back.

They were naturally good at this type of job because they took great delight in tormenting, beating and torturing unarmed, bound and wounded prisoners, but put them on equal ground with any of their captives, and they would dissolve in terror. Unfit to soldier, their placement saved wasting the talents of good men. So if one died from time to time, it was no loss whatsoever.

For the next few seconds, DeGaveston had the small yard to himself, with an open gateway to freedom. The balance of his escort were lounging about somewhere outside that doorway, not suspecting that more than three of their number would be necessary to cart him. However, he knew he did not have much time. The guard who had fled would be at this moment sounding the alarm.

His only means of flight was the old horse, tethered to the cart. The beast looked sturdy enough...but there was no time to deliberate ... he yanked away the strapping, freeing the animal from its yoke, swung onto it's back and dug his boot heels into it's flanks.

The horse turned out to be a miracle. On this command, the once trained beast lunged forward, and with its determined rider clinging to its neck, tore through the gates and into the main avenue of the castle.

The outer compound of this particular castle-prison was considerably larger than most. Being close to Paris, and serving a larger population, it was normally a busy marketplace. It had at one time been a military keep, with towers at each of the four corners of the compound, linked by long earthen battlements. In the center was the castle, Officer's quarters, the mess, the dungeon cells, and a hodge-podge of ugly, squat stone buildings which had been attached over the years as the fort evolved into one of the many garrisons defending the city.

At an earlier time the large open compound had served to marshal and bivouac troops, thus its size, but now, with the suburbs encroaching, it served a more useful purpose — except when there was a hanging.

Fortunately this day there was to be one, and so it had been cleared of all pedestrian traffic in order that the prisoner could be escorted ceremoniously to his death.

Now it served as a clear path to escape. To his relief, not only was the way unpopulated, but the huge archway of the main entrance was directly ahead and wide open, and beyond that, of course, the drawbridge was down. And why shouldn't it be, this was to be an event, and many had come from all around the countryside to revel in the merriment that traditionally accompanied an execution.

This was not the fastest steed he had ever ridden, but obviously more than a wagoner. The brave animal must have seen battle at one time. Several more guards, alarmed by the cries of the frightened jailer, were running to block the gateway from the courtyard. The horse charged undeterred, trampling two of them while DeGaveston was able to pierce the eye of a third.

Relentlessly the noble beast pressed forward, regardless of those who were now clamoring around them attempting to spook the animal and force it to stop. DeGaveston had the advantage of surprise and the unexpected break of seizing an experienced charger. He gained considerable momentum and distance, but he could not outrun the arrows. It would only be moments before they brought him down.

Riding bareback, as he was, with one hand gripping the mane and the other clutching the stolen little sword, fighting was not his best option. He had to ignore the impending onslaught and focus on the gate. It was then that he saw it being lowered, and remarkably quickly for such a large portico.

With that he spotted the lone guard to the side of it, operating the geared drive-wheel and knew his only chance to make it through was to intimidate him into abandoning his post.

Tugging at the horse's mane, their direction changed slightly aiming their charge directly at the gatekeeper. The threat worked. The distance was closing rapidly and the frightened operator saw that he was about to be a victim. He no longer cared about his post and was no longer cranking the wheel. Reacting in terror at the snorting beast thundering down upon him, with its maniacal rider brandishing the deadly little sword, he fled his position.

DeGaveston was going to make it. The huge, suspended door was still open wide enough, and through it they raced, galloping across the bridge and disappearing into a woods about one hundred yards from the moat. Several of the prison militia had mounted up and were in pursuit, but their hearts weren't truly into meeting up with this formidable killer.

They continued in a showy chase for a few miles, but gladly in the wrong direction, and soon returned to the prison with excuses. Although the people were cheated out of a colourful and messy execution, he was forgotten as quickly as he had escaped.

III

At first Philippe was incensed, and probably would have punished those Officers responsible for DeGaveston's keep, had his attention not been greatly diverted.

Literally upon the heels of the ransom for the band of sorry troops, Edward sent a proposal of marriage to the French King, asking for his daughter Isabella's hand in marriage to his son, the Second Edward.

A propitious offer indeed, and one that Philippe could not refuse. In his ambitious eye he saw France overtaking England hopefully, one day, to become his. Philippe's acceptance was dispatched with equal enthusiasm.

Not only did each see this as the solution to end the conflict with France, Edward saw this precocious young beauty as just the thing to one day turn his son's confused young head, and make a man out of him.

At the same time, Isabella was the favorite daughter of France, and this could give Edward a great deal of latitude to manipulate her father, perhaps even right off that precious Throne of his. Knowing that Philippe could be blinded by his own greed and ambition, if the education of his daughter were handled skillfully and she were to become England's favorite new mistress, he could use the Frenchman's weakness against him.

~

In the meantime, while the two Kings were preoccupied each thinking he had outsmarted the other, DeGaveston managed to get back to England with the help of a privateer friendly to Edward. He was granted an immediate audience with his master, who wasted no time in providing for his loyal comrade.

As good a judge of character as he demonstrated in selecting Isabella, the King couldn't have been more off the mark, in choosing his son's newest companion.

Without thinking it through, blinded by gratitude, his charity to DeGaveston senior was to appoint the man's son Piers, nicknamed Perrot, as official companion to the Prince, hoping that the acorn hadn't fallen far from the tree and that the boy would bring a sobering influence into the Prince's young life.

On the surface the young Piers, the same age as the Prince, appeared to be a manly fellow, and impressed the King with his ability in martial arts, his penchant for sports, and his general knowledge of the important issues of the day. Too quickly Edward saw the father in the son, perhaps because he wanted to, and eagerly sent him to the official residence at Langley.

Prepared to close the book on this unfortunate chapter of his son's life, he had no way of knowing that he had just set up the two sides of the vice within which the Heir would be squeezed for the remainder of his life.

Isabella, the magnificent beauty, Princess of France, inheritor of the capricious and cruel character of her notorious father, would prove a wise choice for England. Piers Gaveston, inheritor of nothing worthwhile, would bring the Empire to its knees.

IV

For the next six years, Edward devoted his efforts to consolidating his rule over Scotland. So great was his desire for revenge on Wallace, that any means became justified. He reneged on virtually all of his deals with the Scottish Baronage, and concentrated on crushing any resistance. The only promises he was making were to spare those who had knowledge of Wallace, and were willing to betray him.

Wallace was doing his best to keep one step ahead of the English King, while at the same time make as much trouble for him as possible. Most of the skirmishes encountered by the occupational armies, were of his doing, but none came close to any kind of meaningful victory for the determined Scot.

He never again was able to rally the people as he had done before. Only the die-hards came out to fight, and even though many of the Earls had lost all they had hoped to gain from betraying him at Falkirk, still none would go against Edward.

Wallace tried to even the score for the people, by seeking revenge on two of the lesser Earls who had sworn to support him. They had shown at some distance from the battlefield, only enough to let themselves be seen, and then had ridden away, leaving large numbers of the faithful trapped, to be hopelessly slaughtered.

On one occasion, Wallace had been invited to a banquet at one of the Earl's castles, the latter wanting to make amends.

Wallace somehow had the chance to get to him alone, and when he did, he slit his throat, carving his neck through to where his head was hanging by only a flap of skin. He then marched into the banquet hall, carrying the body, with the head flopping grotesquely slinging blood over those seated, and flung it onto the center of the table, amidst the Earl's wife and children.

On another, Wallace and two of his companions, rode onto the lands of the second Earl and found him hunting.

Without harming anyone else, the three forced him to the ground, and then proceeded to have their horses trample him, their hooves punching holes in his body and smashing his skull into pieces.

Word got out, as Wallace knew it would, and had some small uplifting affect on the people, but it only served to terrify the rest of the Barons which outweighed his popularity and endangered him all the more.

The Earl of Menteith, one Baron who didn't fear Wallace's wrath, enlisted the help of one of Wallace's later companions, a man by the name of Jack Short, who for a guarantee of a large piece of land with income, help concoct a scheme to sell him out.

The Earl's price was a similar deal only ten times the size and a title was thrown in to boot. He could afford to generous to Short.

The trap was set at Robroyston, Short being the messenger with the exciting news that the Council was prepared to rally behind The Earl of Carrick who in turn, all knew, had come out in support of Wallace; Carrick being the most powerful of them all, none of the others were too keen to make an enemy of him.

It was also reported that Carrick would guarantee Wallace's safety if he came to a meeting and so trusting Carrick, Wallace walked right into it. There he was captured without a fight.

The Seventeenth Earl of Carrick also went by the name of Robert the Bruce, and on that beautiful July day in 1305 as he contemplated an afternoon tryst with his mistress, he was surprised by the arrival of Menteith and others.

As they stumbled over their excuses for their visit, an unsuspecting servant joyfully announced the arrival of his hero, one Sir William Wallace. In the few minutes it took for him to catch on, the Bruce was too late to save the man he truly intended to support.

~

On August 23, 1305, in London England, in a public square near The Tower, William Wallace, the warrior poet of Scotland, was hanged, drawn and quartered. The pieces were sent to the four corners of the Kingdom as a grisly reminder of what England does to traitors.

It did not have the effect the King had hoped for.

King Edward the First of England did not attend the execution.

PERROT AND THE PRINCE

Chapter 4
1307 - 1308

1

But never one phoenix perishes then another rises. Out of the legacy emerged the one Scotsman, the one powerful Baron, who regretted his complicity with England.

Guilt-ridden over the betrayal and death of Wallace, and the plight of his people he took up the cause with a vengeance and vowed to take it into the next generation of Kings if need be. His wish was granted.

As Scotland became his, so England also changed hands. As William Wallace had been the nemesis of Edward I, so Edward II was to have his, The Seventeenth Earl of Carrick, Robert The Bruce.

Over these few years, since the humiliation of Stirling, the British Heir had done little to distinguish himself, either at Court or in the field. Edward became infatuated with Piers Gaveston and aside from a total preoccupation in the pursuit of the joys of life with his new companion, his only accomplishment was to infuriate the English Baronage.

From the moment the young Edward met Gaveston, he was completely enthralled by him. And even at his age and station, Gaveston recognized it and took advantage of it immediately.

Although the King was an intimidation he'd rather do without, he saw very little of him and so didn't count him as a serious factor in his ambitious little world. The sisters were something else.

Gaveston was a striking fellow who knew it. In particular a couple of the women at Court had a remarkable talent for sketching portraits and were ever ready to capture his chiseled features and dark brooding eyes. It was always a big day for the others, boys and girls alike, when Gaveston was 'sitting'. All would come to watch, as he would sit so very still, normally uncovered to the waist, while the artist, later it became artists, worked so earnestly and so adoringly at tracing every eye-catching line unable to resist touching him from time to time 'to guide the spirit of their art'.

Hardly did he understand modesty with such obvious attention and tested his vanity at every opportunity. He loved to pose his tall, muscular young body and so would, on purpose, whenever he and Edward and the other palace boys engaged in athletics of an individual nature, strip to the briefest of undergarments "to better perform."

Not only did it have a maddening affect on Edward, it excited all his sisters. They hung on him, and one by one he tempted them into exploratory sexual encounters that, with the energy of their youth, they came seeking almost daily.

There was no way the sisters were going to drum Gaveston out of the loop, regardless of his indifference to, or refusal to jump to their childish demands. It took very little time for him to gain control with both sexes at Court. He learned he could get farther with charm and wit than with petulance, and developed a charisma that few close to him, or those he liked, could resist.

Admirers could be talked into or out of anything he wished. And Edward became the easiest victim of all.

Equally attracted to and capable of the physical connection with men as he was with women, either need meet only two requirements — that they be beautiful, and that they have something he wanted. The young Edward certainly met the criteria, and to Gaveston's delight introduced an unexpected third element, his disadvantage. He was capable only with men.

Gaveston had control.

Although his father was in close service to the King, he personally had never known any kind of wealth or power. But he had grown up around enough of it to know that he wanted as much as he could get. The King's reward to his father was a gift from heaven. His powers of seduction would take care of the rest.

He began almost immediately to make demands. At first, during their teen years, it was confined to jewelry, clothes, horses and other things of value at the moment. But as they both approached young adulthood, the requests were far more imposing. Gaveston had convinced the Heir to trust no one but him, and argued that once the old King died, that he, Gaveston, would be his only protection.

The Heir offered him a knighthood. He argued that as a mere knight, he would have no real power to defend the will of the Monarch, but with lands and titles, he would have status over any opposition.

Edward needed little persuading. But in order to grant lands and titles, he needed the permission of his father, and that he wasn't likely to get without Gaveston performing some major and heroic service to the crown. In the meantime he had to keep his beloved happy with alternatives.

Therefore, his demands and his extravagances were taking a heavy toll on the treasury, and the expenses of the House of the Prince of Wales were far greater than they had a need or a right to be. And all of it appeared to be going on the back of his demanding friend. The anger of the Baronage had become a raw sore. They couldn't abolish the Prince's title or his legal house, without a vote of the Commons, but they could reduce, or even cut off his income — which they threatened to do.

~

It was time for the King to try and do some more damage control. More than a year had passed since Wallace's death. It was going on 1307, and there had been significant changes in Scotland, which needed the King's attention. For a few of the Barons, the love affair with Edward's rule had ended.

For one thing, his one time ally, The Carricks, were now in the person of Robert the Bruce, who had no intention of siding with him, and who, to prove the point, had coldly murdered John of Comyn, and unopposed, ceremoniously crowned himself King of Scotland.

It was a story that Edward did not want to hear. Now ill and feeling himself threatened from all sides he saw it as an omen. It was told that the Bruce had become despondent to the point of madness over his betrayal of Wallace and of Scotland.

He claimed to have had a dream in which he saw his only vindication. The very next day, he sent a message to King John of Comyn to meet with him in a small church near Dumfries. His purpose, he said, was to make amends before his country and his God, and to discuss the situation of Scotland, both were a lie.

The story goes, that each rode accompanied by bodyguards, but when they met at the steps of the church, the Bruce proposed that only the two enter and make their peace with God as their first witness.

The Comyn, being a poorly educated man and given to superstition, agreed that this was a matter best judged before God and bid his men stay put outside, as did the Bruce. With that they walked together to the altar, and as they knelt to pray, the Bruce pulled out his knife and stabbed Comyn to death.

When the news of the assassination reached London, and that the Bruce was calling himself the King of Scotland, Edward saw that the pot was about to start boiling again. He couldn't let the Bruce gain control. This was one Baron who could unite the rest against England.

If there was anything good to say about the situation, it was the timing. No one would oppose Edward's recommendation that he take an aggressive posture, and in all it would give him the chance to vindicate his personal standing. Here at last was a chance to give these boys a taste of manhood.

He would take his son and Piers on what may be for him one last campaign to Scotland. He had hopes that the boy might distinguish himself in battle, however minor, and therefore redeem himself to some extent. Maybe the years associated with Piers would pay off. The young DeGaveston had demonstrated, on the lists, an uncanny ability with weapons, and the young Edward, in theory, had shown himself to be an adept archer, and skilled horseman.

The Heir and Gaveston saw a different opportunity.

They both proved to be the greatest disappointment and the final humiliation. There were no pitched battles, luckily for them; the Bruce wasn't organized enough to take Edward head- on. There were just a rapid series of skirmishes, and mostly with poorly armed, bedraggled gangs of peasants.

None were difficult to beat, but even still the two would hang back at the fringe of the fighting, and take on only those who had managed to stagger, half dead, some limbless, out of the foray, seeking only a place to die.

Off the battlefield it was another story. At night, in the safety of the camp they were both quick to share the ale, and swap the stories with the rest of the troops, but that was as close to the real fighting as they ever got.

After one such small encounter, the enemy turned out to be no more than the farmers from a nearby village. However, armed with only pitchforks, homemade pikes and inferior bows, they fought like titans. Some died, but more were only wounded.

The King sounded recall, ordered that the fighting cease and the enemy's wounded be left untouched. His troops needed no further invitation to leave the field. Fighting with the Scots, even peasants, was something they did not relish at the best of times, but in this case they had no stomach for murder.

He too, had turned away, and was about to head to camp, when the unusual loudness of screaming and wailing behind him, caused him to turn back. At the sight he flew into a rage. There, in the midst of the shameful carnage, which now was nothing more than a scene of prostrate bodies, wounded and dead, dotted by women and children, frantically searching for husbands, fathers, brothers and lovers; were two lone horsemen, wildly hacking and stabbing at everything on the ground.

Piers and the Prince of Wales put on a show for all to see. In the first few minutes of their bravado, two small children had been decapitated, and several women, one pregnant, had been mortally wounded as they huddled over the bodies of their downed men.

Gaveston's final act, as an Officer and a gentleman, fortunately ended in disaster — for him. Spotting a youngster running towards one of the wounded, some distance away from his position. He wheeled his horse, and launched a charge, trampling across the bodies, to attack the child. Another of the wounded, seeing the charge, and being directly in line, gripped his long oak pike, and tripped up the horse, sending the rider flying from it's back.

Gaveston crashed violently to the ground, and tumbled over several bodies, losing his sword. Two more of the wounded, took up the opportunity, and with what strength they could muster, grabbed for anything that would do as a weapon, and began beating on the now terrified and screaming Piers Gaveston.

The King completely lost his temper. Spurring his horse onto the field, he charged his son, and with the flat of his huge broadsword, sent him careening from his saddle into the mire.

The surprised and frightened Heir, at first not aware of who had attacked him, began begging and crying and scrambling madly over bodies to escape, until he realized his attacker was his father. He collapsed, relieved, sobbing and pissing all over himself, grateful to be spared, until he felt the point of his father's sword pressed into his throat.

"You and that other sack of shit will walk back to camp, and if you live to make it, you will pack your things and leave immediately for London. Do not try to see me. How you get there is your own problem, but when, or if you do, you will remain in your house, without benefit of money or friends, until I return. Then I will decide your fate."

He then turned his horse and collected the reins of his son's. Ignoring Gaveston's dilemma at the hands of the wounded, he steered his way to where Gaveston's now stood, gathered those reins also, and carefully, so as not to hurt any alive on the ground, rode away.

He had given up on the future King of England.

//

The two managed to survive the assault of the wounded villagers, survive their trip on foot as far back as Carlisle, and to the utter disbelief and astonishment of the King, convince themselves that they were deserving victors, and heroes of the Scottish wars.

Edward and his returning army caught up with them at a small Baronage outside the city. They had made themselves regally comfortable and were taking full advantage of the respectful Earl's hospitality, when the King descended upon them. He paid his respects to the Earl, and not wishing to disturb the peace of the man's home, concealed his rage, and sat calmly with his company, including his son and Gaveston. His good intentions were shattered when his son opened his mouth.

The young Edward began a pitch that suggested that as his father was growing older, he was losing his stomach for battle. He pointed out that his and Piers' intentions on the battlefield were misunderstood. If ever there had been the perfect opportunity it had been the one just past. When it became his turn, if his rule over Scotland was to be successful, he believed in retrospect that their behavior had managed to assure it. This campaign had been a blessing in disguise – it had been his chance to instill fear and respect.

The King listened, not saying a word, watching his son grow more confident the more he expounded his distorted views. Finally, not interested in hearing any more of the drivel, he rose to leave, which would normally signal an end to any conference, when the Heir asked his father to remain seated, because of one very important piece of business which needed a Royal blessing.

Under the circumstances, The King was beside himself. Where on earth was the boy's mind? He could not imagine what of any business his son would feel justified proposing, let alone asking a blessing.

The Prince's words struck like a cannonball. He announced that he wished to award the province of Ponthieu in France to Gaveston, for his loyal service both on and off the battlefield.

The King flew into a rage. Ponthieu was one of England's most valuable territories. It had belonged to his beloved Eleanor, the Prince's mother, who, on her deathbed, had willed it to remain amongst the royal possessions rather than revert to her cousin, the King of France. It had been a gift from heaven. Not only did it give him a strategic hold in Europe, it was resource rich and of enormous benefit to international trade.

He could not control himself. And without caring what impression he was making on his company, who were watching, including his host, Edward leaped from his chair and lunged at the Prince. He was boiling and grabbed at the first thing he could get a hold of, it happened to be the Prince's hair, jerked him to his feet, and then kicked his knees out from under him. The Prince buckled, and went down, but his father's powerful grip held fast.

The King then dragged him about the room, kicking him, and yelling obscenities, until he came to the top of the crescent shaped staircase which lead down from the great hall to the undercroft. It was there he stopped his tirade, and without hesitation, hurled him down the stairwell. Dangling from his fist was a huge clump of blond hair.

Gaveston fled the room. Edward survived the fall, and together they returned to London. But at the very moment Gaveston arrived at his town house, two of the King's men-at-arms were upon him. He never stepped through his own doorway. They beat him, threw him into the back of a dung cart and delivered the load to the garrison at Dover. By the time Gaveston came to his senses he found himself clapped in irons aboard a ship leaving for God knows where, with a note pinned to his clothing warning that upon penalty of death, he was never to return to England.

When the Prince learned of his favorite's exile, he wailed like a mother for a lost child.

THE FRENCHMAN'S DAUGHTER

Chapter 5

1308 AD

1

On July 7, 1307 King Edward I of England died, leaving behind him an Empire on the verge of extinction.

Long robbed of speech by throat cancer, there were no dying words of wisdom; nothing of comfort passed on to his son and Heir, the young Edward. The weak, indolent and now embittered young man took it as a clear sign of that which he had always believed, that his father hated him, and so he dismissed his father's soul and body, hating him.

Certainly he was not about to grant his father's funeral wishes, and wasted no time disposing of his remains in the Royal vault at Westminster Abbey. He had the coffin sealed before many of Europe's nobility even learned of the death. The Prince did not lift a finger to mourn his passing. So bitter was he, that the King would have lain and rotted in the bed where he died, had it not been for Lancaster.

The Second Edward of England was delirious. Newly crowned, he could now reinstate his beloved Gaveston and lavish upon him all the attention and rewards that his royal heart desired. So anxious was he to greet his lover upon his return, that he set up a temporary Court at the Port of Dover in order that he be there at the precise moment of Gaveston's arrival. His excitement turned to giddiness when from his apartments overlooking the harbor he saw the ship sail in to view.

Not bothering to wait for a carriage, he raced from the hotel, robes flying, and like a love-struck maiden racing to the arms of her returning hero, clambered madly to the docks, shouting his name and weeping with joy.

As Gaveston descended the gangway Edward flung himself into his arms, vowing that they should never again be parted.

At the sight of the King running wildly down Dock Street, waving and shouting, a crowd had gathered but none of it contained any other members of the Royal family or any nobility. His shameful display had not been officially witnessed.

Edward could care less at how he was seen. All that mattered was that he had Gaveston back. He couldn't wait to bestow upon him two gifts which he believed would assure him a rightful place at his side, and a lifetime position at Court.

Back in the privacy of the apartment, after their own reunion was consummated, he announced the first. It had been arranged that Gaveston was to marry Margaret of Gloucester, Edward's cousin, which would effectively bring him into the Royal Family.

Gaveston feigned humility, protesting that the King was too generous, and assured him that the marriage would only be a formality. In secret he was overjoyed. This meant he would be an equal, would have social power and status, and a seat in the House of Lords, not to mention that his new young wife was very pretty, and he had a equal penchant for women as well as men.

Then Edward announced the second.

He was conferring upon him the Duchy of Cornwall, the plum of England. Upon their return to London, it would be made official.

This one Gaveston could not feign. For a moment he could only gape in stone cold shock. " You can do this? You can just give the Duchy to me ..."

"That is correct my darling, I can just give it to you, just like that." Edward was grinning from ear to ear. Pleasing Gaveston was his first concern in life.

Gaveston was not convinced. "Edward, are you sure? Have you thought this through? It seems to me that there is something more to conferring a Duchy than just announcing it. Don't you have to get some sort of permission? What about your family, don't they have a say?"

The questions and the look of concern brought Edward down. He began to bridle like a spoiled child denied his way, not comprehending the implications. "I am the King now. I can do whatever I want, and this is what I want."

Gaveston's easy success with the King had blinded him to the folly of his greed. So far he had been able to keep everything given him, even though others more powerful complained bitterly. Why not this? He took Edward by the shoulders and looked lovingly into his eyes, "all right, all right my dear," he soothed, "If you say you can do it, then it must be so."

Gaveston's words were like a switch with Edward. This was all the blessing he needed for his actions. His excitement returned immediately. "So cherie, you like this little gift I give you, yes?"

"I like it very much." And he did. A light went on in his head. "And do you know what this means?"

Edward was grinning like a Cheshire cat and his head was bobbing with enthusiasm.

"It makes me the most powerful Earl in the land."

When Lancaster heard the news he exploded.

//

London has so few perfect summer days that Edward and Piers saw this absolutely exquisite one as their omen for the future. It was the dawn of their Coronation Day.

The Holy ceremony was to take place at Westminster Abbey. The one mile route from Westminster Palace to the Abbey was lined with thousands of cheering people. It was not that anyone cared for or even liked the King; it was the free flowing ale and the huge party going on in the street that brought out London's masses.

Stretched like a caravan down the length of its center, in a long single file and rolling slowly, were dozens of ornate, open horse-drawn carriages, flanked by handsomely mounted King's Guards adorned in their colorful uniforms of red, gold and black trim, their polished silver breast plates and helmets flashing in the bright sun.

The wealthy occupants of the long line of ornate carriages were also putting on their own show, bedazzling the crowds as they paraded by, decked out in the latest Italian fashions, color, flash and flamboyance being the order of the day.

For the women the primary statement was breasts. Let them spill if you had them; and push them up from your stomach if you didn't. A deeply plunging bodice flirting as close to nipple exposure as possible indicated flair and style. The dictate of fashion appeared to be the winner. Very little was left even to the speculative imagination.

In all respects the day was a rarity.

Very warm and brightly sunny, and people's spirits matched it. Not too often did the city come together to celebrate, certainly not for any occasion of this magnitude, and the crowds were high on the wild street festivities and the glorious exhibition put on by the rich and powerful.

The colorful route was home to a random collection of shops and pubs and crooked building fronts with everyone open for business and all looking to benefit from the day's festivities.

The spectacle of pomp and ceremony was surrounded by bedlam as the huge mob that filled the street and the square leading up to the Abbey shouted, booed, cheered and jeered.

Drunkenness abounded; prostitutes and hustlers plied their trades. Dogs and children ran helter-skelter throughout the throng. And young skilled unseen hands emptied pockets with the ease of plucking fruit.

More Imperial Guards on huge horses and all dressed out lined the route, jostling the crowds as they pressed and guided the enormous animals in their struggle to keep order.

The Royal Mall, as Edward's father had come to call it, was a wide and imperious avenue, and built that way to accommodate the victory parades of Kings, especially his own, and while it made it easier for the Guards to keep order, it also allowed for greater numbers of people to gather. And so it was an impressive site. A roaring sea of humanity against the rich color and spectacle of an Imperial Coronation.

~

At its glittering center, floating grandly in the long line of carriages came the open Gold Landau drawn by its six white stallions, led and flanked by a phalanx of Imperial Guards all on black horses.

Preceding and following were all the nobility in order of rank in their finest carriages each pulled by four horses, none white.

Behind them, mounted on their massive heavy battle stallions, rode the sacred Templar Knights in their formal dress of chain mail armor overcoated with stark white tunics embossed only by the simple red cross of St. George. Behind them were the lesser knights and Officers also mounted, and finally came the invited merchant upper class.

Partying was the order of the day and not confined just to the rabble. Arrogant and oblivious to the public, many of the carriage occupants carried on in their own ribald fashion.

The King was especially drunk. Standing unsteadily in his carriage, clinging to Gaveston, the two waved and jeered back at the crowds, pointing and making rude gestures while swigging from bottles. Each wore an identical cream colored, gold trimmed long carriage cape and from a distance made it hard to tell them apart as they kept stumbling into one another while trying to hold each other up.

The moment enjoyed most by the crowd closest to them began when the horses jerked to a stop in front of the Abbey and Gaveston tumbled, in a clown-like fashion, out of site, disappearing into the bottom of the carriage. The mob roared and screeched hysterically, especially as he appeared almost instantly again above the sidewall of the Landau, laughing with them, his drink held aloft as he shouted, "didn't spill, didn't spill."

Not wanting to be left out of the gaiety and seeing the laughter on the faces around him, Edward took it for appreciation, and opted to keep the entertainment going by staging a grand entrance. With a goblet of wine held aloft in one hand, he impulsively placed the other hand on the side rail of the carriage, and to the delight of the crowd, vaulted with all the grace and style of a circus performer over the side of the carriage and landed like a cat on his feet holding the goblet high to accentuate his dexterity.

So much for a dignified arrival. To complete the show he next, and with a cavalier waive of his free hand, gestured, bowed deeply and extended it helping Gaveston to ceremoniously step down from the carriage onto the red carpet, as if it were his coronation.

But for some, and as it turned out, those most important to Edward's future, in their short sighted attempts to entertain they had made a mockery of the occasion. Their antics became a matter of record.

For every action that Gaveston ever took, there was always an equal and opposite reaction. His monumental ego never failed in its undoing.

Had he provided even a modicum of pleasure through the entertainment value of his antics up to that moment, in a flash he gave it all away. Grasping Edward's outstretched hand he stepped to the ground, his affectation giving rise to more laughter, when suddenly he lurched away from him. His jovial mood in an instant was gone. Staggering away he wheeled around and shouted drunkenly, his finger jabbing the air for emphasis, the goblet of wine in his hand slopping about. "Those ... those bastards... those fucking bastards ... I will be the one walking behind you down the aisle ... I ...I ... me ...not those back stabbing cousins of your."

Edward stumbled after him and clutched him by the shoulder. Looking intensely and adoringly into his grimacing face, and in a low voice choked with emotion and on the edge of tears, he slurred, " You shall my precious friend, you shall."

For a few seconds he held his face close to Gaveston's, then leaned back slowly, looked to the sky, and began shouting in a distorted voice, defiant in the moment. Forgetting the full goblet in his right hand he flung his arm backwards in a wide sweeping gesture, hurling an arc of wine through the air, " to hell with their bloody ceremony ... this is our day ...our bloody day."

Just then an excited group of young men, all attired to the most outrageous extreme of fashion, scurried up to surrounded the King and Gaveston thereby distracting them.

The square was filling quickly with partying guests and by the groupings, the various camps were easily identified. There were those who obviously favored the King and were clustered about him and Gaveston. There were those whose awkward intimidation was well marked, who were well beneath any station and therefore unable to cluster with anybody but themselves; they just gawked.

There were those who were marginally qualified to mix with the bluer blood, but whose overt indifference comically marked their pretensions and total lack of sophistication; they were the least important. And then there were those who had the blood or the merit or both, who had the power – and knew it, and who openly opposed him. That was the most influential group.

To top it all off, the reception was a dismal failure. Too few Stewards were assigned the impossible task of frantically hurrying from gathering to gathering toting heavy silver trays laden with goblets of wine trying to keep everyone happy. And there was not a morsel of food in sight. Gaveston had been responsible for this aspect of the festivities.

The opposition formed a very large crowd. And at its center were the two most important couples in the land. Very important and very dangerous, two of whom were Edward's first cousins, the Earls of Lancaster and Gloucester and the second most powerful men in England; Lancaster in particular, being the next in line for the Crown.

Beside them were their wives, who, for the moment, were the two most powerful women in England.

Both men also shared another element, uncommon to most of their status, and therefore a profound weapon in their social arsenal. Each of their wives was extremely attractive and highly personable and therefore much admired by all of London society.

And normally women who are blessed with such attributes have much to be admired, outwardly as well. Thus they can dress or undress, with magnificent results, to whatever trendy hilt they choose, with any endeavor only bestowing upon their consorts the joyous and copious rewards that glamour brings to power. Needless to say, the two couples were thronged.

~

Lancaster had no fear of the King. He also had an audience and saw it only as another opportunity to share his distaste for him. At this point the wine had the better of his judgment. "I should bloody well do the country a favor and slit the bastard's scrawny throat."

His wife, not so impressed with his loud opinion, hissed at him, "You would do bloody well to lower your voice my dear." There was some chuckling and nodding of heads from those closest to him.

Equally unafraid and slightly more drunk, Gloucester was prompted by Lancaster's outburst to exercise his opinion, "I say get rid of the sodded lap dog, get him to bed with a woman, a real woman, and maybe we'd see some changes in the bloody wretch..."

His voice trailed off as his thought was interrupted by the sight approaching them. It was more than he could take, "awwgh ... who in bloody hell am I fooling ... this is a sodding joke ... this, this..." As his blood rose, so did his voice, "if these two are allowed to go on much longer ... this is the end of England ... it is the end ... I swear it cousin."

Gloucester was usually a voice of reason and managed to keep himself under control most times. This was not one of those times. He was boiling with rage, and he was drunk. Fortunately for the King, Gloucester's wife saw that her husband was about to make a move towards him, and placed herself directly between them, facing her husband, her back to the King. Only Gaveston counted the insult.

Gloucester, on the other hand, knew to obey his wife, especially now.

Face to face with him, she stepped forward into him, deliberately pressing her attractive body against his. A body that Gloucester was more than fond of. His temper was no match for her considerable charms, but she was leaving nothing to chance. From within the folds of her cape and undetected by their closeness, her small right hand had taken a firm grip on his codpiece. She had his attention.

Smiling sweetly and looking straight into his eyes she spoke quietly, "Husband!" and then turning her pretty face towards Lancaster who had momentarily forgotten the King and was now focused on the strange expression on Gloucester's face, "Cousin!,... look at me, both of you, now... please!"

Lancaster, suddenly incredulous, turned his gaze to her in response, a broad grin spreading across his face as he guessed at what she was doing.

Her voice remained low and soft, "if both of you don't shut your bleeding mouths... I swear ... I'll shut them for you ... this is not the time nor ...."

Gloucester, not quite finished with his tirade, began to speak out of turn. "This should be your day Thomas, not that bloody piece of human excrement..."

His words were cut short as his wife's grip tightened.

It was then that Lancaster's wife decided to get in the act and was about to admonish her husband when her hand popped to her mouth. Whatever it was she had to say to her husband was taken from her lips at the shock of the sight that was making its way towards them. The best she could do was gasp, "Oh my God!.... would you look at that...!"

Edward, Gaveston and the group of young men they kept as constant companions were striding slowly towards them, on their way to the Abbey entrance. All were dressed in the newest and most outrageous of Italian theatre fashion, doing their best to startle the occasion.

Never to be outdone, Gaveston had pushed the boundary of style and opted for the most shocking costume of all, only just revealed by the removal of his cape. What couldn't be seen in the carriage was now on full view.

He had donned a high pointed woodsman's peaked cap exaggerated by a long peacock feather which arched over its brim and curved down to his shoulder, a full ruffled blouse with balloon sleeves and layers of lace at the cuffs, a multi-colored fitted jerkin which stopped tightly at his waist, and from there down very little else except revealing skin tight white stockings, no cod piece and hugely pointed doe skin ankle boots.

None of the women were looking at the boots or the cap. He was clearly on display.

Ignoring everyone in an attempt to make a chic statement for the moment, they babbled meaninglessly amongst themselves, as the little Royal cluster strutted through the crowd. By their singular behavior towards him, it was evident that Gaveston was their undisputed leader. Even Edward clung to the arm of his favorite, as might a proud mistress, snubbing his guests, intent on keeping his beloved happy.

~

Hours later and inside the Abbey, things seemed to have settled into a more stately conformation. Edward was seated on the golden Throne of his illustrious ancestor, Richard, Coeur de Lion, immediately in front of but below the huge altar. Bathed in a cone of intense sunlight that for some reason at this moment chose to stream through the high stained glass windows behind the altar, the now Second Edward of The British Empire looked for all that part, regal.

About his shoulders and flowing about on the floor immediately around him was draped Richard's brushed velvet red, gold and ermine trimmed robe. Emblazoned over each shoulder and running the full length of each arm were the embroidered rampant golden lions, reflecting the light and forming a brilliant contrast against the recently installed massive checkerboard of black and white Italian marble tiles that stretched the length and breadth of the soaring nave.

In his right hand he held the gold scepter representing the Empire, and in his left his father's staff of office, hand hewn out of six feet of iron-like stout English oak with it's gnarled, balled top and engraved along the upper half of its shaft with the image of Excalibur representing the strength of his government.

The Archbishop, robed in all his official attire, was standing a few feet in front of him performing the sacred ceremony. They were flanked by at least a dozen clergy.

As the Archbishop was reciting, in Latin, the last of the oath of investiture, from behind the altar stepped another cleric, large and rotund, waddling like a fat goose as he proudly transported on a red velvet cushion the thickly bejeweled heavy gold crown of The Lionheart.

The obese cleric came to a stop facing the Archbishop at a right angle and just a few feet in front of Edward, proudly holding the crown aloft and awaiting the final moment when the Archbishop would ceremoniously lift it from its cushion, bless it and slowly, carefully place it upon the Prince's head. The official act, the holiest and most sacred of the Empire, reserved only for the head of the Church to symbolize God's acceptance and the divinity of the Heir.

Seated just a few paces below the dais and to the right of the Throne were Gaveston, Lancaster and Gloucester. From the looks on their faces the two cousins, once again out of reach of their wives, were once again consumed with rage. A most impressive sight lavished on a most unimpressive wretch.

Suddenly, without a word, without invitation, Gaveston rose from what at the last moment had been set up as a special chair, a post never before stationed at a Coronation, and only a short distance away from the ceremony and strode boldly forward. Struck dumb with shock, no one could move or speak. Deftly beating the Archbishop's outstretched hands to the Crown, he snatched it in his own two hands from its cushion, jostled crudely past the startled Archbishop, and placed it upon Edward's head.

Westminster exploded.

The angry roar from the congregation swept the room like a battle charge. It could be heard across the Thames. Most were on their feet, but none were faster than the drunk, enraged and now out of control Gloucester.

The Coronation was a farce.

The scene at the Throne featured the Archbishop, in shock, stuttering incoherently. The totally flustered rotundous cleric had stumbled backwards into the surging crowd of nobles, tripping up most who had instinctively launched themselves in the direction of Gaveston, and were now a crawling blockade of fallen bodies and expensive robes, while Gaveston was calmly leaning over and kissing the seated Edward firmly on the cheek.

It was to be an expensive kiss. As Gaveston's lips touched the Royal cheek, Gloucester's powerful hand clamped down like a vice on the back of his exposed neck. The other muscular hand balled into a fist, and smashed blindly into the side of his head, narrowly missing the King's face. Once, twice, three times Gloucester struck. Gaveston began screaming. Blood spurted from his mouth and ear.

The suddenness and the violence of the attack, so terrified Edward that he too began screaming. Crouched in a suppliant fetal position in the Throne Chair he was trapped and unable to flee. All he could do was watch in horror as his enraged cousin beat Gaveston to a pulp just inches away from him beneath the altar of Westminster Abbey.

III

Although he had been given a second chance, and a slim one at that, Gaveston did not get the message. If it could be said that he excelled at any one trait, it would be that of the arrogant fool. He lacked the savvy to feign even the smallest measure of remorse; and as for emotion, the only sensation he felt was rage; rage that the other Barons, including that asshole Gloucester, did not grovel.

Order was finally restored in the Abbey. Gaveston's unconscious body was, at Gloucester's command, "dragged like a sack of manure" from the chapel down the center isle of the long nave, and hurled from the steps into the street.

Edward's hysterical protests of the treatment of Gaveston were answered with a slap across the face from Lancaster, who then grabbed the Crown from the young King's head, abruptly handed it back to the Archbishop, and then seized Edward by his shoulders and shoved him back into the Throne Chair.

Edward, too terrified to utter a sound, pouted through the remainder of the ceremony, only too glad at it's end to escape to Gaveston's apartments in Hampton. As for the rest of the guests and the other members of the Royal Family, they too were only too glad to party without him and his disturbing friends.

~

The morning sun had come around in such a way that it had taken the uncompromising position to glare through Edward's uncovered bedroom windows at the two sleeping on the huge four-poster bed. On most any other morning it would have been a welcome visitor. This morning it was a cruel intruder that shone with intensity directly into his swollen, sleeping face, probing at his one working eye to open. It had no intention of letting him sleep further.

As he awoke, so did the throbbing pain in the side of his head. The events of yesterday tumbled in. How he had gotten home, he didn't know. But it was here that Edward had found him, and revived him. He undoubtedly had a head harder than he thought, for Gloucester was surely intent on killing him.

How dare that pig strike him! After all, did he not now possess the richest, most powerful Earldom in all of England? Was he not the King's favorite? Could he not make the King do anything he wanted? His lover, his confidante, his always companion; had Edward not taken him into his arms and wept like a child at their reunion just a year before? And this time, the Nobles could not send him away.

It had not been easy even then. Not even with Edward's father, then alive and then stolidly behind it. The House of Lords still had to trump up a phony mission on which to send him. Now that old goat was gone, and he was now the Earl of Cornwall. How things had changed! Now he could remove some of them, and so he would. Many would pay for the beating he had taken.

It was his right, their victory. Edward was now King and now must be obeyed. He was back in London, back at Court, and with all the power. He could have anything he wanted, and he intended to get everything.

Gloucester may have done the battering, but he had come out the winner. In time Gloucester would pay the ultimate price.

The little reverie was enough for his ego. Having reasoned himself into a better mood, he now only had the hangover to deal with and that could be easily cured with cold ale and big breakfast of roast potato, crispy pork and fresh eggs fried scrambled.

As he lay there contemplating his appetite, in spite of his aching jaw muscles, in spite of the sun's practical joke, he began to smile. The irony of yesterday was that he had fought a battle, and won. Look where he was.

Now it had become a particularly beautiful day. His thoughts suited him, and the more he thought, the more pleased he became. How comfortable and tasteful his London townhouse was. How big his bed was. How deserving he was.

He rolled onto his back and stretched, ready to get on with his day. His arm brushed the body sleeping next to him, and he remembered everything.

"Wake up your Royal Highness." He began roughly tapping the royal personage on the side of the face. "We've got a lot to do and not much time to do it, wake up!"

Gaveston's rough intrusion attacked his dream like a swarm of bees. Edward awoke with a start, flailing, and sat bolt upright. Then just as suddenly, he was on his feet hauling at his clothes in a frantic attempt to put everything on at once. "Jesus Gascon, why did you let me sleep? You know where I've got to go today."

Gaveston lay back, silent, arms folded behind his head, amused at the antics going on before him. After a few unsuccessful attempts to haul on his trousers Edward's burst of energy ended just as quickly.

The King let the wine-stained, crumpled bundle he clutched spill to the floor as the agony of the alcohol still coursing through his veins once again took control. Then came the wave and his knees no longer cared about holding him up. Unable to stand any longer he hugged the bedpost. To no avail. It took only an extra moment before his strength completely gave in whereby, without surrendering his hold, he slowly slid down the length of the polished oak timber and flopped helplessly onto the floor. "Oh fuck," he groaned, "what a hangover. What in hell did we do last night? And what are you laughing about?"

"At you dear boy, at you." Gaveston broke his amused silence. "If your people could only see you now."

"Fuck you."

Gaveston laughed. It hurt his face and he moaned through his laughter. "And fuck your cousin." He patted his sore cheek. "Fuck him, it didn't stop us, did it? Consider after everything that happened, what we did last night at your bachelor party, your coming-out party, your all-in-one-party, old man. It was your big send up. You had a hell of a good time." Gaveston remained propped on his pillows. He couldn't see from his position how the prone Edward laid curled on the floor. But he could imagine and couldn't help laughing in spite of the pain.

Indeed, Edward lay clutching his pounding head. Sobriety was making matters worse. The King had slid down the poster and lay in the fetal position on the cold stone floor in a pile of bed covers that he had managed to drag with him as he crumbled; a resort that he had clung to from childhood when his only companions, female companions mostly, would tease and taunt him with their perverse games and overbearing cruelty.

Then the behavior had garnered sympathy and pity, coming from the small pretty child. Now it only served to make him more absurd than he already was.

The Crown he had coveted for so long was now his and that was good. In spite of the hangover he should be ecstatic, but he was not. The next official duty tipped the scales badly. "You're in a good mood," he groaned. "you're obviously sooo happy that I'm getting married?" It wasn't the idea of marriage that frightened Edward, it was the way that Gaveston had, of late, seemed to be pleased about it, the way he had been promoting it ever since his Royal cousins had ordered the marriage to take place.

He couldn't hide his insecurity and Gaveston played on it.

"I'm not happy or unhappy. It's something you have to do; it's part of your job. I've come to terms with it and so should you, and that's all there is to it. You're a fucking King now and you've got to start acting like it. That means that you've got to make babies so there will be more Kings, and you and I can't do that."

"What makes you think that will happen anyway?" Edward couldn't help pouting. Having a wife wouldn't necessarily mean having babies.

"Why? What do you mean?"

"Because I'm not interested in women. You know that!"

"Oh get serious Edward. How can you not be interested?"

"I'm not, okay. I'm just not."

"Not even pretty ones? Not even when they are close to you, talking to you, pretending to touch your arm accidentally like they do when they're really trying to tell you that you can have them?"

"No, no, not even them." Edward moaned. "Why do we have to talk about this?"

"You have been around beautiful women all your life. All those gorgeous French and Spanish girls your father kept around Windsor. Some of them are still there. What do think they're for my friend?"

"They were for my father. I know that. So what!"

"So what! So didn't you avail yourself of a few now and then. There were so many and so eager to please, and he was never there. How would he know? I know that I played with a few and there were no repercussions."

"Well I didn't, so let it go."

"When you were not quite a teenager, in those middle years, you know, nine, ten, eleven, whatever years; when you started to wonder what women were for. Didn't you ever get a little stiffy going on whenever you saw them naked or when your maids and nannies bathed you? Didn't you find that it felt good whenever they washed your little dick and balls?"

"I don't remember." Edward sighed, wishing Gaveston would get off the subject.

"Jesus, Edward, I thought I knew all there was to know about you. I've always figured you for both sides. And what you did in bed, when I wasn't around, was your own business."

"Thank you!"

"What goes through your mind when you see one of these beauties naked? Surely it gets to you?"

"Oh Gascon, give it up, please!" Edward flopped onto his back, and tried to cover his ears with his hands. His head was pounding, and Gaveston's questions were making the hangover worse.

"What if one was actually working on your post, how could you resist that?"

Edward knew that he would not get off the subject until he got the answers he wanted. Gaveston always got what he wanted.

"Nope. You remember all those parties when you ordered all those whores and then made them strip naked for the whole night ...."

"You bet I do," Gaveston's toes wiggled involuntarily.

"See, I don't even have to look at you to feel your excitement. Well for me, nothing, not even a twinge. I don't feel it, they have no effect on me."

Gaveston suddenly dove over the covers and landed peering down at Edward from over the end of the bed. "So you have never, ever, been inside of a woman?" The humor had left him.

"Honest to God, never ..."

Gaveston laid motionless on his stomach staring down at his pathetic friend, looking so helpless on the floor hugging the folds of the coverlet as a child hugs it's security blanket. "Jesus, all these years we've known each other ... all the wild parties ... I just assumed you were fucking like everybody else!"

"Not once ... not with a woman."

Gaveston rolled over and sat up. Collecting a loose cover from the tousled mess around him, he wrapped it about himself for warmth and hiked to the floor. On his feet he adjusted the sheet for maximum coverage and walked around the end of the bed to stand by his prostrate friend.

For several minutes, he stood and stared at him.

Thoughtful of his good fortune, this brought a whole new meaning to his role as the King's best friend. What he never would tell his pathetic benefactor was that he 'preferred' sleeping with his new wife.

~

She had come to him as a gift from Edward, the daughter of the late Earl of Cornwall, a second Royal cousin by whom Edward could endow and Gaveston could claim legitimate nobility and solve the question of the inheritance of the estate.

Margeurite proved to be an even better gift than Edward intended. Notwithstanding she more than satisfied Gaveston's ambitions, she was everything his sexual appetites desired; beautiful, sensual, attentive to her flamboyant husband's impulsive needs, and never complained of his whereabouts. Gaveston had quite fallen in love with her.

~

"Edward, you are going to have to try it…" He was about to say 'it can be delicious', but he thought better of it.

"Why? What for? I am not interested."

"Look your highness," Gaveston had a short fuse when it came to Edward's childish and petulant behavior, and could feel his temper slipping. Through gritted teeth the order slipped out. "You are bloody well going to do it."

The look of hurt on Edward's upturned face told him he had made a mistake. Though Edward could be manipulated easily by pushing the right buttons, if he felt betrayed, especially by someone he loved, and most especially by Gaveston, he could also crawl into the dark hole his overbearing father had spent a lifetime digging for him, and no amount of reason would prevail, at least not in time for what needed to be done.

Gaveston had to get him back. Exaggerating the best impression of King and Empire servitude, he snapped to perfect attention, and saluted the King roman style by sharply extending his right arm. The action caused the bed sheet he held wrapped about him to drop to the floor. Exposed and poised above his companion, with not only his arm extended, he solemnly pronounced, "Sire, it's for England."

Edward grinned up at him and began to laugh. His depression melted. Only the physical pain remained. His laughter mixed with a long groan and he rolled over onto his side, his head pounding, wanting desperately to be out of this marriage situation.

That is when Gaveston got an idea. In his employ there were several very attractive housemaids, whose obvious ambitions had landed them the jobs. With one in particular he enjoyed a very secret and very intense physical relationship. And she was incredibly loyal. Poor, ambitious, delicious, little slut, he thought. In a way he admired her and felt sorry for her, and others like her, all at the same time.

Pretty, sexy, she had that special effect on men that works like quicksand. The more one resists, the deeper one is pulled in.

And her irresistible and exciting charms never failed in their infinite promise. They kept him coming back time and time again. "What a gift," thought Gaveston. "Such a power these creatures have, and yet what do they win? They set themselves up to be used. And what do they get for it? The chances of crossing over are almost nil."

Yet, he reasoned, "What else was she supposed to do? Not born to any station, nobody was going to give her anything for having any brains, she had no rights, no protection.

Maybe God had been kinder to her than any birthright could. With that face and a body that gave such pleasure, as long as she played their game, men like him and men even more powerful would not want her far from them for very long.

Yes, perhaps for him, no doubt for him, she would perform for the King. After all, he thought, wouldn't that be as good as putting out gets."

Telling Edward to stay, he went off through the house in search of her. He was right. The minute he told her that the King needed cheering up, she was more than willing. Leading her by the hand they were both actually running they were so excited to get her into that bedroom.

Bursting into the room, Gaveston's enthusiasm was getting the better of him, "Your Majesty," he grandly announced as he came through the door, maid in tow, "I have brought you a magnificent gift, nay, a spectacular gift to enjoy as often as you like for a long as you like." And with that he twirled the lovely girl around the end of the huge bed to stand directly over the still prone Edward, and slipped her robe from her body. It was all that she wore.

Edward raised himself onto his elbows. "Oh Christ," he moaned, and flopped back down into the crumpled covers.

Instantly the girl's smile was gone. She began to shrink backwards, drawing her arms in to cover her naked breasts, instinctively fearful that she was doing something wrong.

"No, no, my dear," chuckled Gaveston, stepping up behind her and enfolding her in his arms, he held her fast in front of Edward. It's okay, my pretty, it's okay. He's just not quite awake and has a dreadful hangover," he cooed in her ear. Then, as he held her, he drew her arms apart, putting her on display, eager for Edward to see what a prize she was, hoping for Edward to show some excitement.

The King just lay motionless in a weirdly distorted position, looking, if anything, only threatened.

Gaveston wanted to kick him, hard, anywhere that would hurt, badly. But he knew that would be the most disastrous thing he could do right now. He had only two days to get his indolent friend ready to take a women into his bed, and he wasn't going to fail. "Now Edward, my dear boy, this is no way to behave in front of a lady," he coaxed. "So get yourself up from the floor and onto the bed where she will be far more comfortable. It will be better that way, you'll see."

Expecting resistance, Gaveston was prepared to make it a game and include the naked girl in cajoling and forcing Edward to move, but his plea was answered.

As Edward slowly struggled to rise, to hike himself back onto the bed, he left the covers behind. In his earlier aborted attempt to hurriedly dress he had managed only to put on his shirt, a short one at that, and now the girl was getting a very good look at the King's package.

Although it had never been delivered to a woman, Gaveston saw the instant look of anticipation spread across her face, and knew this one would do her very best to make it work. If nothing else, the new King had inherited his father's good looks and impressive male symbol. The maid was aroused and ready to play teacher. Would the student be willing to learn?

Gaveston watched her staring, and thought, so far so good. "Edward, just lay still, trust me, trust her and go with her on this. Remember, it's for your own good, and it's for England." That remark made all three of them laugh. "Ah," thought Gaveston, "she is not stupid; she knows what she is here for."

Appreciating her wit, he patted her naked behind. She returned an inviting smile to which he grinned back wickedly, "All right my dear, the King of England is all yours."

Slowly she began to crawl across the massive four-poster, stalking the disinterested Edward like a female lioness stalks her prey.

To Gaveston the site was irresistible. How could his friend not be going crazy? Fantasy becoming reality; large firm breasts, lean body curved in all the most enticing ways. God, what a lovely thing she is, he thought. He's got to want this; I know I sure do. Work your magic little girl. He was reaching the point of physical stress himself, and wanted to leap onto the bed with them.

Then he saw what he didn't expect to see. Gaveston could be turned on equally by both beautiful women and beautiful men, and preferably more so if they were all together at the same time. This was one of those special moments, and Edward wanted no part of it.

Her first efforts were going unanswered, and he could see that she was becoming reluctant to continue. It would be necessary for him to move things along.

Already naked; too excited to resist the erotic scene on the bed before him, he was planning to have her anyway after Edward had finished. He would not have to wait. She was still on her hands and knees, hovering over Edward's limp organ as Gaveston crawled up behind her and pressed himself into her. His sudden penetration, although welcome, surprised her and she gasped.

Edward had been laying flat on his back, eyes shut, willing himself to tolerate the lust of this woman. But other than the pleasant sensation of having his penis fondled, there was nothing about it to bring on arousal, until he opened his eyes that is.

Her sudden gasp startled him as well, only to find Gaveston enjoined with her hovering over him. This he liked. Gaveston pressed her to continue to pleasure the King while he fornicated with her. For some reason this worked on Edward. He became wildly excited and began clutching at, and stroking both of them.

Her nervousness gone and forgotten, she had given completely over to the excitement of the moment and was intent not only on her own pleasure, but giving pleasure to both men.

It was now or never. Still gripping her hips firmly from behind, Gaveston withdrew himself and positioned her conveniently over Edward, where she took the King's penis in hand and lowered herself completely on to it.

"Now my sweet," Gaveston whispered into her ear, "straddle him, take him; take all of him inside. You are about to change his world."

The maid was willing and experienced, and coaxed Edward to do with her whatever pleased him. But as Gaveston slipped from his view above him, so did his interest slip away from and out of her. Gently but firmly, Edward pushed the girl off of his mid-section, and motioned her away from him.

She moved quickly to depart. There would be no nonsense or teasing or second try here. Any effort of any kind would be useless and she knew why. Other than volunteering a look, offering to give Gaveston the relief he still seemed to so desperately need, she also knew that it was prudent to leave the room as quickly as possible. The hedonistic excitement so intense just moments before, had completely vanished.

Gaveston gave her a quick shake of his head, indicating that their unfinished pleasure would have to be taken at another time. Suddenly he became very depressed. As he watched her irresistible nudity disappear through the bedroom door, he saw his life going with her.

All of his good fortune was totally at the mercy of the King's good fortune, and the new King had made many powerful enemies; especially within his own family walls. Not a good place to have enemies.

Not a good place to have too many enemies anywhere in Britain. The people did not regard the young Edward as a deity and showed their dislike for him at every opportunity. It wouldn't take much should there arise a popular hero, to put an end to the Monarchy.

And Edward's cousins knew it and baited the hook whenever they could. Lancaster more so than the others, believed that he was the rightful Heir and made no secret of his desire to be rid of the King; and the only person he hated more than Edward was Gaveston.

This marriage was the last hope for Edward and perhaps for England. If he could not at long last demonstrate to his people that he was a real man, a real leader and warrior like his father; able to not only win the hand of the most beautiful Princess in Europe, the daughter of King Philippe of

France; but by doing so, to secure the safety of England and put an end to the bloody barbarian wars, then Lancaster could push him out of the Throne Room as easily as shooing away an annoying dog.

"Edward, do you have any idea of the consequences if you don't go through with this marriage?

The King made no sound.

"We will be ruined, you and I, and everything you have will be taken away. Don't you get it ... you can kiss England goodbye!" Gaveston didn't raise or lower his voice.

So much for both of them lay useless in that bed. Edward lay still, his tears running silently over his temples and back into the bed sheets, his arm draped across eyes to shut out the world. Gaveston leaned sadly against the bedpost. For a long while neither said a word, then Gaveston broke the silence.

"C'mon my dear friend, get up. You are going to France, and you are going to get married. That much you can do. We'll work the rest out later."

Gaveston was about to reach over and pull Edward up from the bed when there was a knock on the door. Grabbing up a bed sheet and winding it about himself, he opened it just a little, "yes."

Standing on the other side was another of his lovely maids, smiling prettily. The little bitch, he thought, she knows already. "Listen my dear," he whispered, "now is not a good time."

"Excuse me your Lordship," she sweetly interrupted, "there is a message for his Royal Highness," and with that held up a sealed document. As he took it she quickly curtsied, stood up, winked at him and without another word, hurried away.

Gaveston closed the door and as he shuffled in the tangled sheet back to the side of the bed he looked at the wax seal. It was Gloucester's. That wouldn't stop him. Without saying a word he broke it and flipped open the folded page. Edward as yet hadn't uttered a word.

Gaveston read every word carefully and then announced. "Do you have any idea what happened at Dundee two days ago ... the day of your blessed Coronation! Do you have any idea?"

Edward peeked out from behind his folded arm and for a long moment stared with one eye at Gaveston before shaking his head indicating that he didn't know.

Gaveston seemed to be waiting for more from him. There was an edge to his voice that hadn't been there a moment ago, which indicated that a sharp answer was expected. His attitude had completely changed and Edward felt it. Quickly he was on his elbows looking anxiously at his friend. "What?"

Gaveston's first response was to fling the paper onto the bed.

Lying on a table not far from the bed was a medium sized, ornately bejeweled Saracen dagger. A souvenir from the late Edward's personal treasure trove. The night before they had been admiring its worth. Gaveston spied it, picked it up and began flipping it over in the air, each time catching it by the handle and each time holding it to admire its artistry and balance.

Edward knew what was coming. His friend ruled and he was powerless to stand up to him.

"I didn't think so," the tone was superior and the words spoken slowly, as he continued to flip the dagger, no longer even looking at it. "Well, your Royal Highness, here's the news." He paused, which just added to Edward's already churning discomfort, and then continued with even more sarcasm, "your Celtic blood brother, the animal they call the Bruce slaughtered the entire garrison ... your garrison .... The whole bleedin' lot of them...."

"How...how..." Edward was stammering; "that's what's in that letter ...?"

"Pick it up, look at it for yourself ...." Gaveston had dispensed with the sheet and the dagger and had put on his hose and britches. As he pulled on his shirt he strolled across the room and settled himself imperiously in a large chair at the head of the same table. Edward's frightened gaze followed him.

For a moment the two just stared at each other before Edward sat upright and read the message. With Edward in shock, he felt smug, in complete control, and placing himself in the chair gave him an even greater sense of importance. It was a gift from Edward; the Lionheart once owned it.

Gaveston remained silent, letting the news sink in.

Edward now sat on the edge of the bed his eyes glued to the dispatch. "What do I do?"

The question defined their lives together. A tiny smile crossed Gaveston's face. "You'll marry this powerful little princess, my boy. Because if you don't this Bruce and every savage like him ... the Welsh ... the Irish ... your backstabbing cousins, the Germans ... all of them will be all over us like flies on dung ... count on it.

"How ... how is it possible. No one would dare to attack England on her own soil...."

"Wake up Edward! ... That was when your bastard of a father was alive ... everybody feared him, and even then he almost lost it to Wallace," Gaveston paused again. He thought he might be going a bit too far. Choosing his words carefully he continued, more softly, "they're not afraid of you...," he stopped.

By the expression on Edward's face, he could see that the words were hitting hard and would only make things worse. This boy hadn't learned much from his father. He took for granted that everyone feared the King, after all they were supposed to.

Gaveston was right. These were words that Edward didn't want to hear. In a high defensive voice he burst out with, "What do you mean they're not afraid of me? I have the same armies, the same generals, the same...."

"Wait ... wait ... settle yourself ... settle ... let me finish. I mean they don't know what you might or might not be capable of. You are not regarded as a warrior, you haven't laid waste to half of the holy land, you have never personally had to lead your armies into battle, and you are new at the job. What I am trying to say is that your enemies will naturally want to test you."

Still seated on the bed clutching the message, Edward seemed placated. "So what are you saying ... I have to go out and attack Wales or Scotland or something just to prove to the rest of the world that I am to be reckoned with ... ?"

"No my dear Sire, no ... at least not yet. But your choice of targets is quite prophetic I must say!"

"Why?"

"You really don't see it, do you?"

"See what?"

Gaveston realized that it was time to help Edward muster all the self-confidence there was in him and had left the chair to sit on the bed beside him. "They may not give you the chance to attack them. It is felt by many, dear boy, that they may be the first to test you. Welcome to your new job."

As much as Edward craved approval, he also trusted Gaveston to get him through difficulties. Again, feeling deflated, he had to accept the possibility. For a long moment neither said another word then he looked at Gaveston and in a weak powerless voice he asked the question Gaveston wanted to hear. "I don't know how to fight a war. What would be expected of me?"

Gripping Edward's shoulder reassuringly, Gaveston replied, "what would be expected of you dear Edward, of you?" He paused and gave him a look that told Edward that all of his problems were about to be absorbed. "Not you dear boy, no, no, no... us Edward, us! ... together, you and I shall run this country."

To say more would be folly. The proclamation seemed to be taking. Edward dressed in silence, and was still silent while they waited for a carriage to be made ready to take him back to Westminster. Gaveston began to think he had gone to far.

Then, out of the blue, as Edward watched from a window as the carriage drew up outside, he announced, "Piers, I have decided that you will be my Regent while I am away."

Gaveston could not believe his ears. He felt that his remark had earned him points, but never would it be regarded as more than a vow of friendship. To be entrusted with the stewardship of the realm, even if it were for only a few days, would forever establish him as the most powerful person in England. He couldn't speak.

Edward raised his voice. "You are not listening Gascon, are you?"

"Yes, yes of course I am ... you are going to be away, I know that ...."

"Then you weren't listening. I said," Edward pronounced the words slowly, "that I want you to act as Regent while I am away in France." The fresh expression on Gaveston's face was enough reward. He began to jump up and down like an excited schoolboy, the disaster of the morning forgotten.

"Regent! My God Edward, ...how ... you can't ... it's impossible ...'.

"You see ... you see," Edward started squealing and dancing about with uncontrollable delight. Gaveston couldn't believe what was happening. He grabbed the bouncing Edward and hugged him fiercely, unable to disguise his joy. That was all that mattered. "Nothing's impossible for me," hollered Edward, "I am the fucking King, and I'll do whatever I fucking well want!"

Gaveston had no control over his own ego. Requited ambition produced in him his strongest emotion. The words were sweet and sweeter still, as he listened to the answer to the most important question. Knowing Edward's inability to straddle tension, he had to be sure that he could pull this off. "I thought Gloucester automatically became regent whenever the King was absent. Is it not the law? Is he not the High Steward ...?"

"Fuck Gloucester," Edward interrupted, "his appointment ended with my father. Besides it's not a lifetime job. Now I get to pick my own High Steward, and it is certainly not Gloucester. For one thing, cousin or not, he's too much like my father and I don't need more of him, and for another, I know he doesn't want me as King. So I'd be a fool to keep him on as Regent and put him in charge so soon after the old bastard's death. Right now, if he gains one more ounce of power, my Coronation will have about as much meaning as another garden party at Windsor."

Edward started through the same bedroom door with things looking somewhat different from where just an hour ago so much hope had seemed to disappear. He stopped and turned back to face Gaveston, "you are Regent, and that is all there is to it."

The words sounded like music.

Hours later, when Lancaster heard them, they sounded like cannon shots.

IV

By the age of fourteen, Isabella de Bourbon was tired of being a child.

The youngest daughter of the most powerful Monarch on earth, Philippe the Fourth, King of France, had started to question the romantic notions she once harbored about men.

In contrast to her pubescent fantasies about gentle knights and bowered love nests, she was discovering all too quickly that outside of her beloved father and brothers, most of the men she knew had somehow developed an insatiable appetite for ignoble thought and deed, especially when alone with her.

Many, whom she had thought of for years as paternal friends and protectors, and others as innocent playmates, were of a recent inclination to want to position themselves too closely, to accidentally place or brush hands where hands ought not to be, and to engage her in discourse of a highly provocative nature.

And none blamed any other. All who knew her, young and old, were of the same opinion. She was exquisite, and even though only fourteen, each discovered with uninvited ease how depravity could occupy such a comfortable seat even in the most righteous mind.

Even Longshanks, although now dead this one year, had been no exception. Just before his death he had had a chance to meet his maturing daughter-in-law and went to his deathbed comfortable in the knowledge that his foresight had paid off.

"By God," he swore, "she'll be the best thing that ever happened to England, and hopefully the best thing for that foppish, bishop's fart-son of mine."

Most advances she could ignore. Some stirred her curiosity, and a select few inspired the same longing.

And not that she was altogether innocent. Some of the experiences were not all that bad. Even though she wasn't entirely aware of everything that was expected of her, there were a few young men whose advances stirred in her sensations that, while scary, were equally welcome.

Fortunately for her, none as yet had weakened her defenses. Refuge was never very far away.

The guardian of the Royal virtue was none other than her tutor and companion, one Constance, a comely beauty herself, only four years senior, who possessed the unabashed charm, clarity and acumen of natural thought to keep her young and exceptionally beautiful charge one step ahead of the hordes of excited male libidos in hot pursuit.

And it wasn't easy. How to prepare for marriage and divulge to one so curious the infinite pleasures that can be wrought between two consenting bodies, and at the same time warn away the very same indulgence that could lead to so much disaster.

And not that there wasn't an abundance of guilt eating away at the double standard she imposed. Constance saw in Isabella's eyes her own hypocrisy.

On more than a few mornings, had Isabella not burst into her bedroom only to surprise her either asleep in the arms of, or grappling in the moment of ecstasy with one or other of the eligible, and from time to time, not-so-eligible, young men at Court? Some of the same who also, unabashedly, demonstrated their smoldering lust for Isabella.

Getting her married was coming not a moment too soon. She was the number one prize in the world, and yearning to be won. Every eligible titled Heir and feudal Baron of any consequence sought her hand. Never mind that she was betrothed. Never mind that marriage was imminent, and never mind that it was to the King of England; some believed that the race wasn't over until it was over. There was no question of what it would do for one's station in life, not to mention the accolades at home. But just to bed this exquisite beauty was worth all the risks on earth.

~

However, Constance got them through it, one precious virginity saved, a day at a time, with all the necessary virtue still in tact. And as the day of the wedding grew nearer the chances and numbers of the dedicated diminished.

Then two things were announced. The King of England had departed London and was on his way to France via stops in Flanders. He desired that the ceremony take place in Boulogne on the Normandy coast, and that he would arrive in two weeks.

The timing at first surprised everyone. Then Philippe speculated that for the King of England, the timing was perfect, to escape his wretched freezing climate.

Anyway, for Isabella the time of year didn't matter. Her husband was on his way. And all of that which she knew was that he was handsome. For now that was the best she could hope for. Her mother, and later Constance, had drummed it into her head that Royals didn't marry for love, they married to save countries, unite allies, expand territories and increase their power, but never for love.

Getting a handsome Prince or King in the bargain was a bonus and usually something that bode well for a healthy marriage. Armed with that understanding she couldn't help her excitement.

Constance, in her own defense after one particularly embarrassing morning, had told her, "that even with normal women they don't fall in love with every man they sleep with. In fact they don't fall in love with any of them. But they sure as hell like most of them to be good looking. It makes having sex more enjoyable. Handsome is good for sex. Love is good for money. And the first thing you are going to do with him is have sex. So what is better?"

That in response to the question, "why is it that whenever I catch you in bed with a man, it is never the same one?"

The three weeks allowed just enough time to alert the hundreds of Royal households throughout the continent who were intended to come and were awaiting the date.

Philippe knew all of his neighboring warlords and minor Kings, and knew that last month's friend could be this month's enemy. But enemies and allies alike had no intention of missing this one. All pressured to seek favor with the French Court. And many of the more ambitious ones saw it as an opportunity to size up the new English King. Rumor had it that he was nothing like his father.

Philippe had the foresight to dispatch a warning that if anyone chose this time and place to make a disturbance, be it King, Queen, Prince or Princess they would be struck dead on the spot.

V

Finally it came time to say goodbye to Paris. For months Isabella imagined it would be impossible, and willed herself to not think about it. But when the time actually came, things happened so quickly and so many of her household favorites were going with her, that her greatest difficulty became the selection of what and how much to pack.

December in London may be a very trying time, cold and damp, bleak and depressing, but not so in the west country of France. The nights were crisp and invited cozy fires and mulled wine. The days were bright and the sun gave just enough warmth.

It turned out there was little time or reason for sadness. And as the huge train of caravans accompanied by legions of cavalry snaked its way across the hilly Normandy countryside it didn't take long for the excitement of the adventure to elevate everyone's mood.

The fun of a rolling party had been anticipated and they were well provisioned for it. What wasn't expected came at every village and shire they passed. They were met with wild cheering crowds offering the soldiers and the travelers wine and cheese and fresh baked bread, just to get a glimpse of her.

She didn't understand the frenzy. To her it seemed reasonable to stop and meet the people. And she didn't disappoint them. Thus the caravan was so slow that the trip to Boulogne took three full days but no one minded. It had been one hell of a party to which everyone they encountered had been invited.

At night, because there were so many of them, and so many followers, no inn was big enough to put everyone up. It meant that they set up camp and make the best of it. Not so much then a leisurely and romantic activity as one reserved for wartime. All insisted that Isabella and the bridal party at least take rooms and be warm and comfortable.

She declined, instead seeing to it that the elderly and the infirmed traveling with them were treated to the comfort. The three days had been a lesson for her as well. Seeing poverty and hardship up close had done something to her. She and her entourage had taken to giving food and clothing and money to those they came upon in need, and help to anyone else who ventured upon or wished to join the happy throng. By the time the train reached Boulogne, the country was in tears.

The castle at Boulogne was her grandfather's great masterpiece. Built as a first line of defense against seafaring invaders, near the rugged southern Normandy coast, it housed a number of functions and as a result was huge. Not only was it the western palace, it served as a garrison, a naval station, a prison and a trading center. Isabella was seeing for the first time the hard responsibilities of a good Monarch. She was also having the time of her life.

~

A Royal bridal shower isn't quite the exercise in debauchery that merits the iniquitous stag party. Although they do have one thing in common. They are both about men. The one is about men behaving ridiculously; the other is about the ridicule of men.

The Queen's apartments at Boulogne hosted the bridal party. Thirty or forty women, of a variety of ages, intent on having fun, were sequestered in four large rooms. Sleeping wherever and whenever they could for the next ten days they had found ingenious ways in which to set up their own individual little nests in helter-skelter fashion, and a never-ending way to keep an enormous hot water bath fresh and on-the-go at all times; and in which they seemed to be at all times.

And the primary topic of conversation at all times; the topic of men. None were sacred. Isabella was learning more about her male relatives and friends than she wanted to know. Not a name came up that didn't elicit a bawdy gesture or remark, especially from the wife or lover.

One cousin got a big laugh when she told them all, "... one day I 'ear him boast to his friend zat I never laugh when 'e get undress. I say to my friend ... because zere is nothing to laugh about ..."

Another immediately came back with, "... ze other night he say to me ... cherie, if I do not make love to you right now, I will die. I say to 'im well you better leave zen so you can die somewhere else ... I don't want you to stink up my house ..."

They were on a roll. "... Cherie, beware ze ones zat carry ze big sword," "and rattle zem all ze time..."

"Zis is 'plus de rien', a lot of nothing, ... so zey can have something big to play with ...,"

"So cherie, because you 'ave seen one, ... you 'aven't seen zem all ...,"

"Ze most important things are monaie an' sex, an if 'e is a young one as well, you are very lucky. But young an monaie don't always keep together... so if it 'as monaie an' it salute you every time ... two out of tree is not bad, ah oui!"

They all squealed with laughter.

~

The French aristocracy tended towards personal comfort and discretion much more so than the English and so their castles were far more welcoming and alluring. And the Royal apartments at Boulogne were the best of the lot.

Made up of large bright rooms, whose walls were dominated by high wide windows that let in lots of natural light, they were furnished in a tradition that was both opulent and festive.

Add to that, Philippe invested strenuously in his magnificent southern wine industry and proudly kept his personal stations well stocked. In the circumstance, this Royal apartment was for the time being the ample favorite. A constant stream of well-wishers descended upon it every day.

Therefore, even in the crowded conditions, one room had to be kept for receiving and entertainment. It meant no futons, no baths, just a good stock of Provencal wines and hearty northern food.

By the end of the first week, Isabella needed a break. Queen Margeurite, the widow Dowager of England, and her aunt and soon to be step mother-in-law, recognized that the girl longed for a change of faces, even if for only a few hours. So she threw a party in her apartment for Isabella to meet some of her new English relatives.

The suites were not so large or lavish, nor did they have the view that Isabella's offered, but they were comfortable and came with their own entertainment. The sitting room windows were directly one story above the guards' courtyard.

As the afternoon passed, Margeurite could see the party was going well and considered keeping everyone on for dinner. Standing alone for a moment inspecting the charmed faces of her successful little fete, she could see that her niece would do well in England. She would need the friendship of these people.

Casually her attention turned to a servant collecting empty goblets from a window sill, and was caught as she observed that the servant seemed distracted by something going on outside.

Margeurite approached, pushed open the window and peered out at the yard below. A group of riders on horses were arriving noisily and with purpose. The animals were lathered, their wet bodies steaming in the cool air.

One of the riders appeared to be bound to his saddle. He was not at all dressed like the others. About his shoulders was a long black cape that had obviously been pushed back by the hard ride and now draped to one side, it's collar turned up. He wore no hat, and Margeurite was struck by his youthful mane of thick black hair.

He appeared muscular and well-formed where, on the exposed side of his body she could see his fitted heavy leather sleeveless vest worn over a ripped white long sleeve blouse; the exposed arm covered with drying blood; and what appeared to be gentlemen's expensive brown tight velvet britches which disappeared into knee high leather hunting boots. She leaned back into the room and called to the others to see.

In a flash the two windows overlooking the courtyard were jammed with curious faces. Isabella was front and center in one of them with Constance beside her.

"What is it?"

"I do not know, cherie. Watch and see."

There were five men arriving. Four of them surrounded the fifth, the one wearing the cape. Inside the yard, the four dismounted. The man surrounded remained in the saddle. From the windows it was plain to see as his horse shifted its position how the man was tied. One hand behind him, one in front and one leg bound to the stirrup.

"Look at his clothes," someone from behind Isabella said quietly, " 'e looks like a 'highwayman, non?" No one answered. The tension held them silent.

The four who dismounted wore the French uniforms of field soldiers. None of them spoke. They had taken positions in a semi circle facing the mounted man, with their short swords drawn.

It seemed nothing much else was going to happen until all of a sudden another soldier, a large barrel-shaped cruel looking man, obviously of higher rank, also clutching a short sword, came lurching through the guard post doorway, pushed his way past the four positioned soldiers and swaggered up to stand just a few inches away from the mounted horse. He appeared drunk, and proceeded to press the tip of his blade against the rider's leg.

This fifth soldier looked like the type of person who didn't need much of an excuse to kill, especially if it was made easy.

The rider didn't flinch, even with the blade cutting through his breeches and into his flesh. He had stared at the ugly Officer the whole time he crossed the yard and he kept on staring down at him, right at him, never taking his eyes off the brutish face.

From where Constance stood it was hard to see their faces, but she could feel that the horrible soldier was intimidated, and was certain of it when he spoke. To make himself seem tougher to his men, he growled his words. "I will untie the bastard. If 'e tries anything 'e is dead."

The other four moved in a little closer, swords poised ready to strike. Liveries had taken their horses away giving them plenty of room to maneuver if trouble happened.

With one hand holding his sword in place, the Officer used the other to remove the leg tie. The rider remained still. The Officer motioned to his men to stand on both sides of the horse and when they were in position he undid the rear wrist tie.

The faces of Isabella, Constance and the others were framed in the window, spellbound. Everyone held their breath; no one dared move. Only Isabella could speak and then only in a whisper, "this must be one very dangerous man. Look ... they take no chance at all!"

The Officer was now very close to the rider's leg, pulling the last rope away from his wrist, the eyes of the rider hadn't changed direction; when in lightening speed the rider grabbed the sword from the Officer's hand and at the same time kicked him viciously in the face sending him sprawling into the dirt.

The other soldiers were completely caught by surprise and for several moments stayed frozen to their spots. This gave the rider time to leap from the saddle where he landed squarely in front of one of them whom he slashed across the upper arm. The soldier cried out in pain and dropped his sword. This gave the rider a second opportunity to take him in a chokehold whereupon he placed the sword point directly at the frightened soldier's throat.

Any advantage for the other two was gone. They had the good sense to stand still. Even with swords pointed, they were not sure what to do.

The ugly Officer struggled to get to his feet. His nose was smashed, his face and eyes bloodied, and obviously dazed by the powerful blow, but not too dazed to begin shouting at the others to kill the rider.

"Kill him ... kill him ... kill him you cowardly bastards...!"

The rider's vice-like hold on the soldier's throat was already choking the life out of him, and then to show that he meant business, the rider cut the soldiers neck drawing a heavy, dark surge of blood that quickly engulfed the short blade. The others would think twice before moving. The entrapped soldier could not control his fear and began to bawl.

The rider grinned at the others. He seemed to be saying 'I'm going to enjoy killing this man, and then I'll kill each one of you'. None wanted to be next. "You ...you fat pig," he nodded towards the Officer, "shut your ugly mouth before you get this poor, stinking wretch killed," with that the rider wrinkled his nose and spoke into his prisoner's ear, "whew ...you do stink ... have you done what I think you've done ... my God man, I should put you out of your misery...."

The Officer remained on his knees, cupping his bleeding face in his hands, and moaning.

The rider continued. "Now ... you ... pig, stay on your knees and listen to me. This man does not deserve to die because you are incompetent... so you will send for your Commander, now! , and when he arrives I will release this man and surrender to him ... not you!"

The Officer, defeated, with one hand still cupping his broken nose, waived at one of the others to go. The soldier turned and rushed into the castle.

"I wonder who 'e is..." Constance whispered.

"...and why they bring 'im 'ere ...?"

The Rider let go of his hold on the gasping soldier who immediately fell to his knees, blubbering, gulping air and clutching his bleeding throat. The point of the sword now pressed against the back of his neck, the rider holding it roman style ready to plunge it down into the man's chest cavity if any one moved to attack.

It didn't take the soldier long to find his Commander. The chief Officer had heard the commotion and was already on his way. And he no sooner stepped through the guard's doorway and Constance recognized him immediately.

Isabella blurted out, "Constance, isn't that the one I saw you ...!"

"Oui, ma cherie, oui," the answer was quick, cutting the girl off. "Shush, ecoutez, listen."

The Commander strode confidently towards the rider, no weapon in hand but obviously not afraid. The rider kept the sniveling soldier pinned beneath him. Constance raised her hand to cover Isabella's eyes, the child had never seen a man die before, let alone by so violent and bloody a method. Isabella caught the gesture and pushed her hand away. She thought for sure the poor wretch was dead and didn't want to miss a thing. The Commander was very brave, she thought, but she believed that this rider meant business.

Then everything suddenly changed. The Commander stopped only a few feet away from the rider and bowed to him. Constance knew his charm and how effective it could be. Would he be able to talk the rider out of killing this soldier? It turned out to be unnecessary.

"Ahhh monsieur, I see you 'ave arrived ... all in one piece I trust. 'ave my men not been an agreeable escort...?" There was a hint of friendship in the Commander's tone.

The rider offered a quick bow to the Commander, then tossed the sword to him, and with his foot shoved his captive face first into the dung. "At your service Monsieur."

Both men reached out their hands at the same time and shook vigorously. The Commander clapped the rider on the back. "You 'ave 'ad a long cold ride ... come inside, we 'ave some excellent Madeira, it will warm you, and we can talk. I will take you to your cell later."

The women above were astonished. Things had been so tense. They had nearly witnessed the execution of a man, and God knows what manner of bloody aftermath, and then in the turn of a moment, the rider became the welcome guest of the garrison Commander.

Intent on the scene below Isabella had leaned well out of the window not wanting to miss a thing, when suddenly her grip on the sill slipped and she started to fall. One of the others crowded in the window was able to grab her but not before she squealed. The rider, about to follow the Commander into the building, turned to look in the direction of the noise and saw the startled faces looking down at him.

'Mon Dieu', thought Isabella, 'e is handsome'. Her eyes went straight to his and she felt herself smiling. He smiled back and something stirred inside her.

"Good evening ... bonsoir dear ladies. I hope our little disagreement here did not upset you...please permit me to introduce myself ... my name is Lord Roger Mortimer, Lord Regent of Wales ... at your service."

With that he bowed, turned away and followed his captor into the building.

As the two disappeared through the doorway, the women could hear the Commander's voice trailing off, "My dear Mortimer, the King will be very 'appy to see the last of you...."

~

The drama was over and with it, the interest of the women. They quickly made their way back about the room all talking excitedly about what they had just seen. All, that was, except Constance. She barely took a step away from the window, hadn't said a word and looked like she had seen a ghost. Isabella took one look at her face, "Constance, q'uest que cest? what is it?"

She uttered the words slowly, "Roger... Mortimer ... ze ... pirate !"

VI

The sea had become rough. Isabella didn't know whether to be afraid or not. Her experience in boats had been confined to punts and commuter barges on the Seine. The ship had seemed awfully big when they were boarding that afternoon. How could the water roll it around like this?

But Constance seemed okay with it. Laughing and squealing every time it lurched and sent her stumbling across the cabin. And if she was okay, then Isabella guessed it was safe. After all Constance had made this voyage several times in her lifetime. And she would make it one more time at least.

It had been taken for granted that both of them were moving. Where Isabella went, so went Constance. Besides there was no reason for her to stay behind. There was no one man, no husband, no estate that could not endure her absence. Edward, at first had been perturbed when he learned that he was to take them both back to London. That Constance was to live in his house; that he was to support her as well.

But his fear of Philippe soon shut him up. A small price to pay for the protective hand of France. Now he need not fear anyone. How blissful it will be for Gaveston and himself. Not to have to deal with war, not worry about armies. All that tax money just to spend on themselves.

With the wedding ceremony just hours old, Edward had unceremoniously announced to Isabella that he had to begin his return to England on that night's tide and could not be persuaded to stay. If she chose to go with him, fine; if not he would send a ship for her at another more convenient time. "I can understand if you need some more time to prepare, but I must go." And just as abruptly excused himself and left the reception, his entourage in tow.

Philippe would have chased after him and struck him down for his rudeness, if it weren't for the fact that he half understood there was a good reason. It wasn't Edward's real reason, but Philippe didn't know that.

It had been rumored all over Europe that the Scottish Warlord, Robert the Bruce, kept it no secret that he had designs on England. And though there was little doubt that Philippe would lend a hand, he would do so only if Edward proved himself equal to the task.

And although the country was in no state to repel an attack let alone wage war, Gaveston had pounded it into Edward's head that his Royal presence gave the impression that he was concerned and prepared to defend himself. Philippe could reason that it was not good for the King to be away longer than necessary. So Edward used this excuse, in effect, to make his escape.

Fortunately for him, Philippe's awareness of Edward's problems stopped there. It was a good thing for the new son-in-law. So instead, for the sake of his daughter he had pledged support to Edward and agreed to inform Scotland of it.

Grateful that his own head was still on his shoulders, Edward played to his good fortune. Quietly escorting his bride aside, but no farther than her father could make out his departing lament, he bemoaned the very idea of separation from his new bride, but his country was in danger. 'Perhaps she should stay; it would be safer. How could he live with himself if anything happened to her? After things settled down, he would send for her and she could begin her life for real as Queen of England, of a strong safe England!'

Philippe beamed with pride as he overheard his courageous son-in-law waxing romantically his concerns for her well-being.

But Edward had underestimated his new little wife. His words only made her all the more determined to prove herself worthy. Was she not her father's daughter? Would she not be the emissary of her father's pledge and march with her husband into the fray; would she not defend what was now hers? Was she not now a Queen? Her mind was made up. Only a coward would stay.

~

How courageous and handsome Edward had looked as he took to the afterdeck on his father's great warship. Two hundred and forty feet long, fifty feet of beam, five mainsails, and forty cannon. The huge frigate was considered invincible.

Below, the cabins reserved for the Royals, dignitaries and senior Officers were spacious with large poster beds, and it was to the largest of these that Isabella had been escorted. Constance was given another smaller cabin right across the companionway. There was no need to explain, Isabella's was to be the bridal chamber.

"Cherie, we must prepare you for tonight. My guess is that this is where you will become a woman in a few hours."

Becoming a woman on this ship involved more work than either of them thought. Isabella and Constance had been as busy as charwomen since they came aboard. It had taken some time to prepare enough hot water for Isabella's bath, carrying buckets back and forth from the ship's galley by themselves, searching the ship's stores for clean linens, and towels. Then to prepare food and drink for his Majesty so that the atmosphere would be romantic and comforting.

Once in the cabin there would be no need to disrupt a night of love-making; to have him dress to go in search of wine or sweets or anything else that his bride desired. No, unthinkable, at least to a French woman. If they had to, they would organize it by themselves.

At first they sat in the cabin and waited. Surely a maid had been assigned to her Majesty. Time passed, and it wasn't until they were aware of the ship's departure that Constance realized that no one was coming. She was furious. How could there be no one on this huge ship available to wait on her new little Majesty? Not willing to sit any longer, she went off in search of staff and ran into one of the ship's Officers.

He was sympathetic but not prepared to deploy anyone to their service. He explained that because it was a fighting ship it was manned by soldiers and the only wait staff consisted of a handful of crude oafs unaccustomed and totally ill-equipped to administer to the needs of Royal Princesses.

They were on their own and would have to make the best of it. And so they did. After some struggling, the bath was drawn, and Constance had consumed enough wine that it had all become a lark.

Isabella kneeled in the small tub and sponged the warm, perfumed water down over her smooth young body. There was no room to sit and stretch out but no matter; rest was not on her mind.

Constance, so much the better for the wine, gazed at her with a maudlin tenderness, praying that she would have it better than most of the unfortunate Royal brides that filled the pit of obscurity across Europe.

She was so beautiful. Maybe she will be lucky. With a body like that she should fill any man to longing for most of his and her life.

Isabella rose from the tub and Constance reached out to hand her a towel. At that precise moment the ship yawed well over to one side and pounded hard against the sea. It then just as quickly righted itself, and proceeded to do it all over again. It sent both of them tumbling across the cabin floor and scared them.

Each grabbed at a bedpost and pulled themselves to their feet. It was important for Constance to remain calm, but that little roll was worse than anything she had ever experienced. Isabella could see that she was frightened. "Hold tight, cherie, just for a little bit. We wait to see if that will 'appen again." Her voice croaked. The ship was, even if for only a moment, right on it's side.

Isabella wasn't going to argue. Even though stark naked, she didn't care if the whole ship's crew walked in, she would not let go.

Constance could see her fear. Isabella's face had turned ashen and she was shaking. "Ecoutez, listen ma cherie, these big ships they construct them for the rough sea. This one, she will never sink. She made to float no matter," she lied. It was necessary and Isabella would never question her knowledge

For a minute or so Isabella just stared wide-eyed at Constance, assessing the information, but not wanting to let go of the bedpost. Constance needed to make light of the situation. The ship had resumed its steady almost comical rolling front to back and side to side seemingly all at once. "Isabella, this may be the position that your 'usband will want you in when 'e is 'ere, mais, but until then I think you should 'ave on your chemise, your night dress, and be waiting, in the bed, like an innocent, a virgin, n'est pas!"

Isabella suddenly was aware of her nudity and the position of her body at the end of the bed, hands wrapped around the post. It did feel interesting though foolish, and it made her laugh.

Constance was right, she didn't yet know what to really expect of sex, that only came with experience, but she at least understood that it was a wise woman who got what she wanted by taking care to bolster a man's confidence, not shake it, especially at the very first time he comes to her.

"Darling," Constance had told her, "men want to think two things, one, that they are the only one who 'as been there; an', two, that you think that it is as big, grande, as it gets. An' so you tell them after a while, after it falls down on the job, an' it will, that the size it does not matter, ah oui, d'accord."

Isabella was giggling as she climbed into bed. Constance would have preferred her to wear a nightgown that was more revealing, but the cabin was cold and it would be unfair to ask the girl to suffer that way, even for love.

Soon they both were laughing as Constance took tumble after tumble in a futile attempt to make the cabin presentable for his Majesty. She would get to her feet only to be sent sprawling onto the bed as the ship took one plunge after another.

"Constance, why does 'e take such a risk to cross the channel on such a night?"

"The mate, 'e tell me that 'is Majesty is very worried an' that e' demands to be back in England by tomorrow."

"I know 'e say 'e is worry about this Robert Bruce, but why to make such a danger for himself an' for everybody?" Her reflective question suddenly raised another thought and just as suddenly changed her mood. " 'E is supposed to want to be with me, non?"

"Oui, c'est vrai, pourqois, why?"

"Why, parseque, why 'as no one come 'ere to see if we are injured, or for that matter if I am prepared for 'im?"

"Cherie, remember you 'ave married a King, not a minstrel, and from what I 'ave heard 'e is à busy King. 'E 'as many problems with his country and some very dangerous enemies"… an' aussi, also, so you comprend, this is a war ship an' I think nobody will think of to come an' see that we are all right. So ma petit you will be patient. 'E will arrive soon. Now you lay back and make the best of tonight, oui, and let tomorrow wait."

~

Isabella awoke with a start. What time was it? How long had she been asleep? She reached across the bed; no one was beside her. She sat up. A lantern had been left lit and although turned down, its eerie swaying light was enough for her to see that no one was even in the room. Constance was gone. Had Edward come and seen her asleep and left?

It was like first awakening from a childhood nightmare. Was she real? Was this real? She wanted to cry out, a nanny would come, and everything would be made better. But that was not going to happen. The adult reality was that she was alone, frightened, but dealing with it, and filled with the sense that something was very wrong.

Flinging the covers back, Isabella hopped from the bed, crossed the cabin, opened the door and stepped out into the narrow companionway. By the dim light shed from her own cabin, she could make out Constance's door opposite to hers She had to knock several times but finally the sleepy voice she heard was familiar... "Oui."

Relieved, she opened it. In front of her was a cubby-space with barely enough room for the door to swing full. Constance lay on a small bunk, and had propped herself on one elbow, a tiny swaying lantern dimly glowed above her head. "Cherie, what is it?" She yawned.

At that moment the ship lurched heavily, and Isabella's own door behind her slammed loudly. It sounded as if the ship had been hit. They both screamed. Isabella had to fight the panic that was trying to take hold. "Something is wrong!"

"What is? What 'appened? Oh, non, non ... could 'e not uhhh? ... you, could you not ...?"

"Non, non, ecoutez ... nothing 'as 'appen, nothing at all ... 'e is not 'ere, I think 'e 'as never been 'ere!"

"Never! ... What do you mean, never?"

"Justament, just that; never. I know I wait, an' I fall asleep, but when I wake just a minute ago, I know 'e 'as not been with me, 'an I am sure 'e 'as not even been in the cabin, I can feel it!"

Constance swung her legs to the floor. "I will go to see ."

"Did you make clear the message...?"

"Oui, cherie, after I leave you I go 'an I tell his own steward. That I think was hours ago." Constance stood up and began to pull a heavy bed coat around her.

~

Only a few days ago, she would have taken this reaction for granted. Somehow, now, watching this unselfish beautiful woman, whom she cherished more than anyone else on earth, rise without hesitation to venture through this darkened ship on this dangerous night, to try and solve a problem that was most certainly not her own, made her feel small, weak, and ashamed. A feeling far worse than panic.

Isabella blocked her way. "Non, non, wait. This is not your task cherie. It is mine. 'E is my husband. It is my probleme 'an it is now for me to bring him to my bed. Now give me your coat 'an just tell me where is his cabin?"

"Please child, I will find out what is keeping him. It is not for you to go about this ship in the dark, on this terrible night. It is dangerous...."

Isabella snatched the coat from Constance' shoulders. "Where is his cabin...?"

~

It had taken some doing, but she found it full aft of the ship. As she had gotten closer it had not been so difficult. The noise of the party could be heard above the pounding of the hull on the water.

Outside the door she steadied herself against the roll of the ship. Standing there, she was alone; there were no guards. It sounded wild inside. All hands were on deck in the rough weather. She jiggled the latch that held the door shut, expecting for a moment that a servant would, as in her own home, appear at the other side holding it open. No such thing. The door swung wide in response to another roll of the ship.

Still with her hand on the latch, the swinging door carried her stumbling into the cabin, whereupon she dropped the coat.

She could not believe her eyes. Before her was a room full of naked men. A sight she had never seen before. Some were engaged in intimate positions which she didn't quite understand and all at the moment were grinning drunkenly in her direction.

The King himself was seated naked, directly in front of her, with a young man on his lap, swigging from a large goblet, obviously drunk as well.

With her sudden and dramatic entrance, the noise stopped abruptly, and it appeared for a moment that the men were caught out. But as she stood there frozen in the middle of the room, the surprise it gave most deserved no more attention than it took to happen. The noise resumed.

There were however a few who appreciated the surprise immediately. Before she could move, a handful of overtly pleased, naked men were crowded around her coaxing her to join them, enthused by the prospects of what lay beneath the flimsy night shift.

One took hold of her arm and tried to place her hand on his penis. More than realizing what he was attempting her to do, she was angered by his impudent hold on her Royal person. A flash of anger brought her to her senses. She tried to pull herself away, wanting suddenly to run from the room, to get as far away as possible. But he held fast, pressing himself against her captive hand.

Then another just as boldly put his arm around her neck, slipped his hand inside the front of her nightdress, and began gently caressing her breast.

Isabella surprised herself. She was not as frightened as she was indignant. And not as indignant as she was repulsed; indignant that they were not afraid of who she was, and repulsed because neither was even good looking.

They were not hurting her, but this was not the kind of wedding night sexual experience she wanted, nor should have to tolerate. It must be a game, she thought; a horrible one, and one she didn't want to play, but a game. After all, everyone was laughing, obviously having fun. Edward seemed amused and unconcerned, and he was her protector.

She had been told about situations like this but never suspected she'd be in one; stories about lone women caught up in a party of drunken men and having to satisfy more than one of them if she cared to get out of it safely. At the time, each tale was told in such a way that she became titillated and fantasized about having such an experience. This offered none of the thrill of those forbidden escapades.

This had to be something Edward dreamed up to tease her, to scare her, to excite her. Well she didn't like it. These men were cochon, pigs. And for the moment, as she stood there, tolerating it, they were closing tighter and tighter around her, touching her, stroking at her buttocks and breasts, pushing their exposed organs against her; the foul odor of their breath and their sweated bodies making her gag and want to vomit. No longer could she breathe and she was going to cry.

Her eyes locked on Edward, believing in him, hoping he understood that enough was enough, that it was time for the joke to be over. And when he saw how unhappy she was, he would end it.

Yes! She was right. Oh dear Jesus, it was a joke. Her heart stopped pounding. Edward was smiling, holding up his hand and motioning her to come to him. Instantly the two men holding her let go and the others backed away.

She started forward. Her instinct was to rush to the safety of his arms where this game would all end. But the boy remained on his lap, even as Edward slopped wine all over him and himself. Why didn't he push the boy away? The joke was over.

"My dear, come join us." Edward's voice was thick and the words were slurred. His eyes trailed from her and she watched him look about the room, grinning at his mates for approval. "Gentlemen, it appears that some of you are pleased with the gift I brought to our little party." He looked back at Isabella, his grin unchanged, "It seems your unexpected arrival pleases our horny friends."

They all began laughing. Edward nodded in appreciation. He loved opportunities to please his beloved friends. He could not lose face now.

"Come little one, come to me." He crooked his finger at her. "Remove your shift ... after all it hides nothing ... and do your duty ... reward our loyal companions with a cherry taste of England's virgin Queen...."

The men cheered his offer. Edward raised his goblet to the room and then turned his attention back to the boy on his lap, and the party continued.

Isabella continued watching Edward, trying to see some kind of sign, something to give him away, waiting for him to finish the prank, to bring it to an end. But he said nothing, there was nothing. He didn't even glance at her. All his attention was on this boy. It was as if she was no longer in the room. Surely there was more. And why were her admirers closing in again, and this time why was one tugging at the straps that held her night-dress in place. Now she was frightened.

~

Abnormal strength comes from fear. Isabella grabbed the one attempting to undress her and shoved him backwards into the others. This cleared a way towards the open door.

Her back was to Edward as she ran and she did not see the goblet hurled after her. "ISABELLA."

She had made the door, but could not resist looking back.

He was on his feet, jabbing at her with his finger, screaming, "Isabella! Stay … where you are … you will do as I say – wife!"

Unlike an adult who may hesitate to weigh the odds, a child, when terrified, will instinctively run for it's life and therefore often has the advantage. Isabella didn't hesitate and took off into the dark, narrow companionway. Behind her she could hear Edward's tantrum, "Come back here you bitch … right now, get the fuck back here … now Isabella, now!" She kept running. "I'm coming after you … and you will be beaten for this … you will obey me you fucking bitch!"

Free of the room and its stink of all kinds of body odors, her mind burning with the repulsive image of her husband naked cradling the boy in his arms, she ran as far as she could before her stomach began to heave. She fell to her hands and knees trying to control the retching. It helped. As the nausea subsided so did the panic.

The cold and the darkness took over and she began to shiver. She was lost. In her flight, the rolling of the ship had not been a problem, now it became an enormous one. She had to find safety. Not in her cabin, that was the first place Edward would look and certainly not here, freezing in this corridor.

Any attempt at standing had suddenly become a joke. Each time she got to her feet it was only to be thrown against unseen walls. How had she made it to here? After several futile tries, crawling seemed to be the only way to move along. Then Edward's voice rang closer, "You slut …you spoiled little French whore …you disobey your King…?" It didn't seem far behind.

By crawling and scrambling, using the walls, the floor, anything to keep moving, her escape took her well into a strange part of the ship and up against a dead-end and a gangway. Up was the only way to go. She climbed it holding one hand above her head. It was the smart thing to do. After a few steps her hand struck something solid but that moved. She pushed against it and like a trap door, it opened revealing a gloom that wasn't as dark as the corridor. She pushed it all the way up and peered over its sill.

A faint amount of light helped her to make out shapes, and as her eyes became accustomed, she saw the outline of a porthole and above it a low ceiling. It was some kind of a small storage cabin, maybe a good place to hide.

She climbed through the opening and crawled onto the floor of the room. That was the last thing she remembered.

VII

When Isabella awoke it was still dark. Her body was warm and comfortable and slow to respond. But as sleep dissipated, the heavy blanket around her became real and so did the body that lay pressed next to her. Had it been a nightmare? Was this her husband? Was this his bed? So why did the room smell like old leather and fish?

No, the night hadn't been a bad dream. It had been real. She was sure of it. But what was this all about? Edward must have found her and taken her here, wherever that was. But she couldn't remember that happening. Her eyes were quickly accustomed to the dark. Assuming it was Edward beside her, he was very still, she sat up to get a better look around and a hand grabbed her mouth.

"Don't, don't fight... I won't hurt you; you are safe.. please don't scream, please your Majesty...."

The scare shot through her like a bolt of lightening. But the words stuck. She calmed just as quickly. Your Majesty! Who? More insanity, another game? Suddenly more angry than anything else, she grabbed at the hand over her mouth. Who was he? He obviously knew who she was. The person held her close from behind. Was it Edward? She hardly knew his voice.

"I'm sorry my Lady, I don't want to frighten you, or hurt you, and I'm going to let go of you now. Please, please don't scream. When you crawled through that hatch you sounded in great distress. I could see you; I have been here in the dark for a while. But I knew you could not see me, and I knew if I spoke you would become hysterical and very easily have hurt yourself. It was better to grab you. I am sorry. But when I did you fainted."

He released his hold. She twisted quickly to get a look at him. Even up close the darkness made it difficult. "Who are you ... what happened?"

"What happened my Lady? To you or to me?"

"To me ... to you ... where am I and why are you here with me? Are we prisoners, yes?"

"Slow down, one question at a time."

The blanket had slipped and Isabella felt the cold. Clutching it around her, she settled back waiting.

"Why are you here ... I can't answer that. I'm here because there is no other room for me on the ship. At least no other room I would care to be in. Certainly I am not going to bunk in with any of your husband's charming friends. And no, I'm not a prisoner and I don't think you are either."

"Why monsieur ... you choose this rat hole?"

"I didn't."

"Well, I didn't either, but now it seems it is the only place for me."

"Can I ask, my Lady, why are you here?"

"Oui, you may ... but stop calling me my Lady."

"Yes my Lady."

Isabella was liking him and smiled at his little joke. "I have made a great mistake and I can do nothing to change it. I run but this is as far as I can go. I am hopeless."

"You discovered your husband's not-so-secret secret?"

"Oui." She tried to make out his features but there was not enough light. "Monsieur, what is your name?"

"I am Roger Mortimer ...."

"Mon Dieu ...."

"What is that ...?"

"I saw you Monsieur. Just the day before yesterday, in the courtyard. You made fools of my father's soldiers."

Stretched beside her, and leaning back against a bulkhead Mortimer had been relaxed. Suddenly he sat upright. "Shhhh …!"

She jumped slightly. "What?"

"Listen, over there … below the hatch."

"Listen to what?" She looked in the direction.

"I hear voices … from below."

She cocked her head and tried. "Non … I hear nothing. Just the wind, the ocean…!"

"Yes m'Lady, there are people below … my years at sea … I know any sound on a ship, in any weather. Life depends on …."

She put her hand up to his mouth and leaned closer to him. "Yes, yes, now I hear them."

The voices were below the hatch. Mortimer whispered, "m'Lady, move back, here behind me." He then slid feet first across the floor to the hatch. Isabella wrapped the blanket tighter and pressed against the bulkhead. They were both silent, waiting for something to happen.

"She has to have come this way. She is nowhere else on the ship. And I'm going to find her. I want her."

"Well I don't care any more, fuck the doxie … fuck all doxies … I'm bleedin' and I need a drink. Did you see what that little bitch's whorin' slave did to me … stabbed me she did .. right in me bleedin' arm … so fuck her if you will … I'm goin' back … besides you can get all you want of that right in the King's cabin … why the fuck is she the prize…" There were two behind the voices, close, loud and drunk.

Isabella lurched forward. "Constance!"

"Shhhh …." Mortimer reached back to her. There were footsteps climbing the gangway.

"I like a wenches wet couch more than cock any day, and I intend to get me that choice little piece before this night's over … I'll be bettin' its right up here … will you lookee here, up here … well, well … is this where you're hidin' me little cock teasin' Queenie."

The hatch opened and in a halo of yellow light a head poked through. At the same moment Mortimer lashed out with his foot kicking the intruder squarely in the face. There was no cry of pain, just a loud crash as the person tumbled back down into the companionway.

"Holy mother … awww Jesus, Jesus, Jesus …!"

They heard running. Mortimer spun around and looked down through the open hatch. In the dull light of an oil lamp hooked on the corridor wall, he saw the unconscious body laying awkwardly on its back at the bottom of the gangway, the face smashed, a pool of blood slowly spreading from beneath its head.

Isabella had crawled up beside Mortimer and was staring down at the same scene. "Is he dead?" Her voice was shaking.

It startled him. "My Lady." He looked to see that she was shivering in spite of the blanket around her. Leaving the hatch opened for the light, they crawled back to the bulkhead. Mortimer adjusted the blanket and put his arm around her. "I am sorry Princess, I am trying to keep you warm."

She didn't resist. "I am frightened ... I am found out ... we are found out. Whoever the other was, he will go back and tell my husband, and then they will come ... I have to find someplace else to hide ...."

"No one will come, not here, trust me."

"Non, non you are wrong. It was madness, he was shouting to have me beaten. He will come." Her teeth started to chatter.

He hugged her closer. "No, he will not come and I'll tell you why. The other, who ran, he saw nothing, and he will not think it was you who did that ...."

"Who then, he will tell something ...."

"He won't know, he doesn't know. All he saw was his friend fall, and he is drunk and a coward ... look, he ran away ... he didn't even care about him."

"But the man, he is so hurt, maybe dead ...."

"I don't think he will even tell, but if he does, your husband will not come here. Not for some drunk who has fallen down."

"But it is his friend."

"No it's not, no it's not, trust me. Your husband has only one friend."

"What if he sends a guard, just to see?"

"Then we are safe."

"Pourqois, why?"

"Because," Mortimer hesitated, not sure how much he should tell, "because a guard will just pick up the drunk, take him back and report exactly that, and that will be the end of it."

Isabella had cuddled against him, her head resting on his chest. She pulled away a little and gave him a sly smile. "M'sieur Mortimer, non, non, you try to make me feel good, merci, tu est un bonhomme," she settled back against him, "but you forget I grow up with guards, toute ma vie, all my life. The guard will look in here; I know it. He will see the man's broken face, know that he didn't just fall and he will look up here."

"Yes, you're probably right ..." he gently brushed his cheek over the top of her head. Her hair smelled fresh.

"What do we do?'

"We wait a little. We'll see if someone comes. If it's a guard and if I know him, all will be well. They are British soldiers and I am a British soldier. If it isn't or I don't know him, we'll see. But I think in a little while we might be able to get you to your cabin."

He made her feel good. "Constance says you are a pirate, n'est pas, is that so?"

She couldn't see the sudden grin. "I was ... sort of ... for his Majesty, the first Edward.

"For England?" Her voice rose.

"Yes, for England," he mimicked her.

"I thought pirates were just for themselves?"

"Some are, but they don't live long ...."

"So who were you against for England?"

"Against all enemies of England ...."

"For a while France was an ...."

"Yes, they were."

"Did you pirate against my country? Against my father?" Her tone was even.

"Well, I suppose there were some ...."

Isabella abruptly sat up, still partially in his lap. "So you murder Frenchmen for this King ...?" She said accusingly.

"No m'Lady, I did not and do not murder anyone for this King." He was matter of fact. "I was a privateer, working for the crown as a soldier. My orders were to capture enemy merchant vessels, seize valuable cargo and take hostages for ransom. I was not, am not, a blood thirsty pirate."

"And how many French ships did you seize?" She sounded skeptical. Pirate stories were the favorites amongst the Court, and the more exaggerated the better.

"Not many, m'Lady ... and none were great prizes...."

"Why not?" She was disappointed. "What about the hostages, ah, oui – there must have been some great ransoms. Only rich people can travel by ship, n'est pas?" She settled back against him. It was warmer.

"Ummm ... yes, there were some ...."

"And the women ...?" French women are tres belle non?" She was fishing. The best stories were always about the plight of the women.

Mortimer knew what she wanted to hear, but avoided the subject, "Your father has a great navy ... how do you think I came to be a prisoner in your courtyard...."

She wasn't easily deterred. "And the people on the ships ... the women ... what happen to them?"

"Put into lifeboats ... all into lifeboats, and sent to safety."

Isabella imagined more.

Pirates were the evil masters of the sea, dashing, romantic; secret heroes. And this one even more so. The women who were taken captive were always ravaged and reduced to wanton sex slaves, never to be heard from again to live decadent lives in opulent secret palaces. She saw herself as his hostage, becoming wanton, trapped in his denizen of evil, his sex slave. It was her fate. She knew it, why else was she driven here? Actually in his arms?

Not sure of what to do, she snuggled closer, nestling her face into his neck and raised her hand up to his shoulder.

It was an awkward invitation but Mortimer was tempted, only, to respond would be folly.

Pressing for something to happen between them, Isabella asked softly, "What if they come for us ...?"

"They aren't coming my dear ... trust me, they won't. Even if your husband now knows about that poor drunk, he won't come. He probably will suspect that I had something to do with it, but he is very afraid of me, and he paid a lot of money for me. None of his pretty boat boyfriends are nearly as valuable to him as I am."

"But won't they want to find me...?"

"I doubt that he will put us together. Right now you are safer here with me than you would be anywhere else on this ship. If they aren't already they will all soon be asleep and then I will get you back to your cabin."

She looked up at him, willing him to take her. "Right now m'sieur I need more than ever to trust you. Without you I know those two would have raped me for certain, and maybe also have killed me. So after tonight what do I do? You will be gone, and I will be at his mercy."

"It doesn't have to be that way."

"Pourqois!"

Mortimer was giving in to the desire to steal away with her. "Right after the ship docks, there is a way for us to escape. I know how to get us off before ...."

"Yes, yes ...!"

He caught himself. "No, no ... I am a stupid man, there is no other way ... no. You have to go with him. You are the Queen of England ... you cannot just disappear ... just like that ...."

For several minutes neither said anything. She laid in his arms, the truth weighing on her, wanting to fulfill the passion. "I think I have married a horrible man ... and I think he will make my life painful ... unless I do something about it."

"What will you do?"

"My father told me that my blood is more royal than Edward's. So I think it is for me to be more of a Queen than he can ever be a King, n'est pas!"

"You will be one hell of a Queen, my Lady."

"But right now, I want to kiss you."

VIII

The morning was bright and cool. His favorite time of day at his favorite place on earth. High atop the main mast flew the Royal Colors of England and of France, snapping brilliantly in the wind as the huge frigate eased her way through the calm waters to come alongside the main wharf at the Port of Dover.

The raised flags were a signal to all waiting that She had arrived.

The Captain had been on the pilot deck since just before dawn. Not that there was anything wrong and not that he was even needed at that hour. But to him the experience of Dover at sunrise was to experience God's mastery.

It confirmed his own simple faith. He wanted nothing to do with the new Protestant inventions, and loathed the inquisitive Papists. He, like most sailors, had made his own Communion with God, and a ship's deck was the only altar they both needed.

The towering cliffs rose out of the western dawn as he imagined must the portals of eternity rise out of heaven. A giant silver ribbon stretched to the horizon in both directions beckoning every Englishman who risked the sea to home and safe harbor.

Now waiting for the stevedores to secure the lines, he marveled at a scene that he had never witnessed before. Even the many times he had ferried the senior Edward, returning from great victories across the channel, nothing like this had ever greeted them.

The port was decked out for a festival. Banners and pennants and flags of all colors, shapes and sizes flew from everywhere. Thousands of cheering, eager people lined the High Street and waterfront. They hung out of buildings, and were perched on every rooftop.

Most noticeable was the large and important group assembled on the landed end of the wharf where the High Street and the waterfront intersect. Protected by an impressive escort of the King's Mounted Guards, were Gloucester, Lancaster, their wives, Gaveston, some of Edward's friends, and other important nobles. Some were on horseback; some had traveled by carriage.

The ship being of such a size took some time to dock. The wait for the Royals to disembark, could add to that time. And in Edward's case, all expected it would be a carefully orchestrated production. The wait therefore was its own event. By late morning liveries were moving about the carriages and horses with serving trays laden with goblets of sherry and madeira and ale; the public houses had opened and the more enterprising keepers had set up barrels right in the streets.

The reception for the new Queen had become one large town party.

At mid-day a new chapter in history was about to be started. With the sighting of the crew moving into position on the decks and along the gangway, and the Cavalry taking their positions along the wharf, the crowd became louder and all eyes were on the ship. Something big was about to happen.

Those stationed in the carriages, drunk or sober, emerged and took up their official positions.

The signal came when the Captain and his Officers marched sharply down the gangway and took up their places at the bottom of it. The first to emerge was Constance. All dressed in dark red in the latest of French fashion, emphasizing a plunging décolletage and fitted to her exquisite figure, she made her way down the gangway to the Captain's outstretched hand.

The crowd was not used to a sight such as this. In terms of style, Paris was another world away from the seacoast of England. But the gaping silence soon turned into cheers and catcalls which could be heard from below decks.

Anticipation had given way to appreciation. As Constance waited on the wharf, basking in the flattery of the crowd and the approving faces of the ship's Officers, the delighted First Officer stepped smartly up to take his place as her escort. The Captain returned to the top of the gangway and as he stationed himself a sudden roar went up from the crowd.

Isabella emerged from the foc'sle, walked directly to the ship's rail and began waving. The fact that she was dressed in the cream and gold of her country's colors, also sporting the same décolletage fashion, made no difference. She was everything rumored and more.

Gloucester and his wife, having taken positions closest to the ship, were not prepared for what they saw. Grabbing her husband's arm, Gloucester's wife blurted, "she is stunning!" And from a guard standing with them came an unsolicited response, "unbelievable."

She continued to wave at the crowd as the Captain took her arm and escorted her to the wharf to join Constance, and together they made their way towards their reception. With every step the crowd become even louder.

Gaveston was in a rage and to make a point, called loudly to a steward to bring him more wine. Gloucester chose to ignore his rudeness, but not to forget it.

Below deck, Edward remained in his stateroom with his entourage. Fussing and preening, his excitement bubbling. Finally he could wait no longer. "Listen to that crowd ... listen everyone. Come, come I must go ...."

Expecting to hear screams of adoration, he stepped grandly through the foc'sle doorway and pranced on deck. A shock wave sounded through the cheering as everyone got a look at his outfit.

"He is hideous," shouted Lancaster, gesturing towards his long pointed boots, which curled up and back at the toes with tiny bells dangling from the tips.

"Look at the breeches, he looks like a Covent pimp," replied Gloucester. They were skin tight with a pleated waistband, which combined with the short fitted jerkin over a ruffled blouse and balloon sleeves gave him the clownish appearance so popular amongst London's street people.

Even Gaveston felt a twinge of embarrassment at the exaggerated duck's peaked cap, which came to a high narrow point atop his head and trailed a peacock feather curling back to touch his rear.

The frenzy of the crowd died as heartily as it started. And no amount of play-acting could bring it back. Edward began waving and gesturing like the paraded Monarch. Some laughed, but most paid no attention. He could see all eyes were on her.

He was about twenty feet behind her as the Royal party approached the top of the wharf. Dozens of little peasant girls had burst from the front ranks of the crowd and were running towards her, each clutching huge bouquets of flowers. This couldn't be happening! It was a plot, a deliberate attempt to destroy him. Bringing her back to England was supposed to be his triumph; Piers had said so.

Despondent, the pantomime stopped as he dissolved into tears unable to watch as she touched them and crouched to greet the shy little ones, while the huge crowds screamed in adoration.

The crowd was wild. Several of the noble women including the wives of Lancaster and Gloucester rushed in to help. She couldn't have handled the onslaught of bouquets by herself, which as it was, she had no choice but to pass back to them as she reached out to touch and hug each of the children.

Lancaster beamed with admiration and clapped Gloucester soundly on the back. "None has ever done this before old boy. Look at the mothers."

They made up the ranks behind, overcome with maternal pride, calloused, overworked hands clutching ruddy smeared cheeks, and eyes streaming with tears, the cheering had become deafening. England was falling in love.

Edward was frozen to his spot, gaping, tears streaming down his face as well. But not tears of joy. Before anyone could get to him, to save him further embarrassment, he caught sight of Gaveston, broke with his group and like a spoiled child ran sobbing, to fling himself against the leg of his mounted friend.

The enraged Gaveston saw it coming and could do nothing about it. "You fucking idiot. What are you doing?"

Edward clung fast even as Gaveston tried to shake him off.

"Let go, stand up, Jesus, Edward!"

Unable to speak, his knees buckling, Edward held tight.

Barely able to control his anger, Gaveston reached down and grabbed the shoulder pad of Edward's jerkin; striking him in public would be unwise. Turning to his companion mounted beside him, he ordered, "This is unbelievable … just un-fucking-believable … quickly, put him in my carriage and let's get the hell out of here."

The crowd had gone quiet watching the astonishing scene, but as Edward disappeared into a large, closed carriage, all the attention was back on Isabella, who remained oblivious and crouched with two little girls.

Glad that the focus was back on her, Lancaster had slipped from his position in the receiving line and was losing more and more of his temper with every step he took towards Edward's carriage. Gaveston saw him too late as he reached for the door handle, his anger out of control. The guards thought twice about interfering.

First one of Edward's escorts and then the other seemed to fly out of the door and over Lancaster's head unseen by him as he charged into the carriage. The guards stationed on all four corners continued to stare straight ahead as if nothing was happening, even though in the stillness of the marshalling area the carriage bounced and jostled wildly. Edward's cries couldn't be heard over the crowd.

Gaveston watched in horror as the silent ordeal seemed to last forever, but afraid to go near. Then suddenly the door burst open and Lancaster stepped out, and went storming back to his own carriage, signaling to the guards to move everyone on out.

~

Isabella was not too keen on leaving. But with the Royal Carriage being ordered off, the reception was over. Along with Constance she had no choice but to take an unceremonious ride with Gloucester and his wife.

"The timing is just right," said Gloucester's wife sardonically, "it is about to storm." In keeping with her sarcasm, indeed, the sky had clouded and it had begun to sleet. Hoping to avoid another display in London she added, "I am afraid this weather will dampen the spirits of the people my dear. There may not be many out to greet you when you get to London. I am sorry."

"Oh please, Madame, do not be. It is just as well … I am very tired … I just as well could have some rest."

Constance could not be silent any longer. In just two days their world had turned upside down, and she was becoming afraid for her mistress, and not at all afraid to speak up to any of these English, noble or not. "Pardon Madame … et Monsieur."

"Yes my dear?" said Gloucester's wife as if addressing an impulsive servant.

"Dites moi … ou pardon … tell me, what is it with this man for whom the King is so, so - uh - emotional?"

"Constance, ferme …!" said Isabella, knowing where Constance was going.

Constance gave her a sugary smile, "ce vraie, pour vous cherie!, deliberately using French.

"Excuse me my dear, but I am not sure that is any…!"

Gloucester could see feathers ruffling. He patted his wife's hand, "It is, my dear … it most certainly is." Looking at Constance, he went on, "that man you refer to is one Piers Gaveston. He and the King have been companions since childhood, and I am afraid to say are unfortunately inseparable.

"Why unfortunately…?"

"It is an unhealthy relationship my dear."

"It is an evil relationship … my dear." Snipped Gloucester's wife.

"Why is that?" asked Isabella.

"Well, let's just say that …."

"Lets just say what, husband?" Gloucester's wife couldn't resist. "Lets just say the truth … they are lovers my child, lovers … do you understand …?"

"Oui ... yes, yes, I understand ...."

"But they are more than that," said Gloucester. "It is not just for themselves, it is very serious and it is the cause for many dangerous problems here in England."

"Your Edward, my dear, is devoted to this man," said Gloucester's wife. "Completely devoted, to the exclusion of everyone else ... and I mean everyone else ... and I am afraid that may even include you. He gives this evil pig anything his heart desires, any title, any income, any estate ... many of our good friends who are not powerful enough to stand up to the King, have had their lands confiscated so that they may become the property of Piers Gaveston."

"He controls the King's every thought, every move."

~

They rode on for a long while engrossed in conversation, Isabella liking this Gloucester and his outspoken wife more and more with every mile, and learning more than she wanted to know about her young husband. Because of the weather, the ride was long and slow. And as the afternoon came to an end, Gloucester assured her that it would be too late for any kind of public reception by the time they reached London. He and his wife would be separating from the caravan to return to their own estate, as they were closer to it on this road.

Their carriage had been trailing the caravan and had come to a halt at a crossroads. So had another just ahead. The couple explained that this was where they would part company, and that the other carriage would take Isabella and Constance on into London.

The King's carriage, already out in front, had taken all the guard and mounted companions, and carried on without even a look back. All the others bound for London followed, leaving the two stopped carriages alone and unguarded save for Gloucester's own two men. Isabella declined the offer to take one of them, confident that she and Constance would catch up to the procession.

It was when the Gloucester's disappeared around a bend beyond the fork of the road, that the two women realized they were alone and with a driver they didn't know. And in the storm night was coming on fast and ugly.

Inside the coach was one heavy blanket, which they had wrapped around themselves and huddled together to keep warm. "Driver ...driver!" called Isabella.

"Ma'am." The voice was surly.

"Ma'am?" Constance grimaced.

"Never mind," said Isabella, and then called to the driver, "Driver how far the distance to Londres, s'il vous plait?"

"A few miles ma'am." Same tone.

"How far ahead is the King?"

"I can't say ma'am."

"Will we catch him up?"

"I doubt it ma'am, the roads is too slippery and rutted for the horses ma'am."

If there had been a way to return to France that very moment, Constance would have taken it, even if it meant carrying Isabella all the way. "Cherie, I think this is very dangerous. We do not even have a sword in here, and I have a bad feeling that the deserted roads in this country are even worse than the deserted roads in France." She whispered, "And that cochon up there is no gentilehomme. I am sure of it ... as for that husband of yours, what kind of man have you married?"

"Constance I am sure that when we get to this Londres, all of this will not be so serious. There will be some explanation, I know it."

"When we get to this place, wherever we are going, I am making an excuse to take you home."

"Non, non, you will not. I will not. We will learn what all this of today is about. There has to be something, maybe it is me?"

"Oui, it is you all right, vraiment! You are a woman! And he doesn't like women."

"I don't understand it. And yes your little joke is amusing. We know lots of men at Court who like other men, but they are also liking women, n'est pas? I see them flirt, and I know that Madame Dumon says she has a lover who sometimes brings other men into their bed."

"Isabella, what you know of Court is one thing, but what you know of life is another. Everybody thinks that sex is just about men and women, but it is not always that way. Some men like both men and women, as there are women who like both; and then there are some men who only like men, only."

"How is that possible? We are born the way we are so that we will want each other. Even without knowing each other. Even without sex, I know that I want a man to love me, not a woman!"

"Oui, that is right and that is what nature intends, but sometimes it does not work that way."

"So you say that Edward does not want me, because he does not want any woman!"

"Oui, c'est vraie."

"How stupide is that. It is just for sex, non?"

"I think it is for more than that cherie."

"I tell you what Constance. I think that when he sees me without my clothes, naked, and you tell me what I should do to his body, I think then he will change his mind, non?"

"Let's hope."

The carriage bounced and jolted through the storm for several more hours. They had it so closed-in to have as much warmth as they could, that neither had any idea of their surroundings or where they were headed. Finally the ride ended. However it didn't improve Constance's mood. Having extricated herself from the miserable little carriage, Constance stood looking at the ugliest building she had ever seen in her life. "Jesu, qu'est qe c'est! What is this merde?"

Isabella was no more impressed. This was England's Royal palace? In front of them was a great stone wall with one tiny door at its base. No courtyard, no grand entrance, no palace guards, no light save two struggling torches on either side of the little doorway.

She didn't expect any kind of a reception, but there were not even any servants, and definitely no husband! Just a half a dozen armed guards marching towards them and the miserable driver throwing some baggage to the ground, and the air stunk.

When the guards were close, they stopped at attention and one stepped forward, bowed politely and curtly addressed them both. "Good evening ladies. I am the Captain of the Guard, and have orders to take you to your apartments. If you will follow me," and with that, made another bow, turned and started back towards a tiny doorway in the massive stone wall that greeted them.

Constance lost her temper. "Pardon m'sieur, vous, Capitaine. Vous arret, venez ici, maintenant … ici!"

The surprised Captain stopped and turned about to face the fiery Constance. She gave him no chance to speak.

"Cette femme … votre lady … est votre Reine, your Queen. You would do well to act like it, you may be very grateful some day that you did!"

The young soldier had no axe to grind with either of them. He was just carrying out orders the way they had been presented to him. The Royal carriage had been there earlier. A man claiming to represent the King had given him orders that two women would be arriving later on and that he was to give them rooms. Nothing else had been said.

The apartments were tiny, dirty and consisted of a handful of dingy rooms, which were all along one side of a narrow hallway. One was for Isabella to sleep, another for Constance, another for two servants assigned to them, and another for eating. It was a blessing neither women had ever seen the inside of a prison.

The two servants said nothing, looked miserable, but went about making things as comfortable as possible. From somewhere, food arrived and both women were so hungry; they ate it without even trying to guess what it was and then fell asleep, fully clothed, on the same bed.

~

For several days the weather remained bad. Both had no desire to go out in it, so busied themselves, along with the help of the two tight lipped servants, in having a bath tub delivered, getting laundry washed, and cleaning the rooms. Food somehow appeared whenever requested.

However, try as she might, Constance could not persuade the servants to say anything more than "whatever you wish ma'am," no matter what she asked. They did tell her that they were in a building called The Tower of London, but volunteered no more on that subject.

Whenever she or Isabella asked about the King, the two acted like they had never heard of him.

As the days turned into weeks, it was becoming obvious that they were confined to this horrid place. No one sent for them, no one visited them, and on the few occasions that they volunteered to go out on their own, the servants were very quick to stop them. "It's not done that ladies go walking about the streets in this part of London ma'am."

Constance agreed with that. All she had to do was look out of one of the windows in their tiny rooms, to see what a misty, gray, dirty place it was. Down below they were surrounded by filthy streets and gritty hovels, and ragged urchins ran everywhere. But she also had to do something about Isabella. The original optimism was gone. She had begun to talk of going home, and was very depressed that none of her letters to her father had been answered.

"I know he wants me to make the best of it here. He wants this country, God only knows why, and he told me before the wedding that this was a better way than to go to war. I love my chere papa but I don't see how I am help from this stinking place, and I write and tell him so!"

It was about the twelfth week, when one of the servants sneaked into Constance's room and left a letter on her bed. When she found it, she quickly hauled Isabella into her room and closed the door. Together they read it. "This is unbelievable ... merde!"

"What is ...?"

"Child, mon Francois ... in this letter ... he makes no reference to any of the letters I send to him! He asked how are we, then ask when I am come home, and ... then he write forever about the parts of me he miss the most. Nothing else ... nothing!"

"Not a word. Nothing?

Constance slowly shook her head no, and handed her the letter.

Isabella's depression had also in good part become mistrust. They were not allowed to explore this 'Tower', prevented from going out, and their questions were lately received with excuses or ignored. She was innocent, but she wasn't stupid. As she re-read Francois letter, their predicament struck her. "How ignorant, these dung eating barbarians!

Now I see – our letters don't get there, they are being stopped ... was your letter opened when you found it, did you see?"

"Non, the seal was in place...yes, I am sure, yes."

"There probably have been others from Francois, but they don't get to us. Listen, he ask why don't you answer my letters, not letter, he says letters – more than one?"

"And he does not say anything about mine!"

"So ... this tells us everything. Three months we have been now, living in this horrible place and every time we ask about moving to this Royal palace they call Windsor, these so-called servants tell us it is not safe, that the King is away fighting, and that this is the only place they can guard us until his return. I am thinking it is all lies. I am thinking that unless we do something we are left here to rot."

"Do you think it is possible that the King has abandoned you?"

"Oui ... c'est vraie ... I do." Constance had never seen this side of Isabella.

ISABELLA THE QUEEN

Chapter 6
1309 AD

1

Edward and Gaveston had taken refuge in the Throne Room at Westminster. It was the one place that Edward felt stronger and somehow more protected from, what he called, his enemies within. And now they both needed all of the protection they could get. Lancaster was out for blood.

So smug they had been, holed up at Windsor, believing that they had eliminated all of their problems, and now those problems were coming back at them all at once.

There were times, as much as he hated them, when Edward was forced to take up his office, and this was one of them. Up to now he always had Gaveston to lean on, so the last thing he needed to see was his normally cool friend falling so completely apart. It didn't do a lot for his own precarious state.

Two fires had been started at the same time, and were about to burn out of control. The worst of them was the one carelessly lit under the French Ambassador. The powerful Frenchman was already threatening dire circumstances, waiting only fifty feet away in the Great Hall and getting angrier by every stalled angry moment, Edward hadn't the courage to face him alone. So he in turn waited for Gaveston to join him who, for some unknown reason, was taking forever to show.

Edward's stalling however didn't match the power of this man's impatience. The Ambassador decided that he had been kept waiting long enough.

His was the matter of Isabella and the wrath of the King of France. While he did not live in England, it would be a dangerous practice; the Ambassador knew as much about it as any foreign dignitary could. And he had gathered all the rumors about this young King. God help him if they are true. Here he sat, rudely detained on a mission of the utmost diplomatic urgency. Hanging in the balance was the very real possibility of war.

No King in his right mind would put anything before that. He should have been admitted upon his arrival. Instead he and his assistant were ushered into the Great Hall where one's only entertainment was to endlessly pace the hard floor of the long stone hall while being treated to rows and rows of portraits of Edward's long dead relatives. He said to his assistant, "Maybe it's a test of one's sanity, but I don't know which is worst, the waiting or the paintings."

To be able to make a joke was his way of letting it be known that the pot had boiled over. It was an insult that had become folly. For a person of his station to be kept waiting at the best of times by any other Head of State than that of his own; there better be good reason followed by clever amends.

With this one however it was sheer stupidity. Not only was there no special consideration for his station or his discomfort, but he had been shunted along with dozens of frustrated others whose hopes of seeing the King diminished with every hour that passed.

Guards or no guards, busy King or not, he was set to march into the Throne Room and confront Edward, when a long robed creature came flying past him, charging the hall, pushing those aside, especially the elderly, who couldn't jump from his path quickly enough; and who barged onto the Throne Room, hurling the final insult by snapping his fingers at two guards who swiftly blocked the way and closed the doors behind him, immediately in the Ambassador's face.

An innocent young clerk who kept post at a small writing desk by the doors and whose job it was to record everyone who was admitted, became the Ambassador's target. In the next instant the slight, prissy young man found himself being dragged across the desk by his huge bow collar, his carefully arranged notes and neatly arranged pens scattered across the floor, "tell your King that I will be back, with the French Army!"

Meanwhile it was an hysterical Gaveston who sailed into the room. "From now on you deal with your cousin … he's out of his mind … he was going to hit me … he was glaring, glaring … at me … the whole time … shouting … spitting." Gaveston was pacing furiously, doing more crying than talking.

Edward was trying to make sense out of the blathering. Something about Lancaster having been in the north and the devastation. "Slow down, slow down. Start at the beginning and tell me what happened … what about Lancaster? I don't know what you are talking about?"

"You know all I am trying to do is to look after you ... I am trying to protect you ... spare you the nonsense and the whining of these grasping, dim-witted relatives of yours ... and what do I get ...!"

"Piers ...Piers ... stop! Slow down and calm down and tell me ... what happened?"

To his surprise Gaveston did as he was told, stopped pacing, took a deep breath and began to relay his story. "A message came yesterday for you to attend a meeting with Lancaster and the Council. He has just returned from the north where it seems he has been these past months. At any rate, I did not appreciate the audacity, demanding that you attend on him, and so I believed it was my place to go in your stead and tell him so."

"I should say ... you did the right thing ...!"

"Well, not so with him. I waited the appropriate amount of time, until all the others were arrived, and then ... as your emissary ... I made my entrance prepared to admonish him for his disrespect to you."

"And ... what happened ...?"

"What happened? Everything happened ... that's what! The man is a pig, an absolute pig! Hear me Edward; I want never to be in his presence again, never. From now on you deal with him ... do you hear ... you deal with him."

"Yes ... yes, I will ... I will ... now, please tell me what happened!"

"Obviously he expected you to enter that room ... they were all there, including Gloucester, and I could see that they were engrossed. And all I heard Lancaster say was that things were in a mess, that there was no one alive, and then he looked right at me, like it was my fault, and said we have no goddamn army.

They kept on talking amongst themselves, I didn't really listen, I was so insulted, but I remained polite and waited my turn. Then all of a sudden Lancaster pointed at me and shouted "Where is his Majesty?."

Gaveston started pacing again but continued talking. "I was horrified, I couldn't believe my ears. Well I wasn't going to take that and so I told him in no uncertain terms. I said 'my Lord Lancaster, I wish to announce that I am here on behalf of his Majesty, and I am obliged to request an explanation for your demand that he attend on you. I need not remind you that an appointment with the King shall be at his pleasure, and that the time and place be arranged with me.'

I want him dead Edward, do you hear, I want him dead. He struck me and he called me a … piece … of … unholy … shit!"

That was as far into his story as he got. The door to the Throne Room flew open and Lancaster roared in heading straight towards them both. He hesitated only a moment when he saw Edward's bladder give out soiling the front of his breeches and forming a puddle on the floor around his feet, but it didn't stop him from grabbing the stumbling Gaveston by the throat. "You are nothing to me, do you understand … and you will never come into my presence again, do you understand … and whenever I send for the King, I will get the goddamn King, do you understand?"

Gaveston was petrified.

"I could kill you right now, but I won't, unless you ever approach me again."

Edward screamed as Lancaster shoved Gaveston backwards into the flaming fireplace.

Gaveston began screaming as he fell.

Done with him, Lancaster turned his rage on Edward. "Where were you cousin, where in the fuck where you?"

"I … I …."

"It was a full Council meeting Edward, not a fucking tea party …."

Gaveston had crawled away from the fire, his clothes burned and his hair singed, but no serious damage had been done, "his Majesty was detained sire … a … a … matter … a matter of personal importance … he only sent me in his stead … and I ….," he was choking, gasping for air, and trying to placate Lancaster.

He should have kept his mouth shut. Without hesitation, Lancaster wheeled and aimed a kick at him narrowly missing his head. "I told you to shut the fuck up. Do not speak, it would be healthier." He went back on Edward. "We are in a disaster. Our northern army is all but wiped out. All have fled our Scottish garrisons, and of what remains, some have turned outlaw and roam the roads plundering; others more loyal have joined the garrison in Carlisle. Now you get yourself cleaned up and be in the Council Chamber in half an hour."

A cleaner, wiser Edward was there in fifteen minutes. Any evidence of Lancaster's murderous tirade was not apparent as he bid the members to acknowledge his Majesty, and asked permission to continue speaking.

"Silence please gentlemen, silence … It doesn't end there. The Earl of Carrick, the one who the Scots prefer to call Robert the Bruce, you all know him … once loyal to his late Majesty … and now calls himself the King of Scotland … well, he has declared all out war on England, and promised the Welsh Barons and Ireland that if they join him, he will take them all to London."

Everyone in the room started to talk at once. All, that is except Edward. The news didn't mean much to him, and besides, what was there to say. If his Commander in Chief already knew the barbarian's plans, then wasn't the matter simple. Just attack Scotland and wipe them out before they can organize. What difference does it make who claims to be the King? He can't be King over me.

He prayed the meeting would not go long. Gaveston was in a dreadful condition and his place was beside his friend.

Somehow Lancaster would pay.

The other Barons each gave their reports; those from the north described the influx of the huge numbers of people seeking refuge on their estates, and those from the south described their pledges of support, Edward did little to hide his impatience. Each took a while and Lancaster was made angrier knowing that Edward was lost on this whole issue. It was time to get his attention before breaking the bonds of restraint.

Raising his hand, the interruption was acknowledged, "Your Majesty, you were not here for the earlier part of the meeting, and before our noble Lords go any further you should know the full extent of the problem." Without allowing Edward the possibility to embarrass himself he continued," it is important to know that this fellow, the Bruce, has murdered or driven off every Englishman in Scotland."

"Murdered? said Edward suddenly intrigued, "how can anyone murder every …?"

"He has done so your Majesty, he has done it. And I have seen the evidence of his heavy hand. All the roads from Scotland are teeming with refugees… and to seal this deed, he has declared that no Englishman shall ever be allowed to live on Scottish soil again. And all those Scots sympathetic to England are being driven out. They are stripped of their lands and titles and put on the road, and any noble of mixed blood is being told to choose or die."

Edward could visualize the terror, and was lost. He wished Gaveston were seated beside him. He would know what to say, what direction to suggest. The room had gone silent. He knew all eyes were on him, waiting.

Gloucester saved the moment. "My Lords, this is the worst news that England has had in years, and I think it too much to ask the King to come up with a plan single handedly and on the spur of the moment. I suggest that we all adjourn to think on this overnight and reconvene here in the morning to formulate a course of action."

Edward was off the hook. The meeting was over and he was more than ready to leave when Lancaster asked him to stay behind. Edward bristled. "You miserable bastard," he thought, "you will never again hurt Piers, and mark me I will find a way to make you suffer."

The room emptied quickly leaving just the three cousins.

It was again as if Gloucester had read his mind and wasted no time in speaking. "Edward ... about Gaveston. Thomas was out of line, but I understand his actions. Wait, let me finish. You have to know, and about this there is no discussion, what that man thinks means nothing to us, to Thomas and me. So do not impose him upon either of us ever again."

Edward tries again to speak. Gloucester again raises his hand to shush him. But this time he continues, "you dare silence your King ...!"

"Yes Edward, I do. It is time that you listened, and you changed. It is time for you to act like a King ... a real King." Gloucester put his hand affectionately on Edward's shoulder, and softened his tone. "Your country is in serious trouble, and you must do something about it, and you must do it now. Do you know that we can no longer defend ourselves ...."

Edward was touched by the gesture, and the last pleading remark took his mind off Gaveston. "What do you mean no longer defend ourselves? We are the most powerful nation in the world, no one would dare ...my father saw to that ...."

"Only in our eyes Edward, only in our eyes." Even Lancaster sounded depressed. "And sooner or later our enemies will come to know it ... and when they do ... yours and our heads will be the first to roll ...!"

"Edward, the truth is that your father nearly bankrupted this country," said Gloucester, nearly whispering. "All those wars with the Saracens and all the fighting with Wallace and the Bruce, virtually wiped out our coffers and killed off thousands of good men. We cannot afford, nor have we had enough time to re-construct. We cannot go to war Edward, we cannot. It would spell the end of all of us."

"So then what do we do?"

Gloucester and Lancaster looked at each other. Gloucester shrugged, "Now is as good a time as any Thomas."

"Okay, so tell him."

Gloucester pulled his chair closer to Edward's and sat down. "The only way Thomas and I see is a strategy that involves you Edward."

In spite of his anger, Edward was flattered by the conspiratorial way in which his cousins were including him. For the first time he felt like a King.

"We can repair our military if we can raise the funds quickly ...."

Lancaster added. "Edward, part of doing that is going to mean more taxes and part is going to mean that our spending must stop."

The smile on Edward's face vanished. "What spending! ... my spending?"

"All unnecessary spending Edward ... all. And yes that includes your spending as well," said Gloucester agreeably.

"What has my spending got to do with a military that cannot manage itself!"

Lancaster saw that Edward had completely missed the point. And under the day's circumstances his fuse with Edward had grown too short. "It is your spending, on that dung hill Gaveston, that has bankrupted us!"

"I do not appreciate ...."

Gloucester knew that if Edward went completely on the defensive, he would shut down and there would be no reasoning with him. Lancaster had spoken out of turn. "Edward, I apologize for our cousin's unfortunate choice of words but there is no easy way to tell you ... only to say that as part of recouping our treasury all the properties you have given to Gaveston have to be returned ... that the lands and titles you have given him have to be returned ... and all the tax income has to stay in the treasury ...."

"No ... no ... you can't ... you can't do this ...!"

"I'm afraid we can ... and we are," said Lancaster flatly.

Edward's face had gone white.

Gloucester took the sting out of their announcement. "It is not just for you dear cousin to pay the price, it is for all of us. We too will turn over our all our income above what we have to live on, and so have agreed all the other Barons. And the same will be expected of the guilds and Burgars and the merchants. It is for everybody to do this, and it is for you to set the example. Your country is in crisis Edward and you must put it first above your friends."

The explanation made sense and calmed Edward. But how would he deal with Piers.

Gloucester offered the solution. "This is not something that you have to tell Gaveston. It is not personal. He will be officially informed as will be others."

As long as Edward didn't have to do the dirty work. It was better this way, let the Court decide who pays and how much. This way he couldn't be blamed.

"So we are agreed?" Gloucester added.

"We are, cousin," said Edward resigned.

"Then there is one more bit of news," said Lancaster, "which is personal Edward, and how you deal with it is strictly up to you."

"Cousin, do you delight in pushing me off a mountain every chance you get?"

"No, I don't. But this is important and I do not want it to get into the streets."

"Very well, what is it that I am to do myself?"

"First I have to ask if you have yet today met with the French Ambassador?"

"No, not yet."

"Perhaps that is just as well."

"Why, do you know something, do you know what he wants?"

"I am not sure, but I think it has something to do with your wife."

Edward felt the familiar stab of fear go through his gut. He hoped he hadn't shown it. "What could he want with her?"

"We don't know, but it is fortunate that you haven't spoken with him yet because there is something you need to be aware of. Our spies tell us that if the Bruce attacks England, then your father-in-law, Philippe, plans to let us exhaust ourselves fighting and then under the pretense of coming to our aid to occupy us and take us completely."

"You are joking! Do you mean that all this time he only looks to be on our side?"

"It seems. Certainly it's plausible."

"Then this marriage of mine, the marriage to bind our countries forever in holy wedlock, is a farce. I have brought the enemy to live within our house." For a day that had started so badly, it was turning out to be a major triumph. Edward had never had his cousins in a corner before. "Cousins, need I remind you that it was both of you who pushed me into this, who said that it must be in order to save our Empire, and all we have succeeded in doing is inviting a traitor into our midst!"

~

The fear that consumed Edward just hours before had miraculously turned to a victory in which he now languished.

After the meeting with his cousins he postponed the French Ambassador, and instead sent for Isabella. If she was, as it seemed of no use to him, then he wanted to dispose of her in as clear terms as he could make. Let the Ambassador take this news back to Paris.

Sadly Edward was incapable of thinking beyond the moment and his own immediate gratification. Isabella was brought to him the following day in just the manner he had prescribed. The word got about London very quickly that the Light Guards, or Longshanks Assassins as they were more affectionately called in a previous regime, arrived at The Tower, precisely at dawn, twelve in all, and without even the courtesy offered a condemned prisoner, took her from her bed and escorted her away.

The servants told the French Ambassador later that as the Guards entered the apartment, Constance, armed with a small dagger, attacked one of the soldiers and stabbed him in the throat nearly killing him. It was the Captain's quick intervention that saved her life. Ten swords were literally falling, about to hack her to death, when he snatched her from harm's way and carried her off to her own room and locked her in.

By his act of mercy, it was clear to Isabella that they were not about murder, but they were not here to indulge her either. She went quietly and was at least afforded the dignity of a carriage as they escorted her to the High Court at Westminster, where she found her husband and Gaveston waiting.

Edward could not suppress his joy at condemning her as a traitor, and ordered her back to The Tower to be held as a prisoner until a suitable time could be arranged for her deportation.

She knew better than to utter a word. The audience lasted all of a few minutes and she was back in the carriage. There was no judge; the hour was early. No Gloucester or Lancaster, or any other voice of reason, no one would have business with the Court at this time of day. It was just Edward and Gaveston seated side by side behind the Bench, and herself standing below the gallery, surrounded by the same guards, while a detached, grinning specter she was supposed to call husband, imposed sentence.

For the first time in her young life she felt real hatred.

II

In the days that followed her sentencing, the servants had thrown in their lot with Constance and herself.

They too had come to know the true spirit of their King as it became obvious he had imprisoned the staff as well. While the four were allowed to keep the same apartments, that was as generous as Edward was prepared to be.

The supply line they had become used to, stopped. It was prison rations and prison treatment all around and nothing more. For anything extra, the servants had to go begging the dungeon guards, and lord knows what they had to trade in return.

It was a big surprise then when one day Gaveston came calling. Isabella assumed that it was to bring news of her deportation, which at this point she eagerly awaited and was disappointed when he announced that he had business at The Tower, and had stopped by merely to check up on them.

Therefore, a horrid foreboding welled up in her when he asked to speak to her alone. Without waiting for an answer, he told the others to leave, and to be certain they wouldn't return, unexpectedly he called for guards to escort them.

Then he took her by the arm and ushered her to her room, whereupon he arranged a chair to face the only window and had her sit down to look out upon the filthy and deplorable streets that could be seen below.

More frightened than she had been since the night on the ship, she couldn't keep her eyes on him as he paced back and forth behind her, every now and then stopping to stroke her hair. And every time he stopped to touch her, the words of his proposition became more unbearable. She began to think that suicide was her only way out.

"So there you have it my dear. No one is coming to rescue you. Your own ambassador has been told that you are, as you say 'encient' and in confinement at Windsor, as it should be and he won't be able to see you for some time. Now this could become the very real situation for you, but only I can help you to get out of here and take your rightful position at his Majesty's side. But you will take all of your orders from me, without question, and, you will accord me all the obligations of a dutiful wife … the ones you will not be obliged to accord your husband. … That is the contract, take it or leave it!"

She wasn't able to hold back the tears. Let him strike her dead. "Get out. … get out … get out!"

Gaveston calmly walked to the door. "Suit yourself my dear, but remember … your future and the future of this Kingdom rests with your decision."

As he departed she heard him call for the guards to release the others. Constance and the two servants, having heard her screaming, came running.

~

"Oh cherie, cherie … ma petite … we heard, we heard every word from that pig's smelly bouche. You don't become his putane, never, I won't allow it."

"Oh Constance, tu est marvielleuse but this one you cannot stop. He will have me. By now my father has been told that I am pregnant and in confinement at Windsor. He will be so happy that if he doesn't hear from me for six or seven months he won't even notice the time has gone by. And by that time you and I will be dead and they will have some excuse for it.

He is right. If I do what he wants, he will give us life and get us to Windsor. It will just take time."

"Then I will give him the sex, not you. Tell him that he can have all of me that he wants, whenever he wants, but not you."

It was out of the question. Constance knew that Isabella would not sell her under any circumstances. So on Gaveston's very next visit she intended to treat him to a surprise that he would not expect or forget.

Usually the servants were the first to know when anyone came calling for Isabella. So Constance had instructed them that upon his arrival to say nothing and to show him to her room instead. Fortunately she was dealing with a man whose whole being was given to immediate self-gratification and above all loved interaction of a sensual nature. Gaveston reveled in the flirtations and titillating social games that delighted the women of the Court, and he saw this little mystery as leading up to something rewarding.

Fully confident that Isabella had come to her senses, and was playing out some sort of French seduction, he waited eagerly. First Constance sent in a servant who, without a word, extinguished all but one of the candles and then left. Next she sent the other who, also in silence, closed the drapes shutting out the light from the window, and then she too left the room.

Gaveston sat still in the semi-darkness, anxious, excited, the light from the one candle putting him in the mood for whatever came next. Constance didn't keep him waiting long.

Once again the door opened and closed, and this time it was her. Through the momentary shaft of light created by her entrance he could see her move into the room, and then for a second as the door closed behind her she disappeared, only to re-appear again in the candlelight stopping just a few feet away from him. She was wearing a full-length cloak with the hood pulled up so he couldn't see her face.

The mystery of her performance was arousing, but as his senses tingled so did two opposing thoughts occur; either he was about to experience the best sex of his life, or he was about to experience a sudden end to his life. But as his hand moved to the small dagger he wore on his belt he got the thrill of his life.

It was as if she read his mind. He was ready to risk death on the chance that he might have her. The time was now. With the sudden spreading of her slender arms into two giant wings, she flipped the folds of the cloak back over her shoulders to reveal one of the most exquisite naked young bodies he had ever seen. "M'sieur, this is what you have come for, n'est pas?"

It wasn't until after she had thoroughly used him up that she confessed. Before taking him to her bed she had instructed him to remove all of his clothing and then she had put out the candle. Gaveston was delighted by the ruse and promised himself that this one would definitely be a repeat. But his plan would not work by accepting a substitute, no matter how incredibly tempting.

Clever girls. He would have to be on his toes. That Constance was a beauty but if she thought that tonight could turn his head, she was wrong. Two were going to be better than one.

The delicious thought only made the plan more interesting. But, he reminded himself, no matter how exciting things became at The Tower, it was essential Isabella become his whore. Yes he could get Edward past this nonsense of calling her a traitor, and yes, he could talk him into taking her into Windsor, but not before he had complete power over her. He must be the one holding her death warrant.

However, he didn't count on losing his mind over her. "Cherie," said Constance, "if you are to be made his whore, then you shall learn to make the most of every advantage a whore can take."

Gaveston had taken to lying to Edward about his absences.

While sneaking to The Tower almost every day, he had been wearing disguises for fear that he would be seen and word would get back.

In short order the four captives wanted for nothing. The larder was constantly full, even the other prisoners were eating better. Hot baths, the thing the four demanded most, were a daily routine. As were clean clothes, fresh linens, and every now and then even new dresses were showing up unexpectedly.

Gaveston was spiraling and knew he was out of control. Even his own beautiful young wife's enthusiasm for sex could not abate Isabella's hold on him. As for Edward, that had become strictly business.

As for Edward! Yes, what about Edward? Gaveston had given him little thought over the past many weeks he had spent groveling at Isabella's bedroom door. It was Edward's own brand of cold water that turned the tables.

Gaveston had masterminded himself onto the horns of a dilemma; even he could see that. Others, jealous of him and equally covetous of the position of favorite, had wasted no time in taking advantage of his distraction, and he had come to discover a dangerous weakness in his so-called devoted friend. Edward's affections were easily shifted to those who paid with adoration.

Gaveston should have seen the signs. Initially the demanding Edward had become altogether too tolerant. It was time to come home.

And it would mean bringing Isabella with him.

Gaveston wasted no time on winning over Edward, although it was a little trickier convincing him to relent over Isabella. He finally persuaded him to understand that the reason the threat of war had dissipated was due to the lie about her pregnancy, and that so long as her father believed that she was at Windsor, the Throne was safe.

"Sooner or later he is going to want news, especially of a birth, and especially from her. We can't hide her forever. I know I thought we could come up with some excusable way to get rid of her, but now I've changed my mind."

But as quickly as the thrill of having things both ways came, it passed. That change of mind began to gnaw on him as well. What was he thinking? At Windsor she would be close to Edward, free from his grip, no longer dependent. And moreover, what if she wove the same spell over Edward. There would be no getting him back.

Isabella was turning out to be a very dangerous game and one that he may not be able to play any more. Already since convincing him to take her in, Edward had taken a step on his own and sent word that she and her Tower household were to be moved. He was listening to others.

Gaveston had to buy time; his carelessness could prove to be his undoing. He needed to do something that would be horribly shocking and to somehow frighten Edward into total submission.

It was the cousins who provided the idea. Their relentless fear-mongering over the notion that a Scottish invasion was imminent set his mind to other possibilities that might just make him a hero. Right now the only thing stopping Scotland from invading, was their fear of French retaliation. The Bruce was no match for Philippe's huge military supremacy. That was good for Edward, so long as Isabella was safe, but it didn't really help him a whole lot.

But what if France were to attack Scotland before any invasion were to take place? What if England and France were to come out together in retaliation for something that outraged them both equally? Edward, the devastated, wounded husband would be way in over his head. Gaveston could just see him, besieged by his own cousins and beset by his powerful in-laws; he would go mad, wouldn't be able to breathe without him.

And what would turn the world on its ear right now? A murder! The murder of Europe's greatest prize – Isabella!

///

She felt cheap.

She knew that Edward's change of heart had come out of fear, not compassion. Gaveston must have scared him badly. What if Edward figured out the real motive? Would it make any difference? Gaveston would have them both together now, how convenient for his balancing act. And the Queen would be a whore in her own palace.

"What if you refuse?" Constance had asked a good question.

But Isabella had given that some thought as well. "If I don't join Edward then I have failed my father. And besides, that is probably what Edward secretly hopes I will do. Then he has no reason to be afraid any more. He will just tell my father that I won't live with him and where does that put me? Edward will get his sympathy and protection. My father wants this country and he will not let those barbarians have it. I will be nothing more than his spoiled embarrassment and he will find a way to keep me out of sight. I have to go the way Edward says."

"Then there is a better way for you to be on the Throne with your 'orrible mari, 'usband, than as 'is good luck charm and Gaveston's slut."

"Qu'est que ce? And what way is that?"

"No matter that we are moving, we are still prisoners and we will be treated like it all the way. Except for one thing. There are two guards who like Pauline and myself; you know, la jolie, the cute little maid that we trust so much. So, I am sure that she and I can seduce them and that way I know I can escape. I will get home and tell Francois and your father the truth and get their help."

"And if you are caught you will be killed, and it is almost certain you will be caught. How will you get to France? Who will help you once you are away from here? Where will we get the money to buy anyone's loyalty? No, no cherie, ... this is my problem. But you are right about one thing; my father must know the truth. We will find another way."

Isabella was not happy when Gaveston showed up the next day. "So you say I cannot move into the palace until more than one month. Why is that?"

"I want to be sure that you will continue to live up to your end of the arrangement. If I move you now, what's to stop you from reneging?"

"You sicken me m'sieur."

"Well perhaps we can do something about that right now ... to change your mind."

"Not today, m'sieur, not today." How she hated his face. Gaveston was buying time. What for?

~

Gaveston needed a back-up plan, and found it in one of Edward's new and very powerful friends. "Well my dear young DesPenser, you must be very proud ... all of your father's estates in Cornwall ...gives you a seat in the House my Lord ...good on you." He found the tall, ferret-faced, skinny fop repulsive. But he poured the wine graciously and smiled.

Lord Hughe DesPenser could not believe his good fortune, but he would die before showing it. An invitation to Gaveston's home! He indeed must be at the top of the King's list. How pathetic that he needed this commoner to enjoinder him. Well, once done, that would be short lived.

As Gaveston raised his goblet all he could think was, "You greedy little rodent, you pucker your smug mouth at me now; when I am done with you that will be your asshole."

Lowering his goblet, DesPenser did not try to hide his condescension, "Why thank you, my dear Piers. Your sentiment is touching ... and so is this very full cup. But I am sure there is more to your invitation than to share your excellent wine. What is it my dear boy? What is it that you want?"

"You know me too well my friend ... but you are wrong about my wanting ... it is just the opposite ... it is I who have something you want ... my dear young Lord."

"Now, now ... your jealousy is not becoming ... and how so ... you have nothing that I could want ..."

"You are wrong my boy ...," Gaveston grinned at the arrogance. There was no point to beating around the bush with this. "I have the King, and I can give him to you ... for the right price."

"What do you mean give him to me!"

"You know damn well what I mean ... put you at his side ... give you his ear ... you know I can do it ... don't be an asshole! ... I'm offering to make real this impossible little dream you have stumbled into ...!"

"And for this generosity... you want what?"

"One little favor ..."

"None of your favors are little, Piers ..."

"I'll put you close to the King because I want you to keep the Queen away from him."

"And how will my being close to him, keep her away ...?"

"Think my boy. Think! Your inheritance ... you now deserve a place at Court ... but instead of that of a rank and file courtier, only I can put you immediately in the highest place ... an advisor to his Majesty, which puts you with him on a daily basis."

"What makes you think I can't do that on my own. I have the privilege of generations at Court, and my family's money can buy whatever ..."

"Don't count on it sire! The King can have your money any time he wants. You will serve yourself better to listen to ways to hang on to it ... and don't underestimate my position..."

"And the King already enjoys my company ..."

"At parties my boy, at parties ... but by dawn they are nothing more than a bad hangover. You understand?"

"So ... how do I affect the Queen ...?" DesPenser was smart to change the subject.

"That will be the easy part ... very easy. As you are not yet a close friend of the King's, so she will trust you, and it is reputed that you have a magician's way with women, so seduce her, seduce her any way you can and all the way if you can, into being your friend and confidante. Keep your relationship with the King businesslike and act sympathetic towards her. It won't take long to gain her confidence."

"Okay, I seduce her ... where do you come in? How does this help me get closer to the King? And, why does this help you? From what I hear, any friend of hers is no friend of his."

"You leave it up to me. The King will appreciate that you are my spy. Be loyal, and you will be amazed where it will take you. I want to know everything the Queen does, and I mean everything."

"Fine, but why? What could she do that will be so important? The King doesn't care anything about her. She will probably drink tea and sew all day. What do you want me to do, tell you every time she drops a stitch!" DesPenser laughed.

"She won't sit around sewing. I know her. I have some power over her, but for how long I don't know. The cousins are demanding that she be moved into the palace. She will take advantage of that and soon be close with them. Count on it. And that will be very bad for me unless I can catch her up to something."

"And what makes you think I can get close enough to her, even if I work there. Doesn't she have some little French bitch that's tied to her hip, who does everything for her?"

"So, you get close to both of them, become their friend. Screw one of them, both of them ... don't you want the friendship of the King?"

DesPenser raised his wine, "Well if you think it will benefit the country m'Lord. Anything for England."

For a moment Gaveston thought he might have a true ally. It wouldn't hurt to offer him another round. "Good, very good. And there is one more thing you must do."

"What?"

"You must never let her and the King be alone together. Especially overnight. Do everything you can to keep this from happening."

"Why? And how in the hell would I do that? What, am I supposed to sleep between them or what?"

"No, but it won't be difficult, trust me. Just be sure that it never happens by accident."

"Okay, but why?"

"Because she is a witch."

"A witch! … You mean evil potions and spells …!"

"No … no fool, not in the literal sense. But in a way, yes. She has something about her … she has a power, an effect on men …you will see."

"Will I go mad?"

"Don't be cute .. no … no. But you will want her; I guarantee it. I mean I have seen this, and I believe that if she gets a chance to work her spell on Edward, he too may succumb, and that would be more than very bad for me."

DesPenser can see that Gaveston isn't amused.

"Yes, yes, the more I think of this, the more I think it necessary that you work as close to her as you can get. Either I keep her secluded and isolated at Windsor, or I remove her altogether."

For all of DesPenser's generations of so-called blue blood, he didn't want to push Gaveston any further.

IV

Having stalled Isabella's arrival at Windsor for a month, with a back-up plan in place, Gaveston was in high spirits. And Edward's eager agreement to spend the day riding had been the icing on the cake.

Gaveston could tidy house in one glorious outing. Never were they without the entourage, and never was there a quicker way to put everyone in their place. No matter the occasion, no matter the place, he always created an opportunity to remind everyone who was in charge. A simple touch on the King's arm to separate him from the group was all it took, and as usual it worked this time as well.

"So my dear Edward. What say you to a holiday?"

"A holiday?

"Yes. A holiday. And I think it should be the south of France .. yes, yes, definitely the south of France. The weather is perfect there this time of year!"

"I ... I guess so. I really don't know."

"Why do you hesitate dear boy? It's not like you need anyone's permission!"

"Well no, but things are awfully bad here right now, and I don't think that the Council would be very pleased if I were to go on holiday, and especially if you and I were to go together."

"Au contraire dearest. Not you and I ... you and your wife. They will be very pleased when you announce that you are taking your wife on a holiday to France, and, that for a while you will be the guest of his Majesty, the King of France. They will welcome such an idea, trust me."

"Take my wife! What in God's name for? If I am to go on a holiday, why would I want ...."

"Edward.. shut up. Don't be so thick. Right now a visit to France is the best thing for all of us. Need I remind you that it may be necessary if you want to save your bleedin' Throne."

"So why do we need her?"

"Because, you twit, without her, you won't be very welcome in France. I doubt you will even get an audience! Sometimes I don't believe you Edward!"

"Philippe is angry."

"Why do you say that?"

"I think he has found out how she is living. The Ambassador is demanding to see her and demands an explanation."

"What?" Gaveston nearly jumped out of his saddle.

"Yes ... here, read this." Edward reached into his vest, pulled out a letter and handed it to Gaveston. No sooner had he done it then he wished he hadn't, as he watched Gaveston's face distort.

Grabbing Edward's bridle, Gaveston pulled them both to a stop. "Jesus, Edward, do you realize what this means? ... How did he find out? ... fuck, fuck ... this changes everything ...!"

"That's not all I'm afraid."

"What's ... not ... all?"

"I should have told you ... but we really haven't been together alone ... not really alone ... and ...."

"What should you have told me? Spit it out. Now."

"You ... you know how my cousins are ...."

"Yes, yes ... what of them?"

"Ohhhh ... Piers ... my sweet ... I don't know how to say this ...."

"Well I suggest you find a goddamn way ..." Gaveston shoved his clenched fist in Edward's face, "... and do it now... and .. tell .. me .. everything. How in the fuck am I supposed to deal with things if you don't tell me what is going on!"

"My cousins have taken control of the Council with its consent. They have frozen the treasury, and they are demanding that Isabella be moved to Windsor!" It all came blurting out like a pot boiling over.

The wound that Gaveston felt open in his chest couldn't have been done better with a dagger. "This is unbelievable ... fucking unbelievable. How could you let this happen? ... How could you be so stupid as to let this happen ... how could you ...." He knew better than to go any further.

"Piers ... Piers ... darling ... everything I have ever done I have done for you ...!" Edward began crying.

"Oh ... shut up! ... All right. What's done is done. Except for one thing ... where does this put me?"

"She will take over the Royal Household ... officially ...."

"Wha ....!"

"Let me finish ... let me finish. If I don't get it out now, I will never get it out." Edward was choking on the words. "They want to send you out of the country."

It was more than Gaveston could handle. How could Edward let this happen? He wanted to scream, cry, beat on Edward but none of that could happen. Best to ride off, let him suffer, let him get up the guts to oppose those fucking cousins of his. Now more than ever, Isabella was best left up to him. There was no choice now but to go with the original plan.

~

It was a job he would have to do himself. There would be no one for hire to kill the Queen of England.

But there would be plenty to blame it on. Gaveston was surprised that no one questioned his presence in the dungeons below The Tower. When he had questioned the Sergeant as to the location of the Scottish prisoner, the answer had been quick and polite. This was going to be easy. Could he have the key to the cell? Well, no that was not possible, but the Sergeant would be pleased to accompany him if he wished to see the prisoner.

That would be fine. Gaveston had another plan. As the Officer momentarily looked away to lift the key from a hook on the wall, he felt an explosion rip through his body and looked down to see the thin bloodied shaft of steel emerge through his tunic from inside his chest. It was the last thing he saw.

It angered him that he had to struggle to remove the blade. It was amazing how easily it slipped through the man, and how difficult it was to extract. There was something to invent, a blade that removed easily. What an advantage in battle!

He then hurried on to the cells, encountering only two more guards, separately, on route. But their deaths were just as easy. Both knew who he was. It was the prisoner who was going to be the challenge. In all likelihood the man would not recognize him, but would he believe that he was being rescued and could he be convinced to run.

Was his disguise good enough? The guards had accepted him with such ease in spite of the clothes he wore. He had purposefully not dressed like a gentleman and instead worn the heavy outer oilskin coat and broad low hat of a traveler. If anything, he wanted to look the part, like an outsider, a tough who had come to rescue this man, not to trick him.

He couldn't afford to have this step of the plan fail. But as he opened the cell door, the inmate shrunk away from him, not knowing what to make of it. Gaveston had to be convincing and so stepped well into the cell to not block the doorway, and motioned him to leave, waving the dagger towards the opening. The prisoner still hesitated. "Go, get out, you are free." He growled. "No one will stop you. I have seen to that."

The prisoner's eyes searched his rescuer for a reason, but he found none. It was the temptation of the open door, the glimmer of a chance of escaping this hell and the urgency in the stranger's voice. What did he have to lose? He was a dead man in here anyway. Only when he encountered the two bodies as he ran down the corridor, did he think the chance was real.

Gaveston followed and watched him vanish through a tiny exterior doorway. The task half done, he then made his way up the long flights of stairs, to the levels above the cells.

The upper corridors were vaguely lit by stout candles which cast just enough glow to enable Gaveston to pick his way carefully and silently over the stone floors.

Fortunately it also enabled him to spot the hulk of the guard asleep at his post at the bottom of the stairs leading to the apartments. His heart began to pound. Ever since the arrangement, this post was to be deserted at night. Why the guard now? Whose idea was this? Edward maybe? His fucking paranoia – I've created a monster! Gaveston's mind was racing.

Any noise of any kind now, would alert everyone above. For the first time all night he felt panic. This he hadn't counted on. It wasn't going to work. He should get away now. The prisoner would still be blamed for the others; it would be as if he was never there. 'Fuck, fuck, fuck!'

Think!

He couldn't turn back. For one thing, the day guards would be on in another hour, and once those bodies were discovered there would never be another chance, ever. And as soon as that news got to Edward, he would freak. She would be moved today.

If he didn't do this, what would be left for him? She had to die and die now.

So just kill this fellow and be quick about it. Look how easy and silent the other three had been. And why? No hesitation, complete surprise. This was no different.

The mission was all but over. The strike was true, and the man never woke up. Gaveston never could remember climbing those last stairs. The next thing he was in Isabella's room standing over her as she slept, his dagger in his hand, staring transfixed at her beautiful face, a porcelain mask in the moonlit room.

"Who's there, who is it?" Wide, frightened eyes were shining up at him. He hadn't blinked; he hadn't moved a muscle.

The impossible was happening. Instead of plunging the dagger down, his reflexes took another direction. The knife went into its scabbard and he began tearing at his clothes and climbing onto the bed with her. His only out would be to claim insanity. Her screaming gave him his excuse for running.

V

Edward's lavish surroundings were a complete surprise to her. Up to now her only exposure to English hospitality had been the dingy prison quarters of The Tower and the stark institution of Westminster. The Royal apartments at Windsor were more like her own back home.

This was only the second time she had seen him since the wedding. He didn't appear to have changed, and once again she was on trial. It was difficult to hold her temper. It wouldn't take much.

"So it is not enough that he is being sent away, but now you come with this absurd tale that he tried to attack you! What do you hope to gain by this?"

Isabella could not believe her ears. Three witnessed him in her bed, four dead guards, and she is accused of maligning him. Her jaw tightened. "Nothing sire. Everything you have been told is true …!"

"I suggest my lady that you think carefully before you continue. Our Lord Cornwall is the most valued member of our Court. This does not bode well for your demands on Windsor."

Her demands! She felt the explosion. "Your Majesty!" She was on her feet and heading right at him. "I may call you husband, may I not your Majesty … for that is indeed what you are?"

Being alone with her was not a good idea. She had come to kill him. "If you must," he said timidly.

"Thank you husband … dear." My, this was a turn. Taking advantage of him was easy; he was a coward! She slowed her charge, but not her tone. "No one respects your Court more than I … and Lord Cornwall is no doubt as valued as you say ... but are you not concerned as to why Lord Cornwall was in my bed chamber in the first place?"

"Well ... I ... until ...."

"Husband, how a man is at his daily endeavors, and what he becomes when he is alone with a lady may demonstrate distinctly opposing sides of his character. And I tell you, dear husband, his Lordship is no gentleman."

Edward had found protection behind a chair. "Your accusation is serious. Would you say the same to his face?"

"Without hesitation."

Relieved that Gaveston would no doubt put her in her place, he hurried to the door and called for a steward to send him in. Unable to face her any further he remained in the safety of the open doorway until Gaveston arrived.

Edward's fear and discomfort was written all over his face. Gaveston knew that he would have to play the bully, only how far he should go would depend on her. "What is it Edward? What do you want?" Haughty familiarity would be a good start.

Edward's relief is visible. "My Lord ... our Queen tells us that on the night before last you were in her bed chamber in The Tower, and that you tried to rape her. Is this true?"

How sweet you are dear Edward, thought Gaveston. Victory was his. All that he needed do was act the contrite victim. He let out a long sigh and slumped into a chair, as if defeated, no longer able to fight on, to defend himself.

"Well my Lord ... what say you?" Edward was trying to appear in charge.

"Majesty," Gaveston bowed his head and mumbled, " ... this is your good lady Queen. What can I possibly say that will convince you ...?"

"Just tell us the truth my Lord ... no harm can come for that."

"Majesty, it is true, I was in the Queen's bed chamber on the night you question ... but I was there for the very best of reasons. The night you speak of and as you well know is the very night that an inmate murdered four guards and escaped the cells, not two floors below her Majesty's chambers."

"Yes, yes ... exactly my dear boy ... that was indeed the night!" Edward was jubilant over the reply.

"Yes ... thank you your Majesty, thank you. ... well, fortunately for her Majesty there was a fifth guard, one of my own appointments, who narrowly escaped death and had the good sense to find me at my townhouse. I immediately came to The Tower to investigate, I felt it my duty to check upon her Majesty. I went to her chamber to find her well and awake, and as I made to leave, she begged me to stay ... and ... and ...need I go on your Majesty ..."

"Finish the story my Lord."

"Well ... she tried to seduce me ... and ... and ... I'm afraid I was tempted Majesty, and I ... I must have been bewitched ... I don't remember what I did, but the next thing I know I was on her bed and she was screaming" ... (Gaveston gives Edward an imploring look) ... "and I ran out. I swear Majesty, that is what happened." (Gaveston bows his head). "I am so sorry Majesty, I am so sorry."

Edward looked fondly at his marked friend. How much was truth and how much was fiction he didn't care, "I have heard enough Lord Gaveston. You need say no more."

Surly now he would be safe from her father. How could he expect England to put a whore on the Throne, daughter or not. "As for you my Lady, your lies will not favor you at this Court. You are no better than a common whore. You are unfit to be our Queen. ... you would have done yourself well to have kept your mouth shut and saved your station.

This good gentleman, and so he has proven, has until this moment, until forced from him, said nothing to me of your behavior, obviously to protect you. But you do nothing to leave well enough alone, and thus undo yourself. You will not be back in France soon enough. May you rot in hell..!"

As Isabella went to speak, Edward raised his hand to stop her. Gaveston remained seated and bowed. "Say nothing my Lady! Absolutely nothing ... lest you chance treason."

Edward's face was in striking distance, as Isabella lunged for him. "No my Lords, no ... lest you rot in hell ...!"

A shriek came from him as he bolted for the door.

"No Edward, no! Wait." Gaveston had leapt to his feet. "Don't call the guards ...!"

"Both of you listen to me, and listen well if you value your lives," her voice was a snarl. "This little play that you have just put on, it will be your last. As you were having your fun, so I was having mine. Edward, your good Dowager stepmother and lest you have forgotten, my aunt, now knows everything and you can be sure is at this very moment telling the French Ambassador.

Do you have any idea how quickly the news will get to my father, never mind that your dear cousins undoubtedly already know as well. Your party is over gentlemen."

As Edward watched Gaveston cover his face with his hands and double over, the ugliness of the same uncontrolled fear gripped his chest. His best effort was to softly call for the two guards stationed in the waiting hall. "Escort our Queen to her apartments."

~

Edward was impressed at his own calm in spite of his raging cousins. Overnight it had been him consoling Gaveston instead of the other way round, and this morning he felt quite prepared to deal with anything they could dish out.

Gloucester was ranting. A message had arrived from the French Ambassador demanding an immediate explanation of Isabella's circumstances and containing a clear threat of consequences.

There would be no dispute about Isabella taking her rightful place. Gaveston was to be out of Windsor and out of England this same day.

And last but not least, "As of this moment Lancaster is taking over your office. From now on you will be seen but never heard on any issue, and starting today you will sign every document I give you. Beginning with Gaveston. He is banished and all his titles are removed and restored to their rightful owners, with one concession. As he is your friend and was dependent on you, Lancaster and I have agreed to assign him a task in order to make a living, for however long that lasts."

"What do you mean 'however long'?" Edward was ill.

Lancaster could not resist speaking up. "Whatever all that was about at The Tower that night may never be known. It is certain that a prisoner did escape, and could have murdered those men, but where is the mysterious fifth guard who so nobly warned Gaveston? At any rate, for now we won't point fingers. So let's just say that if you ever want to see your friend again, he bloody well better prove himself."

"And how is he to do that?"

"We have a job for him," said Gloucester.

"One that he will take, or he is on his own," added Lancaster.

"What job is that," whispered Edward.

"Assistant tax collector in Ireland."

Edward gasped, "that is a death sentence ...!"

"Not if he is doesn't sleep," chuckled Lancaster.

"Now, what I am about to say is not negotiable," said Gloucester. "Gaveston was put on a ship this morning, ... no .. no .. no .. not a word, it is done. ... he will be in Ireland in a day or so, but we will decide if and when he ever returns. I have already taken away all his titles and lands ... and Edward," he takes a powerful grip on Edward's shoulder and grits his teeth, "I am now the official Regent of England. From now on you do as I say and only as I say."

Edward couldn't help the cry that came from his chest.

"So now, enough about him. We have problems to solve. The Ambassador wants an immediate reply to this or he guarantees that Philippe will march on England. I have to answer him today ... telling him what he wants to hear!

So I have taken some steps which I hope will save all of our necks. I have sent an army of servants to help her Majesty move in with instructions that she may buy anything her heart desires, and set up her household in any way that she desires."

Edward turns in his chair to speak.

"Say nothing Edward," say nothing. I am saving your life ... once again.

VI

For the next week Gloucester's and Lancaster's wives made themselves indispensable to Isabella and Constance. Countless servants of all kinds were made busy cleaning and furnishing. Dressmakers arrived every morning and were kept busy until every evening. There were chefs to be interviewed, artists, musicians, and personal staff – all to be French and all friendly to her.

One month later Isabella received a visit that thrilled her beyond her wildest dreams. The Dowager, her Aunt Margeurite, followed by an enormous entourage of all classes of nobility, descended upon Windsor from her palace in Hampton, "You have wasted no time my dear ... what a delightful change ... I am so proud of you!"

Isabella could not hold back the tears. She had not seen her Aunt since the wedding.

The beautiful woman, so like her own mother, so gentle, so opposite the toughness of her father, cradled her in family arms and let her have her cry. "There, there child, I am here now, and my stepson will never get between us again – not if he knows what is good for him."

Margeurite knew this, the youngest Royal gem, better than all the rest of her divine nieces and nephews, and had she not married The First Edward, this was the one of her widowered brother's children who she would have raised as her own. "Listen child ... or should I say your Majesty ...," that raised a giggle and stopped the crying, "I have some wonderful gifts for you, all the way from Paris, and I want you to show my servants where to put them. You may arrange them so that we all can see."

As Isabella left the room, Constance piped up with, "these rooms are just a little bit of it Madame!," she beamed, "the whole palace is changed ... she 'as removed all of the scum that lived 'ere with his Lordship ... all those whining, preening peacocks that strutted up and down these halls are gone! ... now we have a proper staff with good people ... and do you know, she is put bathing tubs in every bed chamber ... and a laundry ... and best of all (she claps her hands) we have a chef from Paris who knows how to care for and prepare magnifique repas ... !"

"Not only has she put this house in order, ma'am" complimented Gloucester's wife, "she has put this country in order."

"Oui, yes I have heard," replied Margeurite. "I've heard news of her, spreading like a fire through all of England ... they even talk of her in Paris ..."

"Ahhhh ...oui madame ... you mean the children and the widows ...isn't it wonderful ...," exclaimed Constance. "Almost every day we visit orphanages, work houses, charities and hospitals. She 'ands over bags of money. The people they love her.

Everywhere we go they wave at our carriage, and she waves back. She even stops all the time to see the children playing and to see that they have food and clothing. We spent nearly one whole day at St. Martens just because there were so many children, and she wanted to see them all. I watch the faces of the parents, I watch her guards. The people they love her so."

"And did you know that she has set up a Royal account at The Tower to feed crippled soldiers ... there are so many abandoned, and so many widowed by the wars in Scotland ... my husband is so proud of her," said Gloucester's wife, dabbing at her eyes.

"Oui, she goes to the hospitals to find out from the wounded soldiers how she can help their families ..."

~

The Bishop of London was a large greasy man, who perpetually stunk of wine and a body odor that could only be described as rotting meat.

The fact that he was unaware of it was testimony to his character. And his choice of ecclesiastical garments did nothing for Isabella's piety. In a parish so cruel to it's innocent devout he paraded his grotesque torso about in the most expensive garments money and intimidation could buy.

Accented by layers of gold jewelry for every occasion, on this particular evening he was showing off in grand style, draped in robes better suited for a coronation, of scarlet velvet trimmed in ermine, and sporting enough rubies, diamonds and emeralds to shame a Sultan.

Isabella hated him, and loathed the frequency with which she had to endure his company.

It seemed that for every social event that required her attention, the church also had it's hand out on the event. And this one was no exception.

She and most of the Barons' wives, now her in-laws, had arranged a magnificent play tournament where all the working-class and poor children of London had been invited to a day of games, competitions, and free food and clothing contributed by the merchants in return for tax relief normally due the Queen as income.

It also gave the older children a chance to rub shoulders with the merchants, shop keepers and barrowers on the lookout for apprentices. And the scheme, now in its second year, had become immensely popular throughout southern England.

Unfortunately, it also had attracted the Church. But for an entirely different purpose.

Priests showed up in droves to extort as much in the way of contributions as they could from the poor, wretched, but superstitious parents. It was the will of God they cried, that so much should come to them all at once. May they rot in hell if they ignored His goodness.

So what they were able, in many cases, to secure in the way of a future for their children with one hand, they were driven by guilt to hand to the church with the other.

At her town banquet held on the eve of the festival to celebrate the children too young and too small or too crippled to participate in the games, she had been disturbed to find the Bishop seated at a table at right angles to her own. Constantly in her eye line, bedecked in his expensive robes, drunk, and shoveling great handfuls of food into his mewly mouth; without once ever inquiring after the hungry and tortured little bodies for whom the laden trays were intended.

Her wine-fed anger swelled to the breaking point.

The goblet left her hand before she realized what she was doing, but not with any regret.

Constance clapped with glee as it struck him squarely upon the side of the head, sending him reeling in his chair, and drawing blood. He squealed like a pig and ejected a revolting great mess of food that slobbered down the front of him. "Let's see you charge her you fat disgusting bastard," she shouted.

The entire square saw and heard everything.

"My Lord Bishop!" Isabella cried, infuriated by the thick, gaping jowls, food hanging from his mouth, "I wish to say this now so that these many good people gathered, who pay taxes in true faith, may know and witness what I expect from you. ... The alms you collect for the poor, shall henceforth go to the poor ... do you understand Bishop, or you shall come to know that misery in hell about which you preach so fervently!"

Surprised by her own fervency, she was suddenly aware of the silence around her, and watched quietly as did everyone else as the Bishop fled from the table.

"Good steward, pour my cousin another goblet of wine, she seems to have spilled her last one," Lancaster's jovial roar triggered a return to the festivities.

~

The Second Edward, King of England, Flanders, Wales, Ireland, and Belgium had become a drunk.

If it had nothing to do with the bottle, he ignored it: his wife, his duties, his life. He wasn't missed.

Needless to say he never attended anything with her nor spent any time with her.

Thus her only and constant companion was Constance. "It has been two years now since those days in The Tower, and I think sometimes we are still in prison. I know we have this lovely palace and these beautiful gardens, but we also still have those walls. No matter where we go it is always the same, we are always surrounded, always guarded. Cherie, would you like to go home to France?"

"Don't tease your Highness."

"I do not know about this place any more. It is always rain, my nose it is always wet. ... Do you long for Marseilles? Oh how I wish to visit ma cousine en Monaco."

"Can we not take a vacance?"

"Oui cherie , oui ... or better yet, we take a vacance, and I make a gift of this country to mon pere," Isabella giggled, "for that I think he will give to me Monaco." She twirled at the idea.

"Why not, who is to stop you. These people should make you a saint ... you would be saving all their miserable lives. Votre pere he could have this country any time he choose."

"Now you tease me cherie." They walked in silence for several moments. "Most of all I hate this cochon, this marriage. I wish he would die."

"As he ever tried to be a husband? Has he ever come to you and ...?"

"No never. He leaves me completely alone .. and for that I am happy. That is not the probleme."

"Ah oui! It is the opposite. You need a man." Constance laughs and jabs Isabella in the abdomen with her upright finger, "oui, oui of course ... you need this ... and lots of this ... plus encore, oui , oui."

For a few seconds they play, slapping and jabbing at each other. Then Isabella becomes serious again. "Do you remember on my wedding night, on the ship, when I went to find Edward?"

"Oui, oui ... those horrible creatures came to ma cabine ... you know I stab one of them."

"I know cherie, and I am sorry ... that was my fault."

"What was your fault, what do you say. They came after moi. I took care of them."

"They were looking for moi, cherie. If they hadn't been they would never have found you, and you would never have been in that dangeur."

"And why do you think that. What makes you think they didn't come for moi anyways? Do you think the men don't want this body? ... cherie, this body has forgotten more tricks than you will ever know ... besides this body is spectaculaire ... and I can prove it." Constance began to unbutton her blouse.

"Ferme ... ferme ... I know the men desire you. They don't hide it when they look at you. ... Be serieuse ... I try to tell you something."

"D'accord, ... I am sorry ma petite. Dites moi ... tell me."

"That night I go to Edward's cabine an 'e is with many other young men and they are all having the sex with each other. They frighten moi. They tell moi to come and give them sex. Edward 'e gets angry and orders moi to make sex with any who wish it. I am so scared, I run and I run over the ship and I find a small cabine to hide. And then cherie something happen."

"What!"

"There was a man in this cabine ... a beautiful man ... so strong, so sure ... he protect moi ... those two men who came after you ... he nearly kill one of them ... and I make love with 'im."

"Oh, cherie ...."

"You know 'im ...."

"I do ...!"

"You do ... you tell me his name just the day before the wedding ... 'e was in the courtyard ... the Pirate, M'sieur Mortimer."

"You ... him ... really doing it? Oh attendez, what ... what was 'e doing on the ship ... a stowaway?"

"Oui ...oui, really, and non 'e was not hiding. Edward paid a big ransom to ma pere for him. 'E is what they call a privateer and has value extremement pour le militaire des anglaise."

"So ... 'ow many times ... was he good ... was he big?" Constance holds up her hands as if describing a fish.

" 'Ow I am to know what you know ... all I know is that I felt wonderful, marveilluse ... several times I feel such a rush of pleasure, I think I want to faint ... and 'e want my body all over, and I want him all over moi."

"Oui ... he was good."

"You know we did it even in the morning just before I have to rush back to ma cabine and get dress for the arrival."

"Cherie! You mean when I come to your cabine to help you dress you had just come from this man?"

"Oui." Isabella giggled.

"Where is 'e now ... why don't you keep this lover somewhere secret for yourself .. I will help you. No one will ever know."

"I don't know where 'e is. And we depart the port so quickly I don't see him again."

"Do you want me to find him cherie. I can do that you know. No one 'ere will care if I am searching for a man ... 'ell they would be surprised if I wasn't!"

"I won't tell you not to do it, but I think it is hopeless. 'E is probably back to sea, or maybe 'e is dead."

"Non, non cherie. A pirate that famous. If 'e were dead all England would know it. 'E is being kept silent. I will find him."

VII

Edward could manage one event. He seldom felt needed, let alone powerful, except on the morning of a hunt – especially this one.

And tradition and protocol demanded that he lead the famous ride, so named after his family and so, out of necessity, all attention was devoted to him.

Lancaster's huge estates south west of London always served as the ideal location. His immense popularity gave reason for the hundreds of participants annually gathered and generosity attracted the thousands of spectators, who came from miles around.

All riding were on fine horseback, milling about while dozens of servants risking trampled feet or a sudden kick from one of the skittish beasts, hurried about toting huge flagons of wine to keep glasses full. The equally many conversations all going on at once and over the din of dogs barking, made up a wall of sound and excitement. It had taken on the playtime atmosphere and the size of a country fair.

For all of his warrior years and grisly battles, Lancaster liked the foxhunt the least. "It is the worst spectacle of English depravity there is Madame." The annual event was pure fun and would be almost impossible to cancel, but over the years he had tried to shift the emphasis to something of a more humane pursuit.

Joking with Gloucester one year he suggested, "why don't we just tag all the priests in the county, give them a head start and test our skills as archers. It would be good practice for war, and save a hell of a lot of wear and tear on me poor dogs."

"Don't you be concerned, this year my dear," his wife replied, her words a little sloppy, "things will not as be as they seem."

Madame Lancaster had a plan to save the foxes.

And with each successive glass of sherry the plan became less focused and more brazen. Her partners in crime, who consisted of most of her female companions, became not only braver but more plentiful as one by one they extinguished bottle after bottle of the sweet amber liquid.

"Ladies, any moment now, just as they release the foxes we shall position ourselves in front of the men and as the bugle sounds we shall bare our breasts. Can you just imagine the hullabaloo? There will be so much confusion and hollering and yelling, that the dear wee creatures will be long gone before the hunt can be reorganized. And we shall keep our bosoms exposed for as long as it takes, no matter how hysterical our dear men become. Agreed!"

"AGREED!"

~

It was a delightfully crisp, sunny morning, with Edward more sober than usual. His pretty friends in their colorful outfits seemed to cheer him. And he was the center of attention until everyone was distracted by a rider charging at full tilt along the estate road towards them.

It turned out to be a messenger who rode up hard, bypassed Edward and handed a dispatch to Lancaster. He briefly read it and then spurred his horse into Edward's group pushing them aside and grabbed the King's bridle.

The two moved away from the others and for several seconds stood their horses still and were in conversation. Then without a word or a wave they were gone, horses galloping, off down the same road, the messenger in their wake.

~

The hunt was a bust.

Partly thanks to the King's sudden departure and partly thanks to Madame Lancaster's brave plan.

Although no bare breasts were directly involved, the ride was halted because a great many of the women were found to suddenly fall asleep or be badly in need of sleep; either way most having to be carried by their husbands, mates and servants and deposited in bedrooms through the manor house.

Once dismounted and otherwise occupied, it then seemed wiser to the men to continue enjoying Lancaster's fine wines and the special festive atmosphere on this exquisite country morning.

~

"So you will let him return!" Edward was like a schoolboy.

He and Lancaster had ridden as far as Windsor where there were other messages waiting, exchanged their horses for a carriage, and were now on route to London. "He has done good work cousin, that you cannot deny!"

"I am not one hundred percent convinced that I should, but yes, my boy, I will let him return. It seems he has done a remarkable job, one I never remotely expected and I am afraid he has come up somewhat of a hero to the military. Our generals want to applaud him. I hope he is a changed man."

Edward could just imagine. Gaveston's good work in Ireland. No longer disgraced. He was now a hero, a conquering hero. He would plan a return for him fit for a Roman General. The report was clear, "His outstanding work at collecting taxes has made the difference such that the army's conditions are in complete turnabout."

"Oh cousin … how can he be anything less. How can anyone but a changed man make so outstanding a contribution to the country? He has single-handedly refinanced the army. He should come home to a hero's welcome … and I shall see that he does!"

Isabella's innovation was a complete hit.

She had one in Paris, and she would have one here. No one with means need be or would be dirty. The heated indoor bathing pool at Windsor had become a daily ritual. Never before had a male staff of a Royal household seen so many unabashed, unclad pretty female bodies parading around with such wanton regularity. And never had the unclad females seen so many active male essentials parading around with such obvious appreciation for their female essentials.

All bathed nude. Isabella, Constance, all on her staff and those who worked in the household were required to bathe every day. Certain hours were for the women only and other hours for the men, to accommodate those who were shy or inhibited, but the mornings were for any and all who were not bothered by shyness and wished to bathe, male or female, and were content to do so nude.

Twice a day the water was changed and heated, thus every morning and afternoon it was clean and ready for its eager bathers.

Made completely of mortar-packed quarry stone the twenty by thirty foot pool held about five feet of water deep and was carefully sealed to prevent leaks by spreading resin-filled mortar over a carefully chiseled and interlocked ledge limestone. The water was drawn in a continuous flow to the pool along a gutter called an aqueduct which was a man made, stone and mortar creek that stretched from the adjacent Thames River to the specially built pool room in the palace.

It wasn't an original concept, Egyptian farmers employed it to irrigate their crops along the Nile River over three thousand years earlier and down the later centuries the Romans built monumental aqueducts on a grand scale throughout the whole of Europe.

By partially submerging a huge wheel suspended in a frame and anchored by large stone blocks along the shoreline of the river, and attaching buckets around the perimeter of the wheel, it was possible to lift water efficiently and continuously. Above the wheel was constructed a sluice into which the buckets would dump their contents as they were inverted going over the top of the rotation of the wheel. The sluice would then carry the contents to the aqueduct. Often the current was enough to rotate the wheel, but at times when it didn't have the force, a pulley system came into play, which attached to the sluice framework and could be used to operate a continuous belt of ropes, which in turn rotated the wheel.

By using horses or oxen marching in a circle to operate the belt, the water supply was available any time if desired. And running a palace of this size it eventually became the case.

The flow was stopped only when the belt stopped. But as it turned out to be good exercise for the horses, and other innovations had come about to serve other needs for water throughout the palace, the wheel industry at Windsor achieved notoriety as an employer and full time operation.

The other particular innovation which came about in league with the pool were the small furnaces constructed around its base, which worked like the fire beneath a kettle. So efficient were they that the pool heated remarkably quickly, and once hot the coals could be stoked low so as to maintain a steady temperature throughout the day.

The pool parties became famous with the nobility and the hangers-on, and the morning bath became the most comfortable place for Isabella and her staff to discuss the day's business.

This day the subject was not a happy one. Gaveston was returning and Isabella wanted him stopped. "Surely we can find someone in Ireland to kill him?"

"I am sure that we can," said Constance, "but it would cause big problems. He is very populaire right now."

"There must be someone that we can find. I hear they are all crazy on this whiskey, and I know they all hate the English. There must be one who is willing to slit his throat!"

"There is no need. This popularity will not last. He will not be in this country for one day, and he will do something stupide. I know it. The best thing is for you to do nothing. Don't let anyone know you even care. The country loves you. That won't change."

~

A month later Edward threw his lavish party. It wasn't quite on the scale of the affairs once thrown for conquering Roman generals, but it was extravagant.

As predicted, Gaveston's short-lived popularity came to a sudden end the same night. The party was the icing on a cake already baking out of control. In the short month since his return, his ego was well returned to its old level, if not higher. It took only the regretted accolades of the assembled Baronage to put him over the top.

"So Highness, you must be very happy now that he is returned?" One of Edward's new favorites observed to him as he held Court over the partying mob.

"He is a hero," boasted Edward.

"So there must be more in store for him besides this." The favorite gestured in reference to the party, "What have you planned for him next?"

"Windsor of course. It is his. He has earned it, he will run it."

"And Cornwall?"

"It will be restored, of course!"

The conversation was not lost on others close to them. The already deteriorating party was the perfect forum to leak the news that Gaveston would be running the Royal Household and that he would be reinstated as the Earl of Cornwall. Along with Gaveston's tasteless and insulting jokes, it took no time at all to ruin most everyone's evening and drive most of the Baronage home.

Edward was delighted that the crowd was thinning, leaving just their friends to party on. It would be a great night after all. Gaveston was back!

~

The next day Gloucester called a secret meeting in his chambers at Westminster to which Isabella was invited along with Lancaster and other Barons loyal to himself. Informed by Gloucester that his cousin may be late, the group waited and Gloucester fielded the assault on Gaveston.

"Why do we not just have the bastard killed?" Some opted for a quick fix.

Gloucester saw the more practical side. "Edward can make any pronouncement he wishes, but that will not make it so. Cornwall is safe from Gaveston."

"Lets make it even safer ... I say let's kill the bastard!"

"Which one?" The off-hand remark invokes a round of laughter.

"Lord Wessex ... be careful of whom you speak. Treason is still a hanging crime. ... On the other hand, no one wants rid of Gaveston more than I. He is my embarrassment ... I granted his return."

"My Lords, he has moved into Edward's rooms with him, and together they have announced that they want my household and moi out of the palace."

"Your Majesty, don't be concerned. It is only talk. None of the guards at the palace will do anything without my order, and by tonight you will hear nothing more of these Royal announcements."

A knock on the door quieted all of them.

"Who is it," called Gloucester.

"Me cousin," the familiar gravelly voice came through the crack made by the slowly opening door.

"Welcome Lancaster. While we have been waiting, we have been sharing some unholy plans for our nephew's playmate."

"Yes good friends, I am sure our points of view don't differ. His return has opened old wounds and he will be dealt with, especially for your sake your Majesty. But I have to change from the subject that I know you wanted to discuss to one that has kept me late. Right now there is news of greater weight than any Edward and his playmate could devise. I hope you are ready for this. Our spies in Scotland have informed us that the Bruce is preparing to invade England."

~

Any command to attend from Lancaster plunged Edward into a painful depression. So he was relieved to discover that he was not the whipping boy this time.

"Well, you don't expect me to go."

"No, I don't. You wouldn't survive. But perhaps Gaveston would. After the way he handled himself in Ireland ...."

"No, no ... cousin, please no. Besides, after the way my father made such a fool out of him, in front of most of those Scottish Barons when we were last there, he would be in as great a danger as I. They would not take him seriously. They would kill him for sport."

"Yes, I suppose you are right." "Damn," thought Lancaster. "If it wouldn't make things worse, it would be a good way to rid ourselves of the shit." "Well then who Edward? It has to be a peace mission. There is no other way. We are not strong enough yet to fight a war ... with anybody ... and especially when we wouldn't have the element of surprise."

"Right now I can think of no one cousin. But if we take one day. Give me a day. I will compose a list of names and you do the same. Surely there is someone."

Gaveston was still shaking even thinking that he was considered a candidate for this mission. "It is a good thing I am back dear boy. They may hate me, but they are jealous ... and stupid. Without me none of you in-bred bastards could think your way across the road. What are you doing trying to solve national crises? The answer is right under your nose ... under our noses, you twit."

"What is it?"

"Send her, you daft bastard ... send Isabella!"

ROBERT THE BRUCE

Chapter 7
1312 AD

/

The carriage containing Isabella and Constance had arrived at the inn designated, just a mile from the Scottish border.

The hour was late, and the small band of pitifully inept guards that accompanied them had, with every mile closer to Scotland, turned virtually insane with fear. Gaveston guessed as much would happen when he hurriedly picked them after persuading Edward to dismiss the legion sent by Lancaster.

As the carriage pulled into the courtyard by the entrance to the inn, a stocky, middle-aged rough looking man and a slender, hard looking but attractive woman with long hair and huge breasts came out to greet them. They had expected their guests earlier and were relieved that they had arrived.

The guards, having been easily distracted by the alarmingly fetching body of their hostess had deserted their hungry and thirsty horses to the care of the stocky man, and had forgotten the unloading of the carriage as they allowed themselves to be fussed into the draft room. Isabella and Constance were left to help themselves to the ground.

Moments later the woman came running back out into the courtyard. "Oh , tis such an honor to have you stay at our wee inn." Her deep bows revealed an enormously firm cleavage. No wonder the poor dumb fools drooled off after her, thought Constance, she probably delivers what she promises. "Come, come let us get you inside where tis warm by the fire ... and some hot food after such a long ride ...."

"Merci madame ... uh ...."

"Tess, your Highness ... me name's Tess ...."

Isabella saw the man standing in the yard before the others did. He was huge, not fat, shaped like a giant wedge from the shoulders to the waist, with knee high leather boots extending below a knee length kilt.

"Here ... wot the fuck are you about ...!" Tess didn't seem surprised by him.

As he strolled slowly towards the three women several more wedge shaped creatures wearing dresses appeared from the night shadows of the buildings and the stables.

One of the guards picked that moment to come outside to urinate and saw the yard full of strange men. As they appeared unarmed, he summoned the courage to draw his sword and call the others, who wasted no time in spilling out into the midst of the gathering.

"I suggest you put down your fuckin' sword ya limey bastard ... unless you all plan on dyin' here tonight." The big man kept on coming.

None of the others went for their weapons. None even moved from the ridiculous pattern in which they emerged. The one guard who for a moment bravely held his sword looked furtively from side to side to see if he was backed up. Seeing the other men frozen to their spots, he lost his nerve and dropped it. Only some strange recall of duty drove him to move to protect the Queen.

Isabella stepped up beside the terrified guard and glared at the large man striding towards her. "What is this? Who are you?" She gave him a look comparing him to dirt. "I suggest that you explain your fucking self, you ox bastard, unless you plan to die here tonight!"

Another of the kilted men joked. "Campbell said she'd be a handful Michael. Careful she don't make ya cry when she kills ya. It'd be too embarrassin' ta tell yer ma."

Isabella ignored the joke. "Do you know who I am?"

"Aye, ... that we do," said the first.

"Then you will know that I am the guest of his Majesty Lord Bruce!"

"Aye ... and that is why yer comin' wi' us."

Without another word the rest of the Scots charged the guards who had no stomach for any kind of a fight, especially with these brutes, and scattered like mice.

Michael scooped Isabella into his huge arms like she was a toy and carried her to the carriage. Another just as easily picked up Constance and placed her on the seat beside. Both men climbed in after the women. Isabella's driver hadn't moved from his perch atop the carriage since their arrival.

Michael leaned out of the carriage window and called to him, "'Ere you driver," who leaned around and looked down in his direction, "see to it yer thinkin' of her Majesty's welfare lad ... you'll be followin' the lads ahead of you ... and that's all you'll be doin." Michael called out, " when yer ready Brian!" He looked over at the dumbfounded innkeepers who couldn't believe any of it, "sorry Tess me darlin', no offence, but we'll be needin' her more than you, but I'll be back ya lovely 'ting."

As the carriage pulled away into the night leaving the two standing alone in the silent courtyard, Tess wondered aloud, "I'll be bettin' Michael's ma don't know what he's up to tonight."

Isabella and Constance were huddled together like two displaced cats. "Which of you is the one who calls himself Robert the Bruce? ... Some bonhommes that you are, messiers !"

Neither answered. Instead they grinned at the two wide-eyed faces and Michael thought, won't he be surprised at what we're bringing home.

Constance couldn't resist. "If this is the official greeting for a Queen. I wonder how they greet a King?"

~

As Edward stared at the document he shook uncontrollably. "They've taken her, and they don't say where."

"What does that matter? It's good, it's what we want." Gaveston was lounging sideways in a huge chair, a goblet dangling from his fingers.

"You said they would kill her, not capture her. Now they will want a ransom. What if her father finds out? What if they have already sent the same message to him? There will be no sympathy for me, no tolerance of any delay ... count on it! ...," Edward rattles the paper in his hand. "It doesn't say where they are holding her ... it doesn't say how much they want! ... I'm not sure I like this plan anymore ...."

"Everything is going exactly as planned."

"Oh is it! And what makes you so sure of that?"

"Think dear boy ...think! These barbarians would not dare tell Philippe. He would be all over them in a nod and they know it and they know they wouldn't stand a chance. Besides, they need France for this so-called war they have declared on us ... no, no ... they don't want to tell France any more than we don't."

"Okay, so why don't they just tell us how much they want ... or what they want?"

"Because right now they don't know. Right now Edward, they believe that we are planning to attack them ... that she was sent to distract them; to slow them down in negotiations while we sneak up their backside. Now they have her locked up somewhere, who cares, while they wait and watch to see what we are doing. Now is not the time to bargain for her."

"When is the time?"

"Let them choose. Meanwhile all we can do is wait ... and of course worry, for the next word."

"And what do I tell my cousins? Now they truly will kill me."

"Oh my darling ... you are pretty, but you are dumb. Don't you see ... this is your chance to become the greatest hero in all of England? You tell your cousins the truth ... the Bruce has betrayed them ... throw it back at them ...this is their plan, remember, you weren't too keen on it, remember; and now you are distraught ... it has backfired ... and you are going to the rescue ... no matter the cost!"

"They are not just going to hand her back because I charge off ...."

"There is a light in there after all ... of course not ... and that is what makes it perfect. It could take months, years to get her back ... in the meantime you appear relentless in pursuit ... and all the while we have everything to ourselves...."

~

The two women had given up any hope that England would come to the rescue.

For months they remained under what could only loosely be called a guard and although isolated, were made extremely comfortable. However, not a word from London.

Neither had been hurt or mistreated in any way. So what kind of stupid game was Edward playing now? For that matter, what was the game that this man was playing?

Their so-called prison was obviously somebody's estate. And short of being allowed to travel about the countryside, they were pretty much given the run of the place. They had plenty of good food, and even Isabella's penchant for a daily hot bath had been accommodated. But of pure delight was the colorful assortment of local costumes in constant supply. The few Royal garments they had brought for what was supposed to have been a short visit, would not be of comfortable service in a long imprisonment, estate lodgings or not.

It would have been stupidity to deny their appreciation. The local custom was far more sensible than their own.

The outfits consisted mainly of linen blouses and small fitted, light-weight undergarments, floor length smooth woolen skirts and wool socks, soft cowhide or doeskin boots, and long, heavy woolen shawls that could be simply worn draped over the shoulders or wrapped entirely around the body and pulled over the head depending on the weather.

The whole effect was remarkably light in weight, warm and very free. Their breasts were not bound and pushed up beneath the blouses, and other than the short panty-like underwear, their legs were bare beneath the skirts. Both agreed that they quite liked dressing this way and perhaps all their friends back in France might like it too.

They weren't so sure about the ones in England though. "If it doesn't look like a carpet or a curtain, and weigh about the same, it couldn't possibly be suitable."

And on top of it all their captors had become their playmates. The guards were so polite, some even boldly familiar and none too adept at 'keeping prisoners'. She couldn't prove it but she was sure that Constance was sleeping with that big handsome one Michael whenever she got the chance.

"It has been months and not a sign from anyone. What is it they play? They give us anything we wish, they do not hurt us, but then they tell us nothing!"

"There has been a trick ... I know it cherie. This Bruce, 'e welcome you himself. ... he say that 'e will meet you himself at that hostel ... so why Michael and the others, and why this place for a gaol?"

"My husband is behind this ... I know it!"

"And that cockroach is behind him."

11

Edward and Gaveston were immensely pleased with themselves. Setting up a field bivouac was great loads of fun, living in tents like Arab Sheiks, great meats roasting on spits over open fires, wine under the stars, gypsy camp followers with their entertainment and games of chance, the shouts of passion and squeals of delight from the prostitutes that swarmed the soldier's tents at night.

There was no doubt that the impression they were making, riding proudly at the head of a large cavalry, marching back and forth across the country just south of the Scottish border in search of a way to rescue his helpless and victimized young wife, was making heroes of them both. Certainly the troops were having fun.

"I do say that my ... your ... last message to your cousins was brilliant. Setting up a camp at the border ... you in complete danger ... complete disregard for your own safety ... I may be a genius! ... but you are a hero dear boy. ... Holding back the barbarian horde ... trying desperately to save your beloved bride ... even Philippe is on your side ... for once ... although I think his threat to attack Scotland is a bit much ... I don't really think he'll do it ... sounds good though!"

"So what is our next move?"

"Well ... now that France has declared itself, we will wait an appropriate amount of time ... to see what will happen of course ... her safety must come first ... two or three more months should be enough ... and then we will make a formal demand ...."

"And what will that be?"

"I don't know yet ... but I will come up with something good ... trust me."

"Why do you think they haven't come up with a ransom?"

"Stuck for a price, I should think!"

~

Robert the Bruce was having a quiet day. He didn't like it. Nothing was as the English informer had said.

Prepared to throw them back into the sea from whence they came, he had marshaled his troops and now they waited. None came. Or if there had been an invasion it had been a silent one.

Now determined to know all the facts before he dismissed anyone, he had gone to see for himself, and on this windy, rough, cold day he saw no one.

There was no one there, and no signs of anyone ever having been there. No camp, no army, no navy, not a single ship in sight.

The cliffs overlooking the Irish channel along the rugged, windswept southwest coast of Scotland are very high, affording a spectacular view. From his vantage point he could see for miles out to sea, and almost the same distance to the north and the south along this stretch of coastline.

Below him and to the south was a long, arched beach forcefully protected and framed into a gentle bay in contrast to the wild ocean beyond by two overlapping and enclosing pincers of rocky outcrops. Between them was formed a natural channel which would permit countless ships to sail easily into the bay, lay safe at anchor and deploy thousands of troops. It was probably the best and only point along this coast where an invasion could be intelligently implemented

He and others had ridden for days and not encountered anyone other than their own country folk, and everyone they queried had not seen or heard anything out of the ordinary.

"Somethin's not right Robert. There's no bleedin' attack and there ent goin' ta be one. This fuckin' limey King is fuckin' wi' ya ... and all fer wha' ... now we got fuckin' France pissed at us and that weren't the idea at all ...."

"Aw shut yer fuckin' gob ...."

"No ... you shut yers ... you got some serious fuckin' kissin' up ta do ... I suggest ya get started!"

~

Isabella and Constance had no idea where Stirling Castle was. But it was where they were to finally meet their captor. It didn't fit with their expectations then that they arrived to a reception and accommodations totally befitting a Queen.

His entrance on the other hand was anything but that of a King. At least not the Kings these two were used to.

There he stood before them, all dressed in all his finery of a kilt and sporran, polished leather boots and ruffled white shirt. She wouldn't call him the handsomest of men, but the longer she watched him, studied him and talked with him, the more beautiful he became.

Neither of the women could help but be impressed. The ornately decorated rooms were filled with flowers; servants galore were lined up everywhere and waiting to satisfy their every wish; there was even a group of seamstresses laden with materials of all kinds and instructed to fashion whatever they wished and around the clock if required; nothing had been left out.

And one room had been devoted to a private commode; while in the center of another stood an enormous tanned hide bathtub – they had no secrets obviously.

There was no doubt he was there to make amends, and there was no doubt that she was accepting.

There was also no doubt to Constance that he was smitten, at first sight.

~

What started as an apology became a courtship. The guards were taken away, she and Constance had the run of the village, and when she asked about going home, the answer made her think.

He had informed her father that she was safe and in his opinion was the dupe in a plot by her husband to prompt France to attack Scotland. 'Personally your Majesty', he wrote, 'I believe Isabella to be in mortal danger if she is returned to England without assurances of her safety.'

She was content to wait for England's reaction. By the time that revelation got back to Edward and his clever friend, it would be an interesting one. Anyway, she was happier than she had been since France, and more than willing to learn more about this incredible man.

Every day he called for her and every day she would eagerly wait for him to make his move. Sometimes they would ride, other times go walking, and always they would dine together.

Once he had her dress as a peasant girl and snuck her into a clan meeting. That was an eye opener. He might have been the ruler of the country, but these clansmen had no hesitation to tell him to go fuck himself if they disagreed.

She would learn how a true leader held free people together.

She would learn everything. Every day was an excursion and a new lesson. The women of the farms and villages impressed her the most. If the men were prepared to spill their blood for Scotland, the women were prepared to spill their souls.

They possessed a swagger and a self-confidence that was provocative, alluring and yet at the same time they were respected in a way that rank and position didn't play a part. She could tell that these women weren't just tolerated.

Scottish men knew their place.

One day when all four were out riding, Michael, Constance, Robert and herself, they came upon three women playing a game on horseback in a small field. Dozens of other people were watching from the sidelines.

The game consisted of placing a small knife on the ground, in the most difficult spot found, and each in turn would gallop madly across the field and without slowing a titch lean to the ground from the back of the horse and try to pick it up; and in the instant it would be in their hand, to toss it to the other rider, no matter her position in the field.

More than once there was a nasty tumble; how the rider wasn't killed was a mystery.

After some time and no end of impressive stunts, the three women rode up to the Bruce and Michael and asked to be introduced.

My God they are beautiful, thought Isabella. She knew she was gaping and couldn't help it. But then everywhere one looks in this country, one only sees beautiful women. Wild creatures, free. And these three, even

with their dirty faces, bleeding knuckles and skinned knees were not
bowed by his presence or, for certain hers, either.

After they rode off, Constance asked, "Are they with a circus to
perform like that."

"No," said Michael, "born and raised right here."

"You joke," said Isabella.

"No, truly, and those three aren't the only lasses that can ride like that
– and you should see them with swords! Boyo, you'll think twice about
gettin' friendly without bein' invited," he laughed.

"Why," asked Constance, "are they those kind of women that just want
to act like men?"

"Not at all my sweet," said Michael, "they are like most clans women.
Some are better and braver about it than others, but most can ride like that
– and fight."

"Why the game, the pick-up like that?"

"A lot of the women will ride into battle with the men, but their job is
not so much to fight, a Claymore gets heavy after a while, but to collect
fallen weapons and see to it their lads is always got a sword in his hand
or a knife. The women have got ta be fast."

"And most can do this?" Isabella was impressed.

"That they can."

These three, elles sont soeur, sisters, oui?"

"Oui," said Robert.

"Elles sont spectaculaire! The men, they must make the men crazy, non?"

"Crazy – crazy. But most they just scare."

"Pourquois, why?"

"Most know with them, that it's be good or be gone."

Constance chuckled, "my new philosophie," she looked at Michael
"we will talk m'sieur."

"T'anks Robert, 'tanks very much."

"Well, I want to be good just like them," said Isabella.

All of her life she had thought of herself as a good rider; she didn'
know the half of it. What had all that been, trotting politely, perched on
the side of a horse, through beautifully scented gardens and Royal deer
parks. Oh that had been impressive. "Robert, teach me to ride, to use a
sword – to fight."

It wasn't long before she got her chance to test her mettle and her newfound skills. She was to see English imperial arrogance at its finest, through someone else's eyes.

"We've learnt that yer husband is sendin' a garrison across the border in a day or two. Probably part of the answer yer waitin' fer. Tryin' ta make himself look good, like he's comin' after ya. You want ta be there to stop him?"

Isabella couldn't wait.

"We'll have ta dress ya up like one of the village doxies, put ya in a kilt. I hope yer legs don't drive them crazy. You'll be the prettiest fighter there." He winked at Constance, "except fer me mate Michael that is. That ugly galoot tinks he's the prettiest ting on earth, and nobody's got the balls to tell him different."

The hour of Edward's arrival was getting closer. She had a wild thought that she wished later she had kept to herself – then no one would have stopped her. 'What if no one recognizes her? Think of the possibilities. "What if she killed him, just went up and chopped his head off or stabbed him or something; would the English know it was her? Surely Robert would protect her, deny the possibility of her being anywhere near Edward – after all she was a prisoner, wasn't she? What would she be doing wandering about, with a sword, in a Scottish village of all places?"

Robert had even admitted that right now Edward's death couldn't make matters worse; might even improve things somewhat.

The Bruce had decided to let the English troops move unopposed a few miles into Scottish territory, a ploy that he shared with the fist villagers with whom they would come in contact. He then hid most of his men around the little town, and had others, including Isabella, masquerade as the towns people to act terrified at the sight of the English.

She stood her ground with the other tough clans women, she felt their equal, eager to play the brazen peasant hussy staring down the colorful soldiers as they jangled into the village. There they were, Edward and Gaveston, all decked out in their finest shining armor, hanging back letting the advance column take all the risk. No one recognized her.

"What's this then," said the first Officer, "a village of only women? Where are your men?"

"You've kilt them all, yer Lardship, that's what," said one of the women, hoping he didn't see her sword tucked up under her skirt. "And wots left of them is out huntin'," she gave him a big grin. "So what is it you'll be wantin' then me fine young soldier … as if we didn't know," all the women laughed, including Isabella.

"Sergeant," Gaveston's impatient voice could be heard from well back in the ranks. "Stop wasting our good time with this scum. Send her to me."

The young woman could not have walked two steps, let alone the distance to him. The sword beneath her skirt was as long as her legs and the handle was pressed up against her belly. If she moved, the Sergeant would be sure to see it. "I ain't comin' ta no one." She yelled. "You want see me yer Lardship, you get down off yer bleedin' horse and come ta me."

Isabella closed her hand around her sword, as did all the others who were in a similar way.

"Madam! His Lordship intends you no harm if you do as he says," the Sergeant maintained his formality.

The joke was over. "Fuck you limey. Get the 'ell back to England if ya know what's good for ya!"

Swords flashed in every hand, on both sides. Isabella stepped up beside the embolden woman and held her sword high, pointed directly at the dismounted Sergeant's face. He was a brave young man. She was impressed as he stood his ground just inches away from the deadly assemblage before him, and with a hint of recognition, looked straight into her eyes, while raising his hand signaling order in the ranks. No one moved. No one that is except Edward.

"Oh my God, oh my God, I'm going to die," Edward felt the pressure in his bowels. Then suddenly from out of nowhere the village was swarming with armed men. They were everywhere including all around the column. He and Gaveston were trapped. Edward defecated in his armor.

While the Sergeant was hoping to calmly back out of this, he noticed the powerfully built man stepping out of the crowd. In his hand he was carrying an enormous Claymore broadsword with a piece of tattered material dangling from its wide hilt. Behind him he heard, "Jesus, I never thought I'd see it again!"

Staring with equal boldness at the big man with the Claymore approaching him, the Sergeant asked, "what is it soldier?"

"It's been about thirteen years now sir, but I won't never forget it. I was at Stirling and Falkirk and Bannockburn, at 'em all, and I seen him and I seen that sword, and I'll bet me wages it's the one.

"What one, man?"

"You would have been too young then Sir, so you may not know who it is I'm talkin' about, but I'll swear that's the sword of William Wallace."

"You've got that right," said the big man. He had stopped just a few feet from the Sergeant and planted the blade into the ground. From tip to handle it was nearly as tall as both of them.

"Then you must be the Bruce," said the outspoken soldier.

"Never mind who he is," piped up Michael. "What we want to know is what the hell are you doin' here, and who are them two toffs hidin' behind ya there?"

The Bruce knew which was Edward. He didn't know who the other was. "Yes Sergeant, who are they? Tell them to get down and come here to me – NOW!" His sudden shout caused Edward to complete his expulsion by urinating.

"If they don't do it now," said Michael, "then me lads will drag them here, and the rest of you lot can call yerselves dead. Now fuckin' get them over here!"

Edward had to be helped; his legs wouldn't support him. Gaveston wasn't much better, but managed to look braver and act with some authority. "If you are my Lord Bruce," his throat was dry and his voice quivered. "I bring you greetings from his Majesty King Edward and I'm come to ask your price in return for her Majesty." Best to get right to the point he thought.

The man had put his arm around the pretty redhead, the one who had pointed her sword at the Sargeant with such defiance, and who had remained standing there all along looking for all the world like her greatest pleasure would be in killing Gaveston, and drew her close to him. She reached across his exposed washboard stomach and placed her hand suggestively against his belt buckle.

Must be his woman, thought Gaveston. Even through his fear, he wondered what this one would be like in bed. What a stunning creature, half wild like this country. One never saw anything like her in London, the long free mane of autumn hair, the sun darkened complexion, and the passionate eyes. What eyes! There wasn't a moment of recognition.

"He can't be givin' ya a price." Said Michael.

"Why not, we are prepared to pay ..."

"She's dead," said the Bruce.

The remark hung in the air, as if time and animation froze, and there was total silence on both sides. Gaveston expected Edward to say something, but Edward was so afraid that he was going to die, that he hadn't heard a word.

The brave Sergeant spoke first. "If what you say is true sir, then you needn't worry about us. You have France to contend with."

"But we have heard from her father that she is well," blurted Gaveston.

"Well you've heard wrong," said Michael. "Now what say ye lads, I'm fer killin' them all." He raised his sword and a loud whoop went up from the crowd.

"What say you woman," said the Bruce giving Isabella a squeeze. "How about you run this fancy one here through. It don't seem he has much to say about anythin', so what good is he?"

"I'd like it just fine," she said mimicking his accent.

"Well you go ahead and do it then," said the Bruce, "and I'll just cover me eyes here, cause I'll likely faint at the sight of blood."

Isabella hoisted the huge sword she was carrying in both hands and placed the tip against Edward's abdomen.

"Anytime darlin' just go ahead, but just say when, so I don't have ta look ..."

"Then how about right fuckin' now!" She leaned in on the handle and Edward screamed.

The Bruce's hand shot out and caught the grip, "Whoa ... Jesus darlin' ... I didn't think ya was really goin' ta do it."

"Yer fuckin' right I was," she continued with the accent.

"And darlin'," said the Bruce, "you'd better be watchin' yer tongue. Do ya have any idea of who yer stabbin' here?"

"Who gives a shite ..."

"It's the King hisself, the bleedin' King of England."

"Does that make him important? ... maybe I should stab him twice then?"

"Ah me little angel, it's time we get you outa these hills."

"Well do somethin' with him," interrupted Michael, "he smells so bad I can't stand it."

"Maybe he's dead already," said the Bruce.

"No loss," quipped Isabella.

"You, Sergeant," said the Bruce, "I goin' ta do you one favor that ya would likely never do for us. I'm going ta count ta ten, and you'd better have this here King of yours back up on his horse, and you'd bleedin' well better get yer arses out of here and back across that fuckin' border or never mind me lads here, these women will want to be hackin' every last one of ya to fuckin' pieces."

"First you will be good enough to tell me the truth of her Majesty." Boyo, this Sergeant has balls, thought the Bruce. He deserves a straight answer.

For several seconds The Bruce stared coldly back at the brave young man, hoping to intimidate him. If he was, the Sargeant didn't show any of it. Then The Bruce couldn't fight the urge to grin, this boy's on the wrong side, he thought. "Yer right boyo, I've been fuckin' wi' ya. She's alive me lad, and in fine shape," he patted Isabella's firm little buttock, "and you'll be hearin' from her soon enough. Now get on yer horse, or the sound of yer head comin' off will be the last ya hear."

The rest had taken off leaving the Sergeant alone and surrounded.

"Mount up lads, and follow them – all the way to the border. And make sure they don't take any souvenirs along the way," ordered Michael, "and as for you young Sergeant, get the hell up with them and tell them two toffs that we haven't done any killin' yet today and we don't like lettin' even one go by."

Isabella had never felt better. All the way back to Stirling she carried that huge sword strapped to her tiny waist, and straddled her horse like the best of any man, regardless of what and how much of her was on display. Sidesaddle was a thing of the past.

Women were silly creatures who did silly things, she thought, all in the name of decorum. The Bruce was right; it was much safer and more comfortable to just straddle the beast and go. Riding even at a full gallop was all done with your legs, keeping your hands free and your mind clear to wield a sword or use a bow and arrow. She was ready to charge into any battle with the best of them.

"Tell me all about this Wallace."

///

The apartments at Stirling were not quite on a par with the one's at Windsor, but she and Constance had decorated them very differently, with the comings and goings of men in mind. The Bruce and Michael were guests in the sitting room almost daily but as for in their beds; things there were only half complete, only Constance shared hers.

"Summer in the highlands is short," The Bruce told her, because no one deserves more than a glimpse of heaven once a year. "Come," he said one beautiful July day, "I'll show you what I mean." And with a picnic lunch they rode out alone from Stirling until they came to a lake that made Isabella homesick for her childhood summers on the Cote de Azur. The water was so blue and clear and from a certain angle it sparkled like diamonds in the afternoon sun.

"Can I swim in it?" She had dismounted her horse and was running towards the shoreline.

"Of course," he called after her, "but it'll be colder than the Mediterranean, you'll see."

Scottish women were not so burdened with respectability as were the English, or for that matter the French outside the bedroom, and Isabella loved that aspect of their society. It fit with her appreciation for the lifestyle of her bathhouse at Windsor. There was nothing more exquisite to look at than a naked beautiful human form, male or female.

There was no beach, but there were plenty of huge granite boulders lining the shore on which to sit and dangle one's feet in the water. Off came her boots and her skirt.

By the time the Bruce had tethered both the horses, spread out the picnic and joined her on the rocks she was already wading around in her underwear splashing the refreshing water over her arms and back of her neck. "It's wonderful, it's beautiful, so clear, I even drink some, no salt, is that okay?"

"I'm sure. It's one of the lakes where we get our drinkin' water." She could tell he wasn't sure if he should be looking at her.

"You can't do this in the Thames or the Seine. They are so dirty and muddy. They are sewers."

"It's not too cold?"

"Non, not at all. I want to swim."

"Okay, ... uh ... well then I guess you'll be wantin' me ta go with the horses until yer done." He got up to leave.

"Non, I want us to swim." She didn't dare look at him in case she wouldn't like his expression.

"Together ya mean ...?"

"Oui, yes ..."

"But I don't have nothin' ta wear fer swimmin' with a lady."

Still without looking towards him she removed her blouse and undergarment, tossing each onto the rock beside her. She was completely nude, and stood exposed in the knee-deep water so that he could have a good look.

"Well, that'll be answerin' me next question."

"Oui, I guess it will."

"So I guess that I'll be takin' off me own britches then ..."

"I guess you will."

"Don't you be laughin' then ..."

"It will depend, if there is something to laugh about?"

There wasn't. She saw enough before he dove into the water and surfaced again where it was chest high. As he watched she plunged after him and came up immediately in front of him. He could feel her breasts touching his chest.

"I don't think I can be a gentleman any longer."

"Pourqois, why, what do you mean?'

"I mean this. You are the Queen of England, you are married; I shouldn't have the thoughts for you that I do."

"Why, I do for you ..."

"I don't think I can stop myself right now ..."

"Then don't."

She slid her arms around his neck and kissed him. As she did, he took her in his arms and pulled her body full against his. She felt him become ready very quickly against her abdomen, and so raised her legs to encircle his thighs. As she did he found his way and she gently settled on to him, taking him deep within. For hours they drifted through the water locked in this position.

IV

Their stories were no longer working.

For almost two years Edward juggled his life between London and so-called "bargaining" missions to Scottish border towns and there were always excuses. The most convincing and the one that bought him the most time involved her father. "If he releases her, he fears retribution from France. He doesn't trust that we can prevent that."

When Lancaster sought to get Philippe's word on it, Edward managed to thwart any effort to contact the French King. "If we go to him now he will agree to anything, but demand that we attack instead, and as you've pointed out so often, we are not ready yet."

"No, but with his help it would be possible."

But Edward always had a plausible answer thanks to Gaveston. "The Bruce is scared. He has made a huge mistake and as long as he holds her no one will attack him and risk her life. The one thing we know for sure, he must treat her well, because he knows that if she dies as his prisoner, retribution will be annihilation." He always made his little speech with such passion that for a long while even his cousins were convinced of his frustration.

Lancaster confessed later that the time hadn't done him any harm. "While those two played house all over the country, we gained control – without spilling any blood. He made it so easy."

"Just be sure it doesn't come back to bite you my dear." His wife was always the voice of reason.

"How can it? He can't make a law without the House of Lords; he can't do anything without us! We control the purse, his purse; what he doesn't realize is that we can cut him off tomorrow; throw him out of Windsor if we want; we control the military!"

Gloucester had a partnership role in the "new" government. "Your wife is right, cousin, he still has supporters. We are still a behind-the-scenes government and our only power is ourselves. I'm not sure that all the people are ready to hear that their King is not really in charge, and I definitely don't trust Baron DesPenser. He and the whole group from York don't side with us. Despenser has split the country down the middle and he has lots of money.

Remember soldiers come from the people, and the people need money, every day. Regular pay for many on the channel side would outweigh any loyalty to a bunch of fat Lords who pay off in pigs and chickens.

They don't think like the people on the west who share in the land; they work in the mines, coin is their god. And this DesPenser would like nothing more than to have control, and what better way than to put Edward firmly on his Throne. The silly bugger was happy taking his playmates on traveling parties, that's how we got control."

"Well it was time to get her back anyway. Learning the truth was just opportunity. If it hadn't been for her brother and his temper, we might have had some real trouble on our hands."

"They were getting ready to attack somebody, and our spies were convinced it was us. You did the right thing by going to them before they came to us."

~

Gaveston had heard the rumblings from London for weeks. He couldn't ignore the messengers any longer. He had kept the news from Edward too long now, and the final warning from Lancaster was no longer on sealed parchment. He had come to their doorstep.

Gaveston was at the end of his rope. It had been almost two months since the big news from London,

'The Bruce has agreed to give her up in return for our guarantee and that of the King Of France that we will not make war on him. Make contact with him now and arrange for her immediate return. France's guarantee is only good only if we act within the week, otherwise they will attack us.'

"All right ... all right ... we can't stay here ... we'll take as many who will ride with us and we'll leave tonight. ... By the time they get here in the morning we will be long gone ...."

"I told you that Carlisle was not a good hiding place. So where do we go from here. Where can we go?"

"We'll find a place ... we'll find something ... someone will hide us."

"Where Piers ... where? ... We stalled too long, and what was the point? Did you think my cousin was lying? He is bringing an army ... *the army*, he means to get us ... and he will! It's been two years, two years ... I've lost my country ..."

"Oh no, he won't ... if I have to hide in a pile of dung ... *he has put a death warrant on me* ... taken everything I own ... declared me a traitor ... and you, what of you ... he has told her father that you have been stalling, lying, doing nothing to get his precious little bitch ... you can't afford to be caught either!"

There was a pounding on the door. "What is it?" Gaveston yelled.

"M'Lords," came a voice from the outside, "there are riders approaching ... a huge number of them ...it's like war m'Lords!"

Army or no army, Lancaster came storming into Carlisle Castle, charging his horse in to the center of the great room. There was nowhere to run. Gaveston got the worst of it and wound up shackled by his wrists to the T-bar of a hangman's cart. His face and body were a bloodied, purple mess, and he wore nothing but his soiled underwear.

"There is a frigate in the harbor," said Lancaster to the wagoneer, handing him a solid bag of coins, "you can't miss it."

"I know the one m'Lord."

"Good. Then see to it that he is on that ship and put in irons until they are well out to sea. Two of my men will escort you; they have a letter from me to the Captain. There will be no trouble getting him on board."

The cart rolled off. From a distance it looked like a meat wagon as it jostled along the cobblestone street leading to the docks, its great red and white cargo swinging back and forth splattering droplets of blood on everything it passed.

"What do we do about the King, my Lord," asked Lancaster's First Officer.

Lancaster had slumped into the seat of an enclosed carriage. Still in a raging temper he was exhausted and feared he may have gone too far. The King of England was half dead.

Seated beside him was the Officer, and opposite him was the unconscious Edward shackled by his wrists to the inside walls of the carriage.

Down at the docks, Gaveston had been cut down from the T-bar and the two escort soldiers were dragging him up the gangway. The Captain stood rigidly at the top, blocking the way on board, with his hand extended. One of the soldiers turned over Lancaster's letter. The Captain briefly read it and then stepped aside pointing towards an open hold. Wasting no time, the two continue dragging him and like a sack of beans, and throw him over the edge.

"Here lads, wot if he dies, wot if he's already dead?" asked the Captain.

Without glancing back one answered "throw him into the sea."

~

In three days Lancaster was back in London and Edward was on the mend. The House of Lords had been assembled especially for his arrival.

"Our Generals are receiving her at the border this day. By tonight she will board our ship in Carlisle …!" He is drowned out by the roar from the House. Shouting over it, he goes on, "The threat of war between France and England …," He is totally drowned out.

V

Isabella clung to him and sobbed uncontrollably.

The only life she wanted was over. There was every chance that she may never see him again. In two years England had become barely a memory, she had spent less time there than in Scotland and with none of the joy and passion that was now her life with the Bruce.

Edward was all but forgotten, and she had come to terms with her father's greed. It was his problem, not hers.

Two carriages sat on a high road within easy view of the border, surrounded by thousands of highlanders. Assembled a few hundred yards away on their own side was a fully prepared legion of English soldiers, including archers and heavy horse cavalry.

The young Sergeant who had displayed such courage a year and a half ago was now a Lieutenant and in command of Carlisle. His orders were that if anything went wrong after she was safely in his hands, he was to kill the Bruce. "And I mean anything," warned Lancaster, "it will be your call."

The Lieutenant understood, but he also understood discretion. The exchange would be dangerous for him personally. He was to ride alone, exposed, away from his troops, over the hundred yards or so to the crossing. He was then to escort the carriages onto English soil where the girls would be transferred to a Royal vehicle. He was then to ride back, alone, with the two empty vehicles guaranteeing that no harm would come to the drivers.

It would be at this moment that all hell could break loose. Killing him would be a major coup for Scotland by engendering much needed sympathy from France. He had been Commander at Carlisle now for almost two years, and living that close to Scotland the rumors don't recognize the border. Sailors and merchants from other parts of Europe traveled freely between the two countries and a great many shared with the beds and ears of the highland girls.

Isabella may be the Queen of England in England, but to most Scots she was the Bruce's fancy doxie, for who, as it was turning out, they were not getting any ransom and because of whom they had spent the last two years fearing a sudden and violent reprisal from France. The slightest misinterpretation fueled by her brother's famous temper and they would not stand a chance.

The country worshipped the Bruce, but she had been an expensive playmate.

This would be a good chance to settle a score. For the moment England was taking the blame for her long estrangement.

"Wot the hell are they doing over there, sir," asked his aid.

"I have no idea Corporal, but our orders are to wait, and that's what we will do." He didn't say, 'and kick the shit out of the Scots if they even look the wrong way'. That could be the surprise.

Through the slit in the carriage drapes, Isabella could see the endless rows of red-coated soldiers on the other side of the meadow. "They will believe that you have given in to the threat."

"I don't care," said the Bruce patting her belly. "You and I know why I've given in. One day this one will sit on the Throne ... that is the real victory."

They kissed one long and last time. "Now you must go my love, now." Pulling away from her, he stepped out of the carriage on the side out of sight to the English; not that they could see much with the two vehicles surrounded completely by his men. "Driver, step down and give me your hat and coat. This is not your risk; it is mine. Brian, go get Michael and Constance and bring them here to this carriage."

When the two lovers arrived, Michael looked up and saw the Bruce in the driver's seat. "What in Gods name are ya doin'?'

"I'm takin' the ladies home meself, if it's all the same to you."

"Like shite ya are."

"Eat shite! I'm not sendin' somebody else to do my business ...."

"I'm not talkin' about that. I agree with ya, she's you're date and you can take her home. I'm talkin' about ya goin' alone. I'm goin' with ya."

"Fuck off, you're not."

"Fuck you, I am. You got my date in there too, and I'm makin' sure she gets home safe."

"They're only expectin' one driver ..."

"Well ain't that too bad, they're gettin' two." Michael swung up onto the seat beside him. "Now let's get goin'."

If anybody would recognize him, it would be the young Lieutenant. As for Michael, how could anyone forget that giant? The horses were kept at a walk and when the carriage reached the crossing they stopped.

The Officer was there alone to meet them. Nothing of what was said could be heard from either side. "Gentlemen, do you think it wise to be doing what you are doing?"

"Only if you don't do anythin' unwise," said the Bruce, smiling.

"Oh, it's not me you have to worry about; it's several others over there who know you on sight, and one or two outrank me. Taking you would be considered a major victory. On our side of this border, my Lord Bruce, you are a wanted kidnapper."

"Kill me and ya kill yourselves. Have ya not seen what's standin' right behind me."

"And have you not seen what is standing right behind me."

The Bruce sensed his partner's anger at the young man's arrogance "Never mind Michael. He's right, let's not do somethin' stupid."

"Thank you my Lord. And I'm sure you'll agree that a change in plans is in order. I suggest that you wait here while I go back and get our carriage so that her Majesty and my Lady make the change right here."

"That won't be necessary," called Isabella from inside the vehicle.

"I beg your pardon Ma'am," said the Officer, startled by the unexpect ed remark.

"We will walk gentlemen." The two were already climbing out of the carriage.

The Lieutenant leapt from his saddle and was on one knee by the time Isabella reached the ground. "Majesty, it is not necessary. My Lord, please tell her Majesty that you will permit a carriage ..."

"Isabella, you'll not be walkin' anywhere ...!" The Bruce jumped down from the driver's seat.

"Oh, that was brilliant," said Isabella. "Do you have any idea how many English arrows were just drawn. Now shut up, both of you, and listen. We will walk down this road, and we will walk slowly, and I'll tell you two why. As long as we are exposed and in harm's way nothing will happen on either side. Am I not right Officer?"

"Nothing will come from our side Ma'am, you can count on it."

"And you Lord Bruce?'

"You know that ..."

"Good! So we are the gate in the dam and so we are not moving from this spot until you and your men have disappeared over that hill Robert and you Officer have sent our forces several miles back over English soil.

"But ..."

"No buts from either of you. Now we would be pleased to have a carriage wait with us and that is all. We will catch up with our troops when you both have done what I have asked."

"Then why in the fuck are they movin' about over there!" Michael was pointing to a legion of archers making their way towards high ground above the Bruce's position.

"Isabella, Constance, get back in the carriage, NOW!" The Bruce had his arms around both and was forcing them back.

"What the ... Lord Bruce, please don't do anything, wait ...!" The Lieutenant was on his horse, and shouting at his men to pull back.

They kept on advancing.

Michael was on the ground and had lifted a struggling Constance, into the carriage. The Bruce did likewise with Isabella. "My dear your strategy was excellent, but maybe too late. My men are movin' because they are, and neither is stoppin'. Now when the fightin' starts there's only two ways at gettin' at each other, one is down that hill yonder, and the other is right through here, where we're standin'. Now I'm takin' you two back."

Meanwhile the Lieutenant had charged back to his line yelling for his bugler to sound the retreat. But the soldier stood at rigid attention, the horn tucked under his arm.

"Do as I tell you soldier, or I will hack your arm off and use the horn myself."

"You will do no such thing Lieutenant, he has my order."

Oh fuck! I might have known, thought the Lieutenant, that toffee-nosed bastard Major. The one who never shuts up about being the King's 'new best friend'. "Major, you have to call them back. You could get her Majesty killed!"

"I have orders Lieutenant, orders given to me by the King himself...."

"Well here are my orders Major," the Lieutenant had ridden closely along side him and unseen by others was pushing a dagger through his doublet and into his flesh, "sound the retreat now or you will die. And trust me when I say that I will not suffer so much as even one lash for doing it. The King may be your best friend Major, but Lord Lancaster is mine. Now do it, and when he's done, get off the field and take our troops with you."

At the sound of the horn, the archers drew back. And those ranks that had a bead on the Bruce and Michael lowered their bows.

The Lieutenant was grateful that the carriage was moving very slowly. He kept the blade sticking painfully into the Major's side until the signal was waved to give the field.

"Wot the hell we doin' Robert."

"Michael, if we go chargin' back, you know fuckin' well what our lads is goin' ta do. Let's keep everythin' calm."

"That young lad is comin' back, look!"

The Bruce pulled up on the reins. Now the Lieutenant was on Scottish ground. "You're a brave one lad, I'll give ya that."

"My Lord, as you can see my men are leaving. Will you not turn about and meet my carriage, over there, at the crossing?"

"Aye lad, I will, but no one will be doin' anythin' else until your men are completely out of sight."

"And what about yours' …"

"It's the safety of these two that I'm talkin' about."

"Me too."

"Then you know what I'm sayin'."

"That was close. Thank you sir."

"I'm afraid it's not over yet lad."

THE LAST EMPRESS

Chapter 8

1313 - 1315 AD

1

Lancaster threw the party to end all parties. Isabella's homecoming was the hottest news in Europe, and the celebration attracted every crown from the Russias to Italy, including both of her brothers. Her wedding hadn't achieved this notoriety.

Because an event of this size took weeks to prepare, and days to unfold, the partying went on for days, leading up to her climactic arrival. And because not everyone could arrive at the same time, the palaces, estates, and townhouses began filling and entertainment had to be provided. Westminster proved to be the best spot. In the heart of London, the guests could be kept close, and the hundreds of servants required, could be easily recruited.

Wait staff were kept hopping night and day, as entourage after entourage sought each other's company. Hundreds of barrels of wines and ales were called for, and in particular, young Louis, her oldest brother and France's Heir Apparent, sent in advance of his arrival one hundred barrels of his finest Provencal Corbieres, Cabernets, and Chardonnays including his highly prized and personal favorite from the Chateaux Neuf de Pape.

Wagon after wagon arrived hourly loaded with meats, pastries and treats of all kinds: fruits, breads and cheeses. Huge spits had been fired for days roasting pig and lamb, and there were games and contests from morning until night.

All of the Baronage were there, including Edward, still looking a little rugged from the beating he took, and careful to keep a low profile, lest one of her brothers kill him. For his own safety Lancaster kept him close.

On the fifth morning the rumors started to circulate. Hour after hour Westminster took on a new look, as gardeners, carpenters and craftsmen of all kinds swarmed the palace. It was also the first day of spring 1312 and everywhere it was as if God had chosen London to welcome the season in honor of her restoration.

An English spring day is like every day in paradise. Throughout, a warm, brilliant sun flooded the magnificent palace gardens and the surrounding city, giving birth to every color of the rainbow; and as evening softly came on, the heated, rose-scented dusk claimed every Londoner. Invited or not, the masses filled every inch of Westminster Square.

They were not disappointed. She was back.

Just at sunset, her open carriage, flanked by hundreds of the King's Mounted Guard, made its way slowly up the Mall, accompanied by the roar of a grateful city. She was all in red, her bodice cut very low exposing most of her ample breasts, with her head bare and her long blond hair being teased by a gentle night breeze.

Many in the crowd wept with joy as she waved eagerly and seemed to be smiling at each and every one of them.

Lancaster had Edward by the arm and held him rooted to the steps of the palace. "After they help her from the carriage and she makes her way towards you, you will go to her … you will embrace her … you will escort her to greet all her guests … and you will attend to her every wish … and if I see anything I do not like, you will be back in your chambers … and your recovery will not be so complete as this one."

Constance was the first to greet the carriage. "I never notice until now cherie, your tits are very much bigger than when we went away. You won't fool some of these women. You are going to have to act quickly … I think even today. After this, who know with him … he could disappear for months."

"So what do you suggest I do … take him behind these bushes … he will run like a leetle girl in a convent … and probably scream like one too."

As they moved towards the building, they were separated. Edward did as he was told, and proudly escorted her to a balcony above the gardens to be welcomed by her hundreds of friends and admirers. In a pretense of letting her have the stage, he slipped quietly into a crowd of his friends and a giant flagon of wine.

She acknowledged the cheers and announced that she was joining the party. With Constance once again in tow, they made their way down to the fun.

"We get him drunk, cherie … very drunk … I will see to that … and put him in bed with you … probably nothing will happen … who cares … voila, you are with child!"

"I don't think it will be a problem getting him drunk."

"No matter, I will make sure."

"And what if 'e denies it?"

"He won't cherie … he won't. I think, even he opens his mouth his cousins will cut out his tongue. No, no cherie, there is nothing to worry about … he just wants to be left alone. There is nothing left for him … he won't care if you are pregnant or not, or whose it is … as long as the others think it is his."

They were about to melt in with the guests. The obvious appreciation of the men was not lost on Constance, "Nice choice of dress, cherie … I hear that the Barons, they pay with gold coin."

Without so much as a glance back, as she reached out to take well wishing hands, Isabella answered, "You must have earned a fortune by now."

//

It was September and Isabella's pregnancy was well advanced.

The plan to effect Edward had worked, except not the night of the party. It was two nights later and had been remarkably easier than she had expected. Edward had come to her chamber on his own; somewhat drunk but not inebriated, and professed their need to have a child.

Was he joking, playing with her? Did he know? She had been afraid that he was in some perverse mood and was intending to hurt her and the baby. Thanks to the Bruce, she could use a knife against the best of men, and slept with a Scottish dagger close by. But he had no such intentions, and in a very awkward and almost endearing way, attempted to seduce her.

She didn't kid herself. When it became apparent that he was serious, she knew it may be the only real opportunity to dispel any future doubt on his part. There would be no trouble going through with it, at least not for her. Over her two years with the Bruce she had become a clever and experienced lover. If she couldn't get this husband of hers excited, then he deserved to be a cuckold. It took a few more drinks for his fantasies to work on him, and all of her skills to get the juices flowing, but he came through and quite admirably.

He visited her only one more time about a week later, obviously having been told that it sometimes doesn't take on one try. But this time he needed help and persuaded her that three in the bed would be more fun than two. She was reluctant, but knew also that she might pay with her life and the life of the child in the future. So what if he needed a man to get him excited; as long as he had intercourse with her he could never argue the paternity of the infant.

What she didn't expect was that their partner would be so good looking, and that he would show such an interest in her.

Pretending wasn't easy. The young man gave her as much attention as he did Edward and so adept was he that she had several subdued orgasms prior to Edward's entering her. And then, it took a considerable amount of wine and some extreme exertion on his part to get the job done. No sooner had he finished when he fell into a sound sleep.

Left with the young man erect and eager, she spent the next several hours giving in to his lovemaking. When she awoke in the morning both were gone and Edward never again returned to her bed and never spoke of it.

But going through the daily routine at Windsor was as blissful as she ever expected. Edward was dutiful, stayed at home, and attended to whatever tasks Lancaster assigned. The bathing pool was back in business and there was no one on staff whom she or Constance hadn't chosen. All of his were gone.

In November she delivered a son, who to her surprise was immediately named Edward by the King. It wasn't her choice but the boy had his eyes. It was enough.

The news that Edward senior was coming to see the baby frightened her. But then why shouldn't he? The secret was hers, he couldn't know. But what if he saw the characteristics? God they were obvious! But he wouldn't be looking for them; he thinks the baby is his. It didn't help the panic.

"Oh God Constance, get the baby quickly, quickly. I want him on my breast before Edward gets here." She motioned anxiously for Constance to hurry.

"Of course cherie, mais pourquois?"

"I don't want him to get a good look at the little one ..."

"Why?"

"Look at him Constance, just look! It's Robert, it's like a reflection!"

"Oh cherie, you are crazy, you are just seeing what you want to see. Look, he is like every infant, with the blond fuzz and the blue eyes. They all have blue eyes at birth and if anything will fool your husband it will be that. He has blue eyes."

"I hope you are right!"

Now she had Constance worried. So she was able to breath a huge sigh of relief when Edward departed. He had come and gone almost in the same instant. The baby was feeding happily when he arrived. He stood over them both, looked down at the infant's profile, smiled somewhat indifferently, asked about his health and hers, pronounced his name and left saying he would make it official.

That was how Edward the Second welcomed Edward the Third into the world.

"Isn't it terrifying," said Constance, "how when you know something that you don't want others to know that you are convinced that they know everything."

"I wonder cherie, I wonder?"

~

As 1312 rolled into the next year, they saw less and less of the King. By February Isabella had become a regular fixture in the Throne Room at Westminster. So much so that she had moved her immediate household and the baby to the apartments in the palace in order to be more readily available.

She took to her Monarchy easily, and found the process suited her. Until one day in April when the job took a turn that began to give her nightmares. It started innocently enough. She was alone with Gloucester and Lancaster.

"For more than a year now Majesty," said Lancaster, "since your return there has been nothing. No reports of anything ... not even a skirmish ... not in my lifetime has it been this quiet."

"Wales and Ireland as well ... mark me something is brewing," added Gloucester.

She didn't want to contemplate problems with Scotland. She prayed their musings were not leading up to something. And nothing more was said, perhaps they read her mind?

"Majesty, we have a lovely surprise for you this noon," announced Lancaster.

As invited, she arrived at the House of Lords precisely at noon. After she had been officially received and seated, Gloucester took the floor. "My Lords and gentlemen all. His Majesty, King Edward the Second and her Majesty, Queen Isabella, are pleased to announce this 13th day of April in the year of our Lord Thirteen Hundred and Thirteen that their son and Heir, is henceforth to be known as Edward, Prince of Wales, Heir to The Throne of England."

There was no King present to hear the official announcement, and no one in he House seemed to care in the least. As the members rose to cheer she felt an incredible chill, someone had walked over her grave.

~

Where was Edward? None of the servants had seen him for weeks, not even the young boys whom he occasionally tried to coax into his rooms. "He has not so much as even tried to see the child, never mind me." Isabella didn't like the feelings that repeatedly crept over her.

"What do you care? ... Where is 'e anyway?" Constance was just as happy that he wasn't around.

"I do not know. I have asked and no one has seen him for days."

"Ah ... maybe 'e is dead this time ... c'est ce bon, " Constance changed her voice to sound scary, "maybe his bloated corpse, with the eyeballs sucked out by the fishes, will float by the surface of the river," she changes back, "ah oui ... it is a dream."

"It is an idée you mean. If only we could hire someone to kill him."

"Why, what harm is he to you now?"

"Cherie, be serieuse, if he takes a good look at this child, he will see it is not his. I know you say everyone hates him and no one will listen to him, but if he complain enough, someone will listen and that will be the death of my son, moi … et vous cherie, et vous … and don't think they won't.

D'accord, oh mon dieu … yours will be the most horrible death … l'enfant et moi, they will just chop off our heads and that will be that … mais vous cherie, ohhh ma povre cherie, ma tres, tres belle … they will tear from you your clothes and then they will give you to the prison guards to have there way with you, and then they will slowly torture you until you are mad from the excruciating pain … ohhh ma belle … I can't bear to even think about it."

"I am so happy. Imagine what you would tell me if you could think about it."

"I make the same joke with you, but I am worried. The other day the cousins dropped a little stone about Scotland, from out of nowhere. Why, what were they hinting at? There are rumors, I know there are."

"Cherie, your imagination plays with you. But if you think he should be better dead, I think I could make it happen. Only it is a risk we do not have to take. You are the real ruler of this country. Everyone is happy with you. There is no war, and the Heir has been announced. How they say here … don't stand up in the rowboat."

"Constance, I think Lancaster make that announcement to try and save me and the baby. It was not yet necessary and there was no protocol involved. Edward was not there, and it was a big deal. The Lords are worried about Scotland, I know it; and don't you think that kind of news will mean something to Robert? For sure it will! He was passionate to think that his son would be the next King of England, and I know he wants me to make sure that it happens. The only thing that could turn it about would be if Edward denounces the child."

Constance was the first to hear him.

The Westminster apartments occupied the second and third floors above the interior entranceway to the Throne Room and anyone on their way there would have to pass very near her salon.

She heard the crash and by the time she raised a guard they saw Edward, drunk, storming along the hallway, screaming obscenities about Isabella and his "entrapment as a nothing, as a puppet." When he saw both the guard and Constance he hurled a goblet at them, struggled unsuccessfully to unsheathe his sword while threatening to stab them, and then lurched on by, finally disappearing into the Throne Room.

"No m'sieur, wait," she restrained the guard, "go, get his own people to come for him. Don't let it be on your head if anything happened."

As the guard hurried away, she slunk to a sitting position against a wall in the dimly lit corridor. She could hear him thrashing about, kicking over chairs, it even sounded like a table being flipped over, before she distinctly heard him sobbing in what could only be total despair.

For the first time her heart went out to him, but not her trust. He was in a maddened state and as long as he stayed where he was until help could be brought, then she would leave well enough alone; but if he headed for Isabella or the baby, then she would bring the walls down.

His scream made her jump. "You bitch!" who was he talking to? Was there someone in there with him? Was he talking to her? No, no impossible … he was ranting! "You beautiful, brilliant bitch! You have it all … you have always had it all … he saw to that, the bastard … the fucking, fucking bastard."

She could hear something biting into wood, like a pick against a log. "what faith did you ever show me … none, none … ever … no, instead you gave it to the bitch … and now, look at me, who am I, what am I?"

There was a long silence. She worried that he might be sneaking out. What could she do? Her room wasn't far away, there was a dagger there; would she have time …? He spoke again. "There is no way out. I am a coward; I am a fool. I stab this fucking chair when I should stab myself. He doesn't care … the bitch doesn't care, … that's it, laugh, laugh at the loser," there was another pause. He is out of control she thought, help better get here soon, then his voice seemed to explode, "no, you will die you insensitive bitch … not I … you. You will pay … you will pay."

From then on Isabella and Constance kept the baby close to them. One or the other or both always had him.

Nobody else was trusted, regardless. For all intents and purposes her staff seemed to adore her, but the majority were English and deferential to the King. Even conversations were guarded, and they talked only when they were sure to be alone and the best place for that was in the gardens.

Then came May, England's month.

Everything was in bloom, the rain took a holiday, and the members of the House adjourned to their assorted country estates. It was back to Windsor until the end of June.

"I am glad we are gone cherie. It is almost every night. An he is now dangereuse. Last night he struck two of his own guards, and then he struck Marie when she happen to be in the hallway. She say he call her bitch ... I murder you bitch ... then he run away, crying."

"Someone is pushing him. I know it. He is not in the palace all day; he never comes to the Council, never. Constance, I think you will have someone follow him ... he won't suspect it because we are away ... it is time to know what he does."

///

"Thank you cousins for coming to Windsor. I promise you that we all, you and your wives, will have fun but first we have to talk." Isabella greeted their arrival herself and wasted no time before she told Gloucester and Lancaster the news.

Taking Constance and the wives as well, they all went to her private sitting room, where she dismissed her staff, pointed out the wines, asking the men to serve, and then announced, "I have discovered that Gaveston is secretly hiding in London and that Edward spends most of his time with him."

"But the bastard is under a death penalty never to set foot again on anything English anywhere." blurted Lancaster's wife.

"This time he dies," added Gloucester.

In unison, Lancaster and Isabella were "agreed." Then Isabella said, "Constance, tell them what you found out."

"Somehow they have been keeping house at Gaveston's old apartments in Chelsea."

"How did that get by us?" said Gloucester.

"I don't know? I thought we took those away! Did you find out how long he has been here?"

"Oui, yes, about two months now ..."

"Jesus!" exclaimed Lancaster.

"So cousins, now that you know, what do you want to do?"

"I say we arrest him, now!" shrugged Lancaster.

"I agree," said Gloucester, "right now."

Isabella went to the chamber door and asked the steward to fetch six of her own guards. "Then I will send them now my Lords, and have him taken to The Tower."

Had Constance's spies been more discreet they might have pulled it off. But more often than not people who sneak around after other people, especially notorious other people, and most especially the King of England, can't wait to brag. And London's pubs absorbed most of the bragging, and many of Edward's friends came of London's pubs.

Virtually, as Isabella was breaking the news, so was Edward telling Gaveston of his suspicion that he was being followed. Edward couldn't believe how calmly he had taken the information and how calmly he was going about helping his friend to escape.

As they made their way through the early morning London streets, two dusty tradesmen driving an old cart, plodding slowly on their miserable way to some slavish job, the police escort passed them and the Officer bid them a good morning.

"Jesus, do you think they sent enough?" Edward laughed at his own joke.

"It's not funny, they mean to kill me!"

"Well, they're not going to, they're not going to get the chance."

Even in his fear, Gaveston was impressed with the change in his beleaguered companion. "Since I've been back you have been unbelievable, my rock, making decisions, keeping me steady; I can't get over it! And now this, you've arranged all this, our escape, and it's so clever. Nobody would ever guess who we are."

"Well, we will have to travel like this until we are well out of London. Our horses are hidden at a pub on the Cardiff Road but we won't get there until this afternoon."

"No matter. They think that we don't know. There will be no alarm. Nobody knows if we're at your house for sure, and when they don't find us there, they'll be off to Westminster, and maybe they'll even check The Tower or they will just disguise themselves and wait until we come home! I hope they haven't anything else to do." Edward laughed again.

It had been a smart thing to do. When a few days later the two arrived at the DesPenser's estate in York, they had traveled twice across England. If anyone were to report their whereabouts it would seem that they were everywhere. The police would soon put all the sightings down to cranks and wishful thinking.

"Some soldiers came here a couple of days ago asking for you Edward, wouldn't say why. I told them that I hadn't seen you for months and didn't expect you here at all. I don't think they will be back."

"Don't be too sure, my dear Hughe." Edward didn't volunteer an explanation. He knew well the jealousy over Gaveston and didn't want to give DesPenser any ideas.

He needn't have worried. The next day when he and DesPenser were alone together, an assurance was made that no harm would come to Gaveston. "Rest easy your Majesty, you are both safe here with me. No one will dare take arms against you while you are on my lands. Too many of your own family owe me too much money, and when your cousins learn that you are with me and that I have taken your cause, you will have no more enemies, certainly none that will admit it."

IV

Hughe DesPenser had put Edward back on the Throne.

The plan had been so simple and executed so easily that Edward was embarrassed that he had to learn it from an outsider. All those years of fear and frustration, when a quick stroke of the pen would have ended it all.

DesPenser invoked an obscure law in connection with a new law that brought her birthright into question, giving him, a Lord of the Realm, the right to pass judgment over her claim to Sovereignty whereby he was able to charged Isabella with treason. The very House that had drafted the law to suit itself, primarily to weed out any usurpers who might gain influence over Edward, had made a law that could frame Isabella.

Wife or not, she was French, France was a potential enemy and therefore, he argued, the enemy had distanced Edward from his role and used confidence to deceive his cousins. The motive, he argued, was not that of a protective wife; after all, "did they share the same chambers? Were they seen anywhere together? Why did she only attend Court and never his Majesty? Did she inherit the Crown?"

His arguments, while not necessarily compelling because most had been on the bitter receiving end of Edward's shortcomings and had on the other hand experienced visible good that Isabella spread, did invoke the letter of the law. Technically she was guilty of usurping, and in a sense guilty of treason.

~

Overnight she found herself back in The Tower. In five years she had come full circle, albeit the House was reluctant to move her and recommended house arrest at Windsor. This threw Edward into a rage. Five years of oblivion had wrought changes in him. He had been as low as he could get, he had seen the weakling and he hated him.

No longer driven by fear, a new confidence had come over him. An animal had emerged and taken him over and had come to use itself efficiently, keeping and nurturing only those around him who brought power and who surrendered it to his will. Isabella would be imprisoned and although he couldn't prevent debate under these new jury laws, he demanded the highest sentence, once imposed.

It was a new Edward that came back to Westminster.

Isabella and her household had been rousted out in the early hours of the morning, and by the same afternoon she was under lock and key. Many were sent packing onto the London road with just what they could carry, and like a long procession of refugees were ordered to find their own way back to France, but instead found refuge on either of Gloucester's or Lancaster's estates.

Constance had put up a violent and bloody fight. Edward's guards were nothing like the ones that they had become used to, and when one drunken beast had decided to reward himself with her, he paid with his life. Fortunately for her he had been alone and half naked with her in her room when she killed him. She was no match for him until he was vulnerable, when she plunged her knife through his exposed groin, over an over again.

The bloody and mutilated carcass wasn't found until the household had been emptied, and then it was a sympathetic Officer who had the body removed without reporting it.

And the dead soldier wasn't the only one who felt her sting. When she got away from her assailant and made it to the nursery, she found three others escorting Edward's nanny with him in arms. Two nearly lost their eyes, and the third was hit so badly in the groin that his testacles exploded. She and the nanny, still carrying Edward, almost made it out when she was struck down by the hilt end of a sword. Before she could get up, the two, surrounded by guards, were disappearing into the night.

It was an enraged Constance with bloody matted hair and scrape cuts on her cheek who wanted to take on the entire Tower staff. No one could please her and in turn were giving her a wide berth. Even Isabella was relieved when she went storming off through the prison halls looking for a fight. Constance's mood only made Isabella more distraught.

The baby had been taken from her, and the only reason she was still sane was that Gloucester had shown up in the nick of time and had taken the baby and the nanny with him. Thank God for the friendly guards who came to help them set up. Had a couple of miserable, drooling louts been sent, she wouldn't have given two half pennies for their survival.

The two that went about making a fire and carrying food into the apartment, were older. One felt compelled to talk to her. "Please do not think that we wanted this. My comrade and I will fetch anything you and your Lady wish …."

"I know this m'sieur, I know it," his words were more comforting than he could know, " … and I thank you, we thank you … just remain close and we will feel safe."

"One of us will always be just outside that door ," … he lowered his voice, "and trust me we will inform you if we receive any orders … there are ways out of here … no one will harm you … and m'Lady, no one will hurt the baby. We was told before coming here that the little fella is with Gloucester at his country house. The King and none of those types will dare go out there … don't you be worrying."

Isabella let out a long slow breath, "do you know what hearing that means?"

"MERDE!" shouted Constance, suddenly appearing, "Why are we here in the first place?"

"Pardonnez moi!" said Isabella.

"This is absurd! Who is this DesPenser? He just write a piece of paper ... say you are a traitor ... et voila ... you are arrested ... merde!"

"Calm yourself. Thomas tell me it cannot hold ...."

"What is this hold? We are in here, n'est pas!"

"M'Lady," the guard whispered.

"Oui."

"You could get a message out ... perhaps to your father or someone who can help."

"What are you say ... you would do this?"

"Yes, m'Lady."

Isabella looked at a doubting Constance. The guard looked at them both and understood. "Do not be afraid ... you do not know this but I owe you greatly ... for that matter, a great many soldiers do, m'Lady. This is not a proud day for us."

"Why you owe her?"

"Once when I was badly wounded, I could not earn my keep, and your husband ... forgive me, m'Lady, he is not like his father ... your husband does not pay wounded soldiers ... and so my woman and my children went to the workhouse. We believed our lives were finished, only to find your good charity at work, m'Lady. They were fed and clothed and had medicine, and were safe until I became well enough to work again. There are hundreds of stories the same, and hundreds more like me. Bless you ... I told you there are ways out of here, and I will help you."

"They will not suspect you to help us?"

"No, they think we are just dumb animals."

"Then m'sieur I am trust you with a message. You will go to see a person ... I tell you how to find her ... you will tell how we are here, oui ... and they will take care of the rest, oui. Nothing can be on paper ... it is safer for all of us."

"Oui madame. It is my honor."

"Ah oui ... et vous m'sieur, parlez vous francaise?"

"En peu madame."
"Tres bien. and how you learn it?"
"I was in service in France with the real King, m'Lady."
"Ah oui."

V

Robert the Bruce had to get a message to her somehow. Another coastal border town had been attacked and all of its inhabitants slaughtered. In the middle of the night in a cowardly raid, British troops had smashed into the little village, wrecking everything in site, burning, looting, raping, killing animals, children; anyone and anything that moved.

And there had been a similar attack on its neighboring village only days before that. Unprovoked and unanswered.

There was no reason. These two towns had always lived carefully alongside the English. Livelihoods on both sides of the border were fishing and coastal farming, and for years troublemakers were dealt with on an individual basis. The people were not warriors and were barely aware that there had been great battles fought between the two countries.

So what had changed? And why, with Isabella in charge? Only weeks before he had met with Lord Argyll who had been offered a peace with France and England if Scotland would respect the border. It had been signed by Lancaster himself, and he couldn't have hoped for anything better.

Something had gone wrong, and unless he could get some straight answers and fast, Scottish tempers were going to boil over, right over the border.

Right now Argyll was the only reason there was a Scotland. The stand against England at Stirling, now thirty years old, was the first roll of the die and ever since only accidents of fate had kept it rolling. One of those accidents had been the marriage of the late Duke of Argyll to the sister of the late Earl of Lancaster, which made the current respective Lords first cousins.

And in spite of the bloody and violent hatred between the nations, the two cousins remained friends and honored family loyalty.

Argyll had become as valuable to England as he was to Scotland. It was the only way the two leaders could communicate without either losing confidence with his own people.

"Robert, his head's safer in England than it is here. Don't ya think he might be lyin' to ya just a little?" said Michael. He hadn't the trust that the Bruce had.

"Why would he do that? Edward isn't goin' ta do him any favors. Any relative of Lancaster's is an enemy of that poor daft bastard. No, somethin's happened to Isabella."

~

Edward loved having DesPenser on his side and wouldn't face anyone or any situation without him present. It had given him a power over his cousins that he had not thought possible. As DesPenser had said, "The kind of power they understand, force."

And thanks to his new gang of friends, it had brought to an end the little reign of terror his cousins and his wife had held over him. Once again he occupied his place of honor in Council, and that little French bitch was back where she belonged, and he was about to officially declare war on Scotland.

So why then did his bowels churn every time he had to face Lancaster? The man had been put in his place, with a snap of DesPenser's finger. So why didn't he feel comfortable?

"My Lords," Lancaster had the floor of the House. "The war with Scotland has spread onto English soil. We have no choice but to take up the initiative and re-establish our dominion over these barbarians. I have called you all here to announce that I have already dispatched thirty thousand troops with orders to push through Scotland like a pestilence, until all Scots are dead or begging to serve their English masters."

"We applaud your noble actions my Lord," responded DesPenser, looking smugly about the room, "but do you really believe it will be that easy? My estates are in the north; I have seen first hand what merciless beasts these celts are. They have no rules my Lords, and I believe our men deserve knowing this."

The room was with him. Almost all heads were nodding and there was a rumble of assent. Make this Edward's day and he would be the next Commander in Chief.

Edward never felt his royalty so much as he did when DesPenser placed his hand on his shoulder and spoke the words, "Our King has expressed his deep concerns for his troops, and wishes that they be well prepared. Our King wants this to be the war that ends all wars with Scotland."

Lancaster could see that Edward was on the verge of tears. How sad it was to see this poor young fool so easily manipulated, and how difficult it was to keep from beating this greedy bastard DesPenser into oblivion. But it was only a matter of a few more days, so let the prick dig his own grave, and let the others smile while he is doing it.

Better to have the House united right now. There would be enough trouble later on. "My Lord DesPenser, I have personally shed blood fighting the worst monster of them all, William Wallace, and in the end we got him. England will not make the same mistake twice."

"My Lord Lancaster, you are too modest. It is true indeed that you deserve credit for the capture of Wallace ... and I do not hesitate to add ... and all here agree ... that you are unquestionably the hero of Falkirk ... but with all due respect my noble Lord, the Scots now follow the Bruce, and the Bruce was once one of us, and more gentlemen ... know thine enemy ... and this enemy is mine." By the sounds around him, the room was on his side. No good to let Lancaster get a word in now, "HOLD GENTLEMEN! ... hold, please. Hear me. The Bruce has dined at my table, we have shared battle stories ... we have shared whores!"

Edward beamed at the raucous response to his friend's clever humor.

"Gentlemen," DesPenser continued, "in deference to our learned and most noble Lord Lancaster, I make the supplication that my own experience take precedence in this campaign. My Lords I submit that you elect me to command this Ministry and have full authority for all the measures that need be taken to win this war!"

He had dropped the bomb expecting his supporters to be in favor, but not the majority. But the message was clear; the King was in his pocket. "Edward," he said below the noise, you will never have to worry again."

"But look at my cousin's face ...and some of the others!"

"Fuck them!"

"Go now lad," Lancaster had grabbed his aide by the arm, "put extra guards on her - loyal only to me. Tell her I will be along as soon as I can. I now fear for her life."

Suddenly Gloucester was at his side, shouting into his ear. "Thomas, it is a coup and the stupid bastards don't even know it. Do you realize what this means ... if we defeat Scotland she is dead, and if we don't..."

"She is also dead ... as we all are."

"Then we must take her, now, today, this hour!"

"No, not yet, but we will replace all of the guards at The Tower with our own. They may think DesPenser better equipped to fight the Bruce, but they won't support him in any other way. His only chance to get her is to make it look like an accident, and we won't let that even be a possibility."

"I have an idea."

"What?"

"Go to this DesPenser and make him believe he has your confidence. We need to be included in everything he plans to do, and we need Edward to think that we are all on the same side."

Sometimes Gloucester wished his beautiful wife didn't have brains as well.

Practically from the day they met, they had shared an unabashed passion for intimacy that was the envy of most of their friends, and also unlike most of their friends discovered in each other an abiding partnership where neither put the other in a secondary role.

She told her girlfriends their secret. They discussed things while they were having sex. If they were good enough for each other sexually, then they were good enough for each other in all ways.

Many of Gloucester's most successful decisions were formulated in the bedroom.

But when it came to a debate, that was a different matter; and as for winning one, he was no match for the seduction of her bath time.

"Come and wash my back." Five little words against which he was powerless and that cost him every time. Why did she always have to put him on the spot when she was naked, and especially when she was wet? "Why can't this war be stopped? Why can't DesPenser be stopped? Things have gotten out of control, and you and Lancaster have some fast thinking to do."

This was a different tack. Often when she wanted to voice her opinion on matters of state, which was often, she chose breakfast. He thought, this time she must really think I'm wrong. "He has personally bought half the military. If we do anything right now short of protecting Isabella, we could have a civil war on our hands ..."

"Right now, protect Isabella and you could have a hanging on your hands – yours. Kill DesPenser. Have him murdered. Take away the purse and you take away the problem."

"Not so easy. He has worked out an arrangement for Edward to get his hands on the money."

"Edward isn't that smart. Do you think he'll keep up with a military payroll when he has money to spend on himself and his pretty boys? No, never! Edward will bring himself down overnight."

"Okay, let's say I do murder DesPenser. Right now he is a hero to most of the House. They don't know that he staged those raids in Scotland. He has them convinced that those towns were hideouts full of thieves and murderers, scum who were sneaking into English villages, killing innocent people. I am certain that he staged those too, but he has the House convinced that he knows that corner of Scotland better than anyone alive, because his family once controlled all that territory."

"So now he's started a war, and all for what? So that he can run England on Edward's back and take you out? And you're going to just let him do it?"

"No! But if I murder him, I will be the first suspect, me and Lancaster, and the laws are pretty clear on Barons killing each other; and what's worse is that I put you in jeopardy. Think about it. We are going to war. If I kill him and am convicted, I will also be convicted of treason and that means my head, and means you lose everything: the lands, the titles, the income, and you will be an outcast. The wife of a traitor, where can you go? No one, and I mean no one will welcome you anywhere. Do you want to wind up a street whore, because that is likely all the future you would have."

"Obviously not. Being the whore around here is good enough for me."

"So unless you have any other ideas for me right now, I'm going out of my mind scrubbing this heavenly little body and I am going to lift you out of this tub, take you over to that bed and do some things to it that will give new meaning to your status around here.

"Oh! Are you talking about a promotion or a position."

"Both."

"You're welcome to do whatever you like, I'm always ready to improve my value around here, and as a matter of fact I do have a good idea."

"So do I."

"In a minute, in a minute. Take your hands off of those and let me tell you. Then we will deal with your idea."

"Can't you do both?"

"It's you who can't concentrate. Now listen! You and Lancaster have to get as close to Edward as you can. Make him think that the whole campaign wouldn't be possible without his leadership, and ignore DesPenser as best you can. And, contrary to what you think, you'll only save Isabella if you don't make a big deal out of her right now. Remember, prison or no prison, she is the mother of the future King of England, and the daughter of the King of France; and while Edward and Gaveston are stupid enough, DesPenser is not. Besides he will never go along with anything Gaveston might suggest, even if it's just on principle. He wants Gaveston out and himself to be the boss, and if anything happens to her there will be nothing left to be the boss of.

He knows his charges are groundless and he has only so much time to make his mark before her hotheaded brother finds out that some hit Baron has put her back in The Tower. He will turn this around because he needs to be her savior not her assassin. See his plan, make war on Scotland, become a hero, Edward looks good, blame Isabella's incarceration on Gaveston, rescue her, France is happy, kill Gaveston, he has the King all to himself, he has England all to himself."

"And you figured this out all by yourself …?"

"It doesn't take a genius to see through these greedy little insects. Even you could have done it if you'd take your mind out of your pants."

"Well I think you are a genius, which means I get two for the price of one. So my lovely little warrior, what good does all that do us?"

"None, unless you and Lancaster stay close to Edward for the time being. You are still his cousins and you are third in line. It means that you are still the spare and the House won't let any outsider interfere with that as long as you are seen to be loyal, especially now. Your best move is to keep Edward off balance. Whatever DesPenser advises, have a good alternative. And recommend DesPenser to lead against Scotland."

"What? Wait now missy, everything you have advised up to now makes sense, but here you don't know what you are suggesting. Lancaster is the Commander in Chief and ..."

"It doesn't mean he has to lead this time. You question my reason; well reason this. DesPenser is not a warrior, he will botch things up and you and Lancaster will be called upon to save the day. Who will have the edge?"

"Okay, okay, I see it. But what if we lose. It doesn't seem likely, but what if?"

"We don't want to think that way ... but if we do, then there may not be an England and none of the scheming will matter to anyone. So don't think that way."

"No, no, if we lose at Bannockburn, then Isabella will be the key to everything, our future, England's future, history."

"Still, don't put any good men on to guard her, they are all needed. Put some old worn out relics on her station, and act like you are content for a while."

"In this way you don't make sense. My sweet, you only sound as if you are jealous ..."

"I am saving your pathetic hide, that's what I'm doing. We'll get her out of there soon enough, and I will tell her what we are doing. But right now, especially now, if you or Lancaster do anything to help her, you will be perceived as traitors and everything you said will come to pass, win or lose. So who's whore do you want me to be, yours or some drunken sailor's?"

V/

"Robert, there's a girl here, from England, a young lady who says she has a message from Isabella. She got through with Tess. She says she has ta give it you or she's willin' ta die; she won't give it nobody else."

"Well send her in and we'll see what she's got ... and if she wants ta get ta heaven that bad, maybe she'd rather go there with you, after all I been hearin' about the way yer spendin' yer nights ... oh! Ya won't be havin' ta see her in after all ... Tess me darlin', how are ya. Nice of ya ta wait until yer invited darlin' ..."

"Shut yer gob Robert, I'll not be waitin' on the likes of you, not after all the times you couldn't be waitin' ta get yer horny hands on me ..."

"Well if yer not be watchin' that mouth of yers, you'll be payin' for this visit too ..."

"And you'll be talkin' with a higher voice too ..."

"All right Tess me precious, tell us what you've got ..."

"What I've got is this little lady come from her Majesty with some bleedin' serious news that you'd better be listenin' to ... go ahead darlin tell Mr. high and mighty, what you've got."

"Sir, I have a message from my Lady, her Majesty, and she said I'm to deliver it right to your hands Sir, and she said Madam Tess would help me." The girl curtsied and then stood very still.

The Bruce looked at her and smiled, she couldn't have been more than twelve or thirteen. It took a lot of guts to do what she was doing, all alone and he wondered if he would let one of his daughters take on a mission like this, she must love her mistress very much. "Have you eaten anythin girl, Tess?"

"No Sir ...."

"No Robert, she wouldn't take a bite. Just wanted to get the message through to you."

"Well you've done that lass and you've done it well too, so Tess let get the two of ya fed and tended, and then tomorrow ya can get on back.

"Tomorrow is it Robert. I'll first be tellin' ya about tonight, and all the ideas you'll be forgettin' ..."

"If I'll be gettin' any ideas about tonight, you'll be the first to know Tess me girl. Now get yer pretty faces out of here so I can read the message, and darlin', did she tell ya anythin' ta say to me?"

"No Sir, just to give you that. If I knew anything it could come to hurt me."

"Brave girl, you're safe here lass. Now off ya go and get some hot food in ya."

Michael had already started reading, and the second the women had left the room he blurted out, "Isabella's in The Tower..."

"What the bleedin' hell ya talkin' about ...!"

"Ya, she's been accused of treason, fer bein' French ... here read!"

"Fuckin' hell ...!"

Dearest:

I am once again a prisoner in The Tower of London. My husband and his friend Lord Hughe DesPenser say I am guilty of Treason. It doesn't matter that I am his wife; they have accused me and say that I have estranged myself from him and therefore by implication have declared myself his enemy, and because I am French, so must I have the desire to take his place in the name of France. Yet it is he who won't live with me and so they use it to blame me. You know he likes only his pretty boys.

So be it. Now I need your help my darling. I need you to tell my father about this. I also have to tell you that they are going to make war on you. This DesPenser has all of the Barons convinced that it is in England's best interest that they once again take control of Scotland.

God be with you.

He is safe.

Isabella

The Bruce kissed the letter. "Thanks darlin'," he whispered. "All right Michael," he said aloud, "we know about the war, but this takes us one step farther."

"What step?'

"We've got ta get her out of there!"

"What the hell you mean, get her out of there. She's in the fuckin' Tower of London."

"I know, but that's no reason ta leave her there."

"That ain't right around the fuckin' corner neither. What're ya plannin' on doin', fightin' yer whole way down ta London from here, climbin' The Tower, puttin' her over yer shoulder and fightin' yer whole way back?"

"If I fuckin' well have ta …!"

"Well just in case you've forgotten, we got a fuckin' war to fight right here in the meantime, and we kinda need ya for that. How about ya go get her after …?"

"Ya know what I mean Michael. I'm not totally daft. First we get someone off right away ta tell her father, and we go talk ta Carnarvon. There's got ta be someone down there who will protect her. Then we go and kick the shite out of these limey bastards."

~

Edward had lost his country. "It is hideous ...I can't stand it ... I can't stand to think about it... did you know that Roman Generals, even Emperors, were expected to kill themselves over far less than this ... it was the honorable thing to do ... !""Oh shut up Edward ... for Christ's sake!" The absurdity of the words only made his position clearer. If anyone's life was at stake, it was his own. Gaveston knew he would have to flee or he would definitely be killed.

"Shut up ...you shut up! There were thousands and thousands of bodies everywhere ... acres of them ... dying, dead. There was a river of blood ... a river ... running down the slope of that hill ... and the rats ... the rats ... already ... thousands of them too, with the ravens and the vultures in a mad feeding frenzy!"

"Edward, don't, don't do this to yourself!" DesPenser put his arm around him.

"We are finished ... annihilated ... there is nothing left!" For him the omen was Lancaster's body, the lifeless form glowed strangely in the dull light as it lay prone on a stretcher across the room from him, under the draped, bloodstained white linen sheet.

Who was he kidding, this cousin was the backbone of England, trusted and respected all over Europe. It was not to himself that the English listened. What was the way to hold it together?

For the first time in his life he felt an inkling of his father. He would take Lancaster's body home, and somehow make amends for that. As for England, it was in a shambles and had to be rebuilt. "Hughe, you are the only one here who has not lost everything. Your estates are still your own, your lands, your income, so we will come to live with you ..."

"With me your Majesty? ... I am honored, but you have no need to do that."

"Yes we do, Hughe. You are our only hope. But first I have to do something very private. I have to take Lancaster home, and I have to meet with Gloucester, or all our lives won't be worth a damn."

~

Gloucester's wife had broken the news to Isabella.

There was no way that anyone could get her out until after the war unless she could figure some way to do it on her own.

That got her thinking. She and Constance had had nothing but time and had taken a really good look around the place. And come to think about it, one thing that struck odd were the guards, they were all old and half drunk most of the time. Not the toughest of security. Maybe the weakness, and the way out, was right under their noses.

The ones closest to them were their personal day guards whose roles as jailers had turned to those of protectors and watchdogs. To her personal delight others on The Tower staff were not permitted into the Royal apartments without good reason and a search, and the two had gone so far as to put their lives on the line every day by first tasting every bit of food delivered. She learned that the two old fellows had known each other since they were children, as street orphans, and had been pressed into and served in the military together most of their lives.

They had no families, and had pretty much been tossed on to the scrap heap of useless soldiers to fend for themselves, when every able bodied young man was called up for Bannockburn and London was left to be defended by those too old or unable to fight. They had no love for the King or any of his friends.

If it hadn't meant death for them, they probably would have let her go as she pleased, but there was at least some pay back in the comings and goings of her maidservant. She had become part of their team effort in the care and feeding of her Ladyship and was never questioned as a matter of course.

Her errands were no longer escorted, and lengthy absences often ignored, even those that took days. There had developed a comfort level amongst all of them that could become Isabella's escape route.

And certainly these two were the keys. "Guard, s'il vous plait, … dites moi … where are all the young men who were to be stationed here?"

"All sent to Scotland, m'Lady, … to fight in the war."

"A war! With Scotland! When? Why do they send everybody?"

"Oh, this is the big one, m'Lady. They say this is the war to end all wars... It is just us, the old ones who are left to defend London."

"So Jean and the others, they are gone?"

"Yes, everyone .. all gone."

"Mon dieu! ... So how do we know what will happen?"

"It will take days, even weeks for news m'Lady. We can only wait."

"Hmmm... so who is it that you guard here, now ... c'est moi?"

"Oh no, m'Lady. We have a prisoner." He beamed. "An important prisoner." He leaned forward and lowered his voice. "A very dangerous prisoner ... but don't worry, m'Lady, he will not get to you ... we will see to that!"

"Oh m'sieur ... I do not know ... are you certain, that we are safe I mean ... after all we are only two floors above this place .. what if 'e escape?"

"He won't, m'Lady, he won't."

"I want to see this dangerous prisoner."

"Oh no, m'Lady, no ... now that would be inviting trouble, big trouble!"

"But if you are with me, what harm? What can 'e do?"

"No! Please, m'Lady. I cannot. If anything happened ...please m'Lady?"

With other than the man she married, Isabella knew that she had an exceptional way with men, young or old, and enjoyed the game of persuasion.

This poor old horny fool could be played like a harp. She fired the first shot. The Bruce once said that her pout could start a war. With just a wide-eyed, child-like look of hurt, men were pressed to make amends. "Just take me to see where the prisoners are kept. After all, if I have to spend the remainder of my life in here, then if I see how they are locked up, I will feel better ... and you will protect me, n'est pas?"

The guard was in way over his head. The huge almond eyes were irresistible. "I will show you, but the cells cannot be opened."

Early the very next day, like a child eager to play, Isabella was at the guard post waiting for the old man to come on duty. Even the night shift, who saw little of her, were content to stay, so charmed by her unexpected appearance.

The jealousy of the day guards was evident and they couldn't resist showing off their familiarity and authority. She needed do nothing more than look perplexed, coy, and helpless. To make them stumble over each other even more she peered inquisitively into the darkened corridor leading to the cells, appearing frightened but helplessly tempted and anxious to begin her adventure.

The old man, perplexed at seeing others so ready to volunteer as escorts, stiffened his back, pulled a walking torch from it's rack, lit it and announced boldly, "take my arm and remain close."

This was the time to make her move. Still peering down the corridor, she used her smallest, sweetest voice, "Who is he?"

"His name?"

"Oui .. his name."

"I don't know, m'Lady… I am not supposed to …."

"Ohhh … please m'sieur!"

" M'Lady, you would not know the likes of this creature. His name would mean nothing to you …."

"Well then, what harm can it be to tell me … oui … oui!" Any other time, she wouldn't have cared who this important prisoner was, but maybe he was political and maybe it could do her some good.

Bolstered by the envy of the others behind him, owning the moment was too important. "He is a pirate, m'Lady. He used to be an English pirate, but now Lord DesPenser says he is a traitor and so he is here, and he is very dangerous. I know nothing more than that … except that his name is Mortimer, Roger Mortimer."

She could not believe her ears. To learn it was a Frenchman or a Scot, even the simplest ally would have been good enough news, but this was beyond her wildest dreams. Of all the people in England who could do her the most good, he was only two floors below. She had to fight to control the excitement in her voice. "A pirate!" she whispered. "They are bad, oui?"

"They say this one is m'Lady."

"I have never seen a pirate … what does he look like?"

"Well, some pirates look meaner than most people. That's cause they're bloodthirsty and only love gold, … but this one looks more normal," he sees the rapt attention on her face, and wants to impress, "except in his eyes, and I've looked in them eyes, they cold, bloodthirsty eyes m'Lady … you'd like to faint if they ever looked on you."

"Ohhhh … I want to see him … I want to see him …!"

"That's impossible … impossible."

"Ohhh … m'sieur … how can it be? You are with me … and you are big and strong … we can go and look quickly, non…?"

"M'Lady, I am sorry, even if I wanted, even for you, this I cannot do."

"Then I think you do not like me." She was pouting again.

"No, no, m'Lady, it is not that. He is here under special guard, with the Commander … sent special by his Lordship … he is the only one to go near his cell … the only one. It would be the hangman for me if I opened it…."

"Well he will show me the scary pirate then … where is he, I will tell him now!"

The old man could not refuse to take her to the Commander, but he warned her that nothing good would come of it. And although as much as he cared for her, he was relieved to be uninvolved in this little caper.

~

Isabella stared down at a large pile of leering fat squatted before her. Her cleavage would be her best weapon here. This fellow was ugly, brutal-looking and it was obvious his only interest in her was what he would like to do to her.

"So, little French lady, you want to see a pirate?" He farted as he struggled from his chair. Not that he intended any respect, he just wanted to get as close to her as he could. Somewhere down in all the heavy folds of cellulite that layered his unwashed groin he could feel his swelling.

The smell made her gag as he came within inches of her and then slowly encircled her in a crawling, insect-like way, dragging his abdomen against her buttocks. His greasy, dirty hand traveled down her shoulder and arm and his fingers brushed against her breast. She felt his convulsion against her hip.

"Oh m'sieur, I do."

"And what is there for me, if I show you this pirate?" His voice was hoarse from the pleasure he had just derived.

"I am French m'sieur … I think I will come up with the appropriate reward."

Taking this as an invitation, he cupped her breast, "When?"

It was all she could do to not run. "Tomorrow m'sieur, tomorrow. I will meet you here, in the morning, oui?"

"I have a better idea!" He kept pressing against her thigh. "What is that m'sieur?" Her eyes frantically searched the tiny room looking for something solid with which to strike him. "Tonight, little frenchy, … tonight. You be back here tonight, when we are alone, and if I get what I want, you get to see the pirate."

"D'accord! Commander, you certainly do not waste time. This is so exciting." Where her prayers being answered or was this to be her last night on earth? She had no way of knowing what awaited at the end of this quest, she would have to take it as it came, and hope that he was alive and strong.

Coyly she slipped from his grasp without repercussion. "M'sieur, do you like brandy?"

~

Isabella had to stomach the trail of the foul smelling, very drunk prison Commander as he stumbled and staggered his way to the cell of Roger Mortimer.

As it turned out this was the worst part of her evening. Getting him so very drunk and avoiding him physically had not been as difficult as she had imagined. He was well inebriated when she got to his office. But now her impatience and repulsion was growing unbearably, and somehow she had to keep him interested as he fumbled hopelessly with the key, dropping it several times while trying to negotiate the lock hole. The worst thing would be for him to become frustrated and give up.

And the noise was sure to bring other guards, between the clatter of metal hitting stone time and time again, and his drunken babble. How would she handle it if others heard and came to help? Somehow she had to hurry him along. Maybe if she could draw his attention away, he would let her open the door. She poked flirtatiously at his shoulder, "So after we see this pirate, we go back to your room, n'est pas… and we…."

"Don't you know it little frenchy ... don't you know it!" He kept on jabbing the key, only this time he got it.

The next move in her plan was the deadliest, for her. Everything depended upon what was behind that cell door. As she hoped, she didn't need to make it. As the lock gave and the cell door swung open, the guard, eager to show off, drew his sword and stepped inside. It couldn't have happened more perfectly. The next few seconds would determine her fate.

From out of the darkness the shape was on him instantly, sending him crashing back out into the corridor and the sword flying. Mortimer went first for the weapon. The Commander didn't stand a chance. Too drunk to comprehend the last seconds of his life, he didn't see the arcing blade and it is doubtful that he felt any pain as the mighty blow cleaved his semi-conscious head in two.

In the next instant her own life could end. She knew Mortimer would strike instinctively. His blood was up and the light was bad. Her voice would be all that could save her, and even then it could be temporary. She could be overheard, and this would be as far as they would get.

"M'SIEUR, IT IS I, ISABELLA!"

VII

"How did you know I was here?" Mortimer lay submerged in the huge tub of steaming water, only his wet scrubbed head was visible.

It had not been without a lot of complaining and reluctance on the part of her servants that such a full and hot bath had been drawn at that time of night, for what appeared to them to be no good reason. How they failed to discover him was a mystery.

As they came and went bringing bucket after bucket of water, not only was she sure they would smell him, even though he was well hidden beneath her bed, but they most certainly would see the pile of ragged clothing burning in the fireplace. But nothing. And even if they did, they were too busy whining to notice.

In hindsight the trip back to her suite was a blur but the events of the night were nothing short of a miracle. She had anticipated the obvious and therefore had Constance tempt their two guards to drink with her in her room. That part had been easy. They were already on good terms. What she hadn't planned for was the possibility of things going wrong. But then what could she have done if there had been obstacles. It was a do-or-die, impulse situation.

But what if Mortimer had been ill and dying? Unable to help himself, much less attack the armed Commander. What if the man hadn't been so drunk? So eager to show off? It was fate. It was all meant to be. The only course was to assume everything would happen as it did.

After they dragged the Commander's body into the cell, there was a single guard they had to deal with on route to the apartments.

Participating in his death thrilled her. As Mortimer hid back in the shadows, she undid most of her bodice, thoroughly exposing her breasts, and approached the drowsy soldier with a tale of how the Commander had passed out in the corridor, and would he come and help. The female body, she thought, reading the fool's mind like a signpost, what a weapon; he will desert his post on the chance that I might lie down with him.

This fellow too died without protest and had been deposited in the cell. They locked up and took the key with them.

"I didn't know that you were here until yesterday. That was the only idea I could come up with."

"Well it was a great idea and I am happy you did. That sack of shit told me a while ago that you were in here, but I had no way of letting you know. I have been here for almost six months. You have no idea how good this feels." He lay still and let the stinging heat penetrate his bones.

"What happened? What did you do?"

"I don't really know. I obviously fell out of favor, but I am not certain why. I had set anchor at Liverpool with a good haul ... you do know that I am still a pirate ... ?"

"Oui, oui, yes ... the guards were very impressed with that. It is why I found out that you were here."

"I am supposed to be in your husband's employ, but then he is not a very loyal employer ..."

"Not a very loyal husband either ..."

"Yes of course! What am I saying ..."

"So what happened in Liverpool?"

"I went ashore to meet with 'the King's' agent and the next thing I knew I was a prisoner. They shipped me straightway here, no trial, and obviously no hanging, not yet anyway."

"Do you know that there is a war on, right now?"

"No, I don't," he sat up partially and looked at her.

"Yes there is, and my guards tell me it is with Scotland, with m'sieur le Bruce and that it is a big one. Every soldier has gone. Only the old ones are left here to protect London and this place."

"That might explain it, my arrest. Are there Welsh involved?'

"I do not know. Maybe! But whose side would they be on?"

"Scotland's, of course."

"I will find out. These two old guards who are put on us are very nice, and they do not like my husband. They will tell me whatever I want to know."

"How did you get in here? What could you have done?"

She told him about the charges and about DesPenser and his incredible power over Edward.

"Gaveston is a babe in the woods compared to DesPenser. Now your husband has some very dangerous playmates indeed. Do you know much about them?"

"Non, rien, nothing. Just that a while ago Edward saved Piers' life and then they ran off together to hide out with the DesPensers. The next thing I know I am charged with treason, and the House of Lords, including my friends Gloucester and Lancaster are helpless to save me."

"The DesPensers have always been trouble in the House, but your husband's father was very powerful and could keep them in check. And after him, the two cousins were more than equal to the task. So as long as your husband was kept in tow the DesPensers had no leverage. How did they get to him anyway?"

"Because I have been stupid and careless," Isabella jerked her little fists, "no, we, the cousins and I, have been careless. Edward has had nothing to do and we have not been watching him."

"Well, they should be watching him now, and very carefully. This family is of some low nobility, truly questionable, but about a hundred years ago, when all the Warlords and would-be Kings were squabbling over this country, they did old King Henry, your husband's grandfather, many favors.

They were a brutal bunch who kept the north east well in line and under Henry's control. Old Henry was grateful and so kept increasing their holdings. He was also probably afraid of them, they were a blood-thirsty lot, but they knew how to deal with the celts, and that mattered more because they were the biggest problem of all.

Now the DesPensers own most of the iron deposits and mining in England and so have big control on the making of weapons and practically everything else that the country needs. Everybody wants iron today; it's the material of the future.

They are very rich, and since Longshank's death have taken to siding with whomever suits their purpose. They can buy control, and that's what they will do with your husband. Trust me, if the Bruce didn't hate them so much, it's very possible they would side with Scotland if they thought that they would wind up the new Royal Family. That would be very bad for England. But it's not possible so they have set their sights on Edward. It's only a matter of time."

"So they now control the House?"

"No, I don't think so, but they know the laws, they have a large personal army and they intimidate the poorer Barons. The vote against you was probably easy to get."

"So I have no power! Even if I get out of here, I can do nothing, oui?"

"No, oui!," he teased her, "calm yourself. There is a lot you can do. For one thing you can bring about a stalemate in the House. You don't know Longshank's law … but then why would you … it's what they used to manipulate you, but you can turn it against them … accuse DesPenser of the same thing … of turning the King's head against the best interests of England .. The House has to hear you …"

"Why didn't Lancaster or Gloucester tell me this …?'

"Because they probably don't know the law all that well either … see, sometimes what you know is more powerful than any weapon …"

"How are you so smart?'

"My father. He taught me to first use my head, then my fists."

"Then how do I get the House to listen?'

"Get a message to Lancaster or Gloucester telling them you have new evidence to support your innocence, and you need to present it in person. That's all they need, you have friends, the House will sit and give you a hearing. The water is getting cold."

"Then get out of it and we'll get you dried off."

"Why, your Majesty ... we! ... you and who are going to dry me off?"

He had shaved clean the infested mat of hair that was his face. God how handsome he was, and the smile he gave her now took care of any resistance she might have put up. "You and I ... unless you prefer not to participate ..."

As she marveled at him naked, his wet muscled body glistening in the firelight, her nightdress just seemed to loosen and fall. She found herself, as if in a trance, standing just inches from him as he stepped from the water, holding out the huge towel that had been draped over a chair.

He spun it about his shoulders like a monstrous cape and as his outstretched arms fanned the huge expanse of linen across his shoulders she imagined before her a great angel. An angel who in the next moment stepped against her and took her in his giant wings. The delicious warmth of the cocoon formed by his arms and the dry layers of fresh linen, her body pressed tightly against his, and the heady scent of his clean skin was all she needed.

They made love through the night.

VIII

Edward's courage impressed Gloucester. But it didn't erase the fact that England was on its last legs. Lancaster's death was the final blow.

Having returned to England with the body, as he did, and facing the music, as he was, endowed him with the right to Chair the Council. But that was as far as they were prepared to go. Edward had suffered a great and permanent defeat. It was time for him to go.

"What made you think that DesPenser could lead us against Scotland?" Gloucester asked, feeling sorry for him and hating him all at the same time. "This is so much worse than Stirling that the two can't even be compared. It wipes out every victory we've ever had." His temper was rising. " The death of our dear cousin is on his shoulders … and he will pay Edward, he will pay… I will make certain of that!"

"He has cost us England," someone yelled.

"Let us hope you are wrong, my Lord," Gloucester replied sadly, "but we can waste no time in making some strong friends." He was staring at Edward who sat silently, eyes downcast obviously unable to look him in the face. It was time.

Initially when the decision was made he thought he would derive great pleasure out of what he was about to do, now he felt only that he was on the worst side of duty and the discomfort in performing the unpleasant task made him sweat. "I have two pieces of business before you, your Majesty, and both are immediate and invite no opposition."

Gloucester averted his eyes from Edward as he announced that from that day forward England and the Empire would be governed by the Council, subject to Ordinances that would require the vote, with himself as Regent.

The King was to have no official powers whatsoever and no access to the treasury. Instead he was to have an allowance. In addition, Isabella would officially head the Royal Household and represent the Crown in all State matters. "I have signed her release, Your Majesty, and if I ever again hear even so much as a whisper against her, you will suffer the consequences.

Furthermore, she has petitioned Lord DesPenser as a traitor and responsible for the death of Lord Lancaster, and this Council is well prepared to accept the charges. They are most convincing, your Majesty."

If anyone in the Chamber felt the least amount of remorse, they didn't show it. Edward had half expected this and knew better than to protest. A kind of detached sobbing racked his body, but had no will to fight it nor the desire to try and feign dignity. It was as if he had left his body and was watching with the same contempt along with the rest.

IX

If anyone wondered who Mortimer was or where he had suddenly come from, they didn't dare ask.

Isabella could not believe the ceremony with which she and anyone she chose to bring were collected from The Tower, and the immediacy at which they did her bidding.

What had happened? Only hours before she and Mortimer were locked in each other's arms, exhausted from their passion but unwilling to let go of every illicit moment they could steal, certain that they were both soon to be dead.

It had been one thing to sneak about the deserted Tower in the dead of night, when the staff were at about one tenth their number and all the exits to freedom were sealed shut. It would be another to actually escape without a great deal of help from both inside and out.

And then Constance, wonderful Constance, ever oblivious to discretion, had burst into the room, waking them mid-morning, to announce that there was an escort arrived that had been sent by Lord Gloucester to take them all to Windsor.

After the initial shock and disbelief had passed, the real problem became where to find clothes for Mortimer? He couldn't walk out naked. "Not that it wouldn't be a beautiful sight," said Isabella, "but I wouldn't want the other women to go berserk."

It was worked out that chef would lend some items, and so it was that Roger Mortimer, under penalty of death, walked unopposed out of The Tower of London and into the bedroom of the Queen of England at Windsor Castle.

And as if the suddenness of her release wasn't overwhelming enough, there to greet her in her massive apartments were a host of couturiers, hairdressers, chefs, maids, and servants of every kind. And in their midst, grinning like a schoolboy, arms outstretched, was her wonderful Gloucester and standing beside him, her beautiful son.

She began to laugh and cry at the same time, scooped the boy up in her arms, hugging and squeezing and kissing him madly all over his little face until giving in to his wiggling and squirming.

There were far more interesting things to do, and other children doing them, in the busy apartment, than to be kissed by one's mother.

"So that is it, mon petit m'sieur, that is all you have for your mother," she beamed at him, resisting his struggles, and tickling his neck by blowing against it.

The boy giggled with delight, nodding his desire to be put down.

"Oui, oui; look at him m'sieur, just like a man. Now he has had his kisses and can't wait to be off with his friends." Barely had his little feet touched the floor and he was off running.

Turning to Gloucester, she threw her arms around him. As she hugged him she couldn't help asking, "are my baths still working my Lord?"

"They are! You can thank my wife for that."

Mortimer played his role to perfection. Acting the devoted steward waiting unobtrusively to satisfy her every whim.

"Where did you get this one, my dear? My, he is very attentive. I don't remember sending him," said Gloucester curiously.

"No my Lord, you didn't. We discovered last night that he was about to lose his position and so we gave him a new one. He is big and strong and we require a man with power and stamina."

"What do you know of him? How do you know if he is trustworthy? Are you comfortable sleeping with him under your roof?"

"Most comfortable my Lord."

After an hour or so of small talk and waiting for Isabella, Constance, and his wife, to go through their antics with the various materials and the shoes, 'goddamn the shoes,' Gloucester's patience began to wear thin.

Granted, the excellent wine that he himself had provided had seen him through, and Mortimer had made sure that his Lordship had never seen the bottom of his goblet, but there were things she had to know, and the day was passing.

Without thinking, as Mortimer filled his vessel one more time, Gloucester uttered the thought, "women, there is no satisfying them," to which Mortimer replied, "bless them."

"My dear Isabella, I do need very much to talk with you," Gloucester finally chided, "can you women not deal with all these things later?"

Her respect for him was boundless. Without hesitation she ordered everyone from the room, everyone except Mortimer, Constance and Lady Gloucester. "These two will stay my Lord. Please trust me and trust them."

With Constance, he knew why, "but your Majesty, this man, you say you just met him and yet you will include him in some very serious and confidential state business?"

"Yes my Lord, I will, and after we are done talking you will understand why."

Isabella was not prepared for what Gloucester told her. Neither was Mortimer. For the first time in all of her ordeal with the DesPensers and her husband, the separation from her son and the months under penalty, she couldn't stop the tears. "You really think that they murdered him!"

"Yes my sweet, I do," choked Gloucester as he watched her crumple to the floor in Constance's arms.

Mortimer knew of the greatness of both of the cousins, this one with him now, and the noble Lancaster. He too felt an emotional surge.

As she listened to how bad things were, and to the details of the disaster at Bannockburn, she was not surprised to learn that there was a strong abolitionist movement demanding an end to the Monarchy. Gloucester went on to tell her that they must be rid of Gaveston and the DesPensers if they have any hope of survival.

"The people love you my dear, as does everyone in the House. I hope it will be enough to turn things around. The abolitionists are making use of some very clever rhetoric to make their case. Your good work is the evidence they are touting to convince the other Barons that when people work together, the country is stronger. And of course to gain their support they assure all of them that their lands and titles are safe by preaching that the role of the landlord is essential in a healthy economy. Only what they fail to say is that they want to be the landlords. Those assholes will confiscate us so fast that we won't know what hit us."

"Ils sont merde! They are worse than the worst King could ever be! Comprenez vous mon chere cousin. Their hunger for power is a maladie. Too much in France we have the Papist tyrants who think that only they are correct and those who disagree with them must die.

Mon Grandpere was a King, mon pere, et maintenant mon frere, toute ma famille, toute Roiaume … et oui, mon mari … I have seen the good and the bad in all of them, and I will take anyone of them over a zealot. It takes a lifetime to make a King, not just some clever words to make everybody follow like sheep."

Gloucester sat down heavily on a settee, feeling relieved to hear this brave young woman.

"You know mon chere, I think if I come with you to the Lords and I tell them that we do away with this Gaveston for good, and we make DesPenser pay for our dear cousin and for Bannockburn, I think we have them with us for good."

If it were appropriate for a Queen to wield the axe, Isabella wanted the job of decapitating DesPenser.

She prayed Edward had nothing to do with it.

X

Isabella took days planning this. Her entrance had to be nothing short of spectacular.

When those two massive oak doors swing open, The House must, in an instant, embrace her as their undisputed leader, otherwise it would be over. They must truly believe in her and make her their Queen of England; not some French Princess, not the betrothed product of some treaty, not the breeder of Royal inventory, but the Ruler of an Empire.

The plan had been for her to make an entrance on Gloucester's arm, but at the last minute she changed it. If she was going to win them over, she had to go it alone. "You will see cousin, you will be proud," she told a disappointed Gloucester.

~

"My Lords, her Majesty, Queen Isabella," the Speaker's voice boomed out across the chamber, and the tall doors swung open.

It would not be an exaggeration to say that House tilted. Not only were they to a man struck by her spectacular beauty, but they were moved by the show of patriotism and at the dazzling way in which she was attired to address them.

It had become customary in the divided England, as a demonstration of loyalty, for Royalists to brandish in as many ways as possible the colors of the Lionheart, and one's choice of clothing was no exception.

The dress was crimson velvet, floor length, emblazoned with gold trim and featured a high wing collar that framed her exquisite neck and face, and closed discreetly above her cleavage in a perfect V.

Her hair had been pulled up in a French roll to emphasize her classic Capetian profile, and upon her head was the light gold crown worn by the Lionheart at Crecy and considered protocol when visiting the House of Lords. She had chosen not to wear earrings or a necklace. Nothing must take away from her dedication.

But what most especially won the day were the long wide sleeves that draped to the floor. As she strode slowly to the center of the room, she held her arms at her sides. The members could see brilliant flashes of gold as the material swayed with her steps.

But it wasn't until she stopped, raised her hands, which were carefully hidden in the velvet folds, and clasped them at her waist, that the entire House was on it's feet, cheering.

Over the entire length of each sleeve was embroidered in gold a rampant lion such that with her hands held at her midriff, they appeared to stand in front of her.

The applause grew to a roar and that grew to a din as the loud cheering was accompanied by the stamping of heavily booted feet. The melee was only brought to an end by Gloucester making the dramatic gesture of leaping atop the Speaker's table and shouting for order at the top of his lungs.

When at last they settled and she was able to speak, her message was short. "My Lords I thank you for this great honor, and I am grateful that you give me this opportunity to speak with you on the most urgent matter.

... I am here to ask that you forgive my husband for his indiscretions and to ask for your sympathy. ... For some of you it is a great obstacle, I know this, ... but I have no choice but to tell you that he is ill, he has been this way for a long time, and now I believe he is in great dangeur.

He is with people who I believe have only one interest, and that is to use him to destroy this country. I cannot let that happen ... and neither can you." She stopped to let her words sink in. In the silence it was hard to tell what they were thinking.

But she had no choice. The gauntlet had been dropped. She had challenged them to support her move to depose her husband. She had to go on. "So I have this to ask of you. ... I want your permission to go myself to rescue my husband ... and I promise that I will do it with all discretion.

... And I ask that you formally charge M'sieur DesPenser," she couldn't bring herself to call him Lord, "with the murder of our dear Lord Lancaster. Of this I am sure that I can prove his guilt. And to permit me to also make his arrest.

There is no need to give our enemies any more excuse to spill English blood. ... From now on I will take the responsibility for the Crown and give my husband the time he needs to recover."

That was enough for them to digest right now. They knew well what she meant by "rescue" and "take responsibility." Gloucester had said, 'balance dignity with humility'.

She lowered her head and closed her eyes, not knowing what to expect. If anything, she expected an outburst of dissention. Either way, there was one thing certain; DesPenser would never make it to trial.

Instead, it started with clapping, which turned to shouts of encouragement to more of the same cheering she had received just minutes earlier.

Gloucester leaned over to his aide. "Isn't she wonderful!"

~

When word reached DesPenser that Isabella was on the march, numbers of his already small militia deserted. There was now rumor in the news that she personally led the army heading in his direction and that, to his men, was proof enough. Most saw defending Edward as a hopeless cause.

On her side it had the opposite effect. Most of her troops saw her presence as justification for riding against the King.

Over the generations the DesPenser estates had grown into a walled fortress of considerable size complete with castle, drawbridge and moat. From the tiny room atop the main tower in which he hid, Edward could see her and her cavalry approaching up the main road. Even at this distance he could see her clearly. Her long mane of sunlit hair stood out like a beacon.

He was cornered.

There she was, prepared to do battle and none of DesPenser's men were anywhere in sight. As her band came closer he could see that she was as ready for combat as any of her men, dressed alike in lightweight close combat gear, comprised of the leather skirt and waist cut jerkin over a breast plate, for easy movement in the saddle, and knee high, chain plated leather boots, their legs, as hers, exposed from thigh to knee.

The only difference was that the skimpy gear worn by light horse cavalry was for maximum mobility and quick action in battle; on her it brought a whole new dimension to female sex appeal, especially the effect lent by the clear sight of her two favorite weapons.

Why was that necessary, he wondered. From his view he could see that beneath the jerkin she was wearing only an open bodiced peasants blouse suggesting that the chest plate was uncomfortable, or was it another example of her unmitigated gall?

While it did nothing for him, he understood that most men would follow a pretty pair of tits before they would eat.

Fuck her! Where was DesPenser? Oh God, it would be so easy to kill her right now. Such an easy shot. One well placed arrow right between those mounds and who would blame him?

The bitch had seduced his England right out from under him, and now the half-naked slut, leading a bunch of horny thugs; she was making war on him! Fuck her!

As Isabella and her troops slowly approached the walled hamlet they could see that the drawbridge was down, and that the main gate was open, but there wasn't a person to be seen anywhere. The place appeared totally deserted.

On an estate of this size, at this time of day, there would normally be hundreds of people about, many of whom worked there, coming and going. Aside from some cattle grazing in the fields outside the walls, there wasn't a person or an animal in sight. And with the exception of the open gate and the bridge in place, it had all the makings of the scene that customarily prefaced an attack of major proportion.

The fortress battened down. Heavily armed troops stationed behind the walls and in the battlements in the event that the ramparts were breached; archers positioned at every turret and high point, cauldrons of boiling oil poised over gates and access points with the added insurance of pike hedges behind each to greet any foe that may break through.

And in the better-equipped forts were often mounted custom-fashioned wall catapults capable of hurling large boulders and fireballs down on the attackers.

None of any kind of this preparation was in evidence. Nowhere in sight was there even one of the King's soldiers. There was something very wrong.

"Wait Isabella. We will hold up here." Roger Mortimer had ridden with her as Commander of this special force, where his special talents were all the insurance they needed.

~

A pirate was a very unique type of fighter to begin with, and a warrior who had been a pirate was the most unique of all. Every sense was a raw nerve. In his world the enemy was on all sides, the man fighting beside you and with you one minute could be trying to slit your throat the next. There were no rules of engagement, no teamwork, no ranks; in the plundering business it was every man for himself.

Often at sea they would encounter what they called ghost ships. Ships that appeared to be abandoned or where all on board were dead, and in some cases they were legitimate. Either worn out old vessels once sailed by brigands who had made a better score and had dumped the rotted ship, often along with the dead; or ships that were supposed to have been scuttled but for some reason the fire had burned out leaving a floating hull.

And then there were those that were death traps laying in wait. No sooner boarded than bloodthirsty cutthroats highly skilled with rapiers and knives, appeared out of nowhere, with usually the surprised pirates taking the beating.

Mortimer had been through all of this and more, and if DesPenser's castle were a trap, he would not be fooled.

From his little hideout, Edward could watch her every move. About a hundred feet from the drawbridge the troops had been signaled to stop. The only time she would be out of view would be if she crossed the bridge and came in through the gates in the castle walls.

But once in the courtyard she would again be in sight. "Where was DesPenser?," he thought. "Damn him! Now would be the time to strike. A few well-placed arrows from the battlements and Isabella and her men wouldn't stand a chance."

But nothing happened. She and two or three others seemed to be having a discussion, none of which he could hear, and then incredulously he watched as cautiously she and the same few rode on in alone. Why did the soldier next to her look so familiar?

Mortimer took the lead and was the first to enter the courtyard. What greeted him was a large and completely deserted square. All of the buildings were aligned along three sides, and all as high as the outer walls, obviously the rooftops served as battle stations; the fourth wall providing the access way through which they had come.

On any other day this enormous courtyard would be the perfect marketplace serving the entire countryside for miles around; so why not today?

Because today it was the perfect trap.

It could easily fit nearly the entire battalion, and once all were inside a hail of arrows from the surrounding rooftops could wipe out a great many men before they could even dismount.

Isabella and the others had followed closely on his heels, so all were within the sound of his low voice, "turn, turn about, all of us out, now! Go!"

No one asked why. The words were no sooner spoken than they all were headed for the gate with Mortimer now taking up the rear. One desperate arrow gave him his plan.

The shot wasn't fatal. At least not for Mortimer; it struck him in the thigh, not penetrating even the length of the tip, but it would prove fatal for most of DesPenser's force. As he recoiled from the sudden and unexpected stab in his leg, his horse reared dumping him just yards short of the protection of the portcullis that straddled the wide gate.

But from his position on his back on the ground he could see a soldier hidden above in the gate mechanism, ready to drop the bars. It had been a trap. "Lower that you piece of shit, and you die. You are out here alone with nowhere to run, think about it," he shouted.

His voice caught the others attention who stopped and looked back to see what was going on. When Isabella saw Mortimer lying on the ground, an arrow sticking out of his leg and blood running from the wound, she leapt from her horse and ran to him.

"No, no," he waved her back, "it is not serious, I'm okay." With that he yanked the arrow from his body and scrambled to his feet to show her. "You others come here to me! Isabella, go now, tell the Lieutenant that all are to dismount and we will take this place on foot ...EVERYBODY STAYS CLOSE TO THE BUILDINGS.... Now go! Go!

You, up there, get down, now!, and tell us quickly are there any others up in this tower ... the truth now or these men will hack you into little pieces ..."

Isabella had sprung back into her saddle and was racing the few hundred yards towards the band who, now aware of the trouble, were in turn racing towards her.

When they met and she relayed Mortimer's order, there was no debate from the Lieutenant. The command spread quickly through the ranks, and in seconds were three hundred heavily armed troops, all on foot, jogging towards the castle gate with Isabella out in front.

It was there that they met the wounded Mortimer who instructed them to occupy the front battlements by climbing up through the portcullis tower, and then under the protection of the inner wall barrier to take each of the buildings, that flanked the sides of the square, one at a time from the top down.

Not only would the element of surprise favor them, but that way they could take out the archers first and swarm the combat soldiers from above. Those in each successive structure could only wait to defend themselves unless they wanted to take to the yard in which case they would be the victims of their own trap.

DesPenser's strategy had turned against him. It was a rout. Rather than surely die for a few shillings, as the result of an ill-conceived enactment of systematic slaughter, and a cause for which they had no stomach, all of DesPenser's men flooded out of the buildings into the square yelling that they surrendered, and plead for mercy.

Mortimer held Isabella back from leading the men any farther. It was grand that she wanted to prove worthy, but that was never in doubt. They knew their job, had done it many times, and didn't need her help.

As the yard filled, Isabella walked amongst the kneeling and squatting men studying their faces. It would be a viable way for any one or all three to make an escape. For one thing, many were blond and fully bearded as was Edward, and if he had donned scruffy clothes as many of these mercenaries wore it was likely he could slip out of here. Many of these men would ultimately be released.

As for Gaveston and DesPenser, she was probably the only one who would even recognize them which would make their escape even easier.

After a search that convinced her they weren't amongst the prisoners, she looked to the Keep at the end of the compound. They had to be in there. The four-story structure was immense and covered the entire width of the market square. On the ground floor and exposed at either side of a broad and ornate exterior staircase were his Lordship's stables, livestock pens and cold cellars; the stables and pens were empty.

The cut stone staircase led to the second floor and a massive double paneled oak door. It was up these stairs that she made her way. Her own troops were searching below. If they found anyone she would know soon enough.

One push on the door and a panel swung open easily enough. All right, she thought, here goes.

From the outside in the daylight it seemed as if she was stepping into a black hole in the side of the building, but immediately inside she found herself staring across an enormous room with a ceiling that was at least two of the remaining three stories high; from which hung a circular chandelier big enough to eclipse the center of the room. Beneath it sat the only piece of furniture, a round oak table nearly as big surrounded by a variety and number of equally sturdy looking oak chairs.

To the left was a fireplace large enough in which to stand; and to the right began a long broad circular wooden stairway that curved its way upward clinging to the walls and exiting right to a landing on the third level and disappearing left through the ceiling on the fourth.

The opposite wall was a cascade of heavy draperies which hung from the ceiling to the floor undoubtedly used to cover the long narrow windows which would, out of necessity, be inserted in that particular wall, and which, if not in use by archers to defend the house, did little to afford much light and a great deal to freeze out the inhabitants.

The drapes alleviated some of the latter problem. The construct of the inner stairs was therefore no accident as a variety of these windows could be reached by it at different heights. The last vestige of safety was here in the main house, and it on it own was a fortress within a fortress.

With her lightweight rapier style sword in hand, Isabella started across the Great Hall. If there was any threat to her right now, it could only come from one of the three. But her instincts told her that they were hiding, somewhere in this building, and it would be in each of their best interests to pray that they not be discovered.

The slow step-by-step click of her boots on the stone floor echoed back at her. Even though common sense told her otherwise it was as if someone was following. She called out Edward's name; it came back as a ghostly echo.

Fear was winning. She wanted to give in to it and run back to the safety of Mortimer. It was becoming greater than the desire to find Edward. Yes, she would go back and get Mortimer and some of the men and together they would search. Yes, that was the smarter thing to do.

But was it? Would it not risk Edward being killed? And if she went for help, chances were that's exactly what would happen. Besides herself, there was only Mortimer who shared her purpose, and there was no counting on him, he lay wounded. As for the men, they were there for one thing only, to do that for which they were trained and paid – to fight and to kill. If Edward, who she imagined by now was hysterical and desperate, did anything stupid like attack anyone who might come upon him, he would die.

No, she had to go it alone.

The voice made her jump.

She wheeled around thinking it was one of her own men behind her, but there was no one. The rising fear came all at once, and she spun back around, sword poised, again no one.

Then she heard it again, a soft voice from a dark alcove by the fireplace.

"Looking for your husband my Lady?"

The figure who stepped into the diffused light of the room was Gaveston. She thought she was looking at a corpse. The skeletal face gray and drawn, eyes sunken in black holes, his lips thin and pulled like those of a cadaver. She began to shake uncontrollably as he slowly walked towards her, and her only comfort was to back away from him with the sword raised to shoulder level pointing right at his chest. "I will kill you, I will."

"And then how will you find him?" The corpse grinned at her. The teeth leered big and dark, like a horse's. "Put the sword down, it won't be necessary. There is no one else here but Edward and I. Come, I will take you to him."

Isabella kept her distance behind him, the weapon held ready as she followed up two flights of stairs to a small bedroom on the fourth floor.

All the way a voice inside grew louder and louder, warning her not to follow this man. Why did she feel like the prisoner? It was supposed to be the other way around; after all she had the weapon.

The calm, purposeful way in which he lead, like an arrogant houseman showing a visitor the way. Not like a frightened captive prodded along by the fear of death. He had a plan, that was a certainty; so she had better come up with one too, and quickly. There would be only one way to deal with this. At the moment she encountered Edward, she would also stab Gaveston.

It would solve two problems. Hopefully it would end his miserable existence, and if not, even if he were only wounded, it would make dealing with Edward a lot easier. To have to deal with getting both of them out of the house would in all likelihood be impossible. For one thing Gaveston would have the courage to resist and Edward would certainly feed off it.

There was no Edward. Just this evil man, leering with those awful teeth; grinning like he had just won. An anger like she had never felt before chilled her, mind and body. Without thinking or hesitating she flicked the point of her blade in his face and drew blood. "Cochon! Your games are over, you pig. Now where is he?"

Something she hadn't noticed before. Gaveston was wearing gloves. The next thing she knew he had grabbed the blade and the sword was parting from her hand. She lunged to try and hold on to it, and that gave him all the opportunity he needed.

In what seemed an all-in-one movement, he dropped the sword and grabbed the front of her soft cotton blouse, easily tearing it away. Before she could pull herself away from the attack, the back of his gloved hand smashed across her face, sending her sprawling to the floor.

"Now my little French whore ... you will give me what I want .. and then I will give you what's left of your husband. His mind is gone, thanks to you ... you whoring bitch."

One pull on the thong which held his codpiece in place and he was fully exposed and coming at her laying on the floor.

She kicked out at him but he was fast and managed to kick back, very hard and squarely into her knee. For a split second the pain was all consuming, and that was all the break he needed.

He was down on his knees, yanking her legs apart.

She tried flailing and twisting her body, but he was too strong for her and had wedged his knees between her thighs. Then she felt the blows, again and again, her stomach, her ribs, the side of her face; the pain was incredible. Was she struggling, fighting back, where were her arms, her hands, her feet, she didn't know. All she started to feel was herself spinning, her mind trying to take her to another place, if only this weight wasn't holding her down, pressing on her, something probing and jamming at her, pushing, pushing, entering her, no, no, unwanted; fight it, stop it, tighten, harder, harder. Someone was screaming, unbelievably; it was deafening.

Suddenly the weight pinning her down was gone. The pressure, the probing, gone, all gone; just a voice, a sweet voice, gentle, soothing; she felt herself floating and settling onto something soft.

As the voice penetrated the confusion, so did everything else become clear.

Her body and head ached beyond anything she had ever felt before. Even, as a child, when she had been thrown from her horse, so may times, it had never hurt like this. If this is what the surviving soldiers felt like after a battle, no thanks. No wonder women didn't want the job.

How did she get on a bed? And Mortimer, her beautiful Mortimer; sitting beside her with the wet cloth, so soothing, gently against her face. She reached out and softly touched his. How? Why was a better question? What had happened?

"The lieutenant saw you going into this house and came to get me. The medic was stitching my leg and so I told him to go after you. The next thing he was just about at the top of those stairs when he heard you screaming bloody murder from in here. He came running and found this piece of shite beating the crap out of you and trying to do something else with you ..."

Yes! Her hand sprung to her mouth, and her lips began to quiver. She could feel the tears coming, "Oh my darling, I am so sorry; oui, yes, 'e rape me I think ...." Whenever she became upset or excited, her accent thickened.

"No, no my sweet, our good Lieutenant got here in time," Mortimer leaned over and kissed her.

She wrapped her arms around him and hugged him to her. Her body hurt, but not so much as it felt wonderful to hold him. "But 'e attack me there," she whispered, "I could feel 'im ... I fight 'im my darling, I fight 'im, but 'e 'urt me so much." She couldn't hold back and started to cry.

"It's all right, it's all right," he stroked her hair as she clung to him.

Then suddenly, getting control of herself, she leaned back to look him in the face and sniffled, "I need a bath, yes, oui, that is it, a bath ... to wash 'im away, to wash everything about 'im away ..."

"I don't know where we'll find a bath here my sweet, but I have taken care of some of that for you."

"Some of what cherie?"

"Some of your problem. That is why I know he didn't rape you."

She looked at him, still not understanding.

"I washed you ... down there ... your underwear was torn away and you were bleeding ... our Lieutenant was very discreet and left the room ... and I cleaned you up. That is how I know. He spilled some of himself on you, but that is as far as he got ..."

"This piece of sheet, quelle moyen, what do you mean?" The remark from earlier suddenly struck her.

Mortimer jerked his thumb towards the floor beyond the end of the bed. "Zat piece of sheet!" he mimicked.

She had to sit up to see, and what she saw made her gag. She very nearly threw up. Sprawled, or perhaps a better word was spread, across the floor in an enormous pool of blood and gore was what was left of Gaveston. His head had been cleaved in two from the top to his neck, and its contents littered the room.

"Oh mon Dieu, I 'ave to leave, I 'ave to, maintenant, now!" Pain or no pain, broken ribs or not, she was on her feet. It was more than horrific. She had never seen anything like that, ever.

~

Edward was found.

Thank God no one had hurt him, and when she and Mortimer arrived in his room he was sitting at a small angular table which contained a few scraps of bread that didn't look any too fresh, and a mug half full of stale beer, staring dully at the floor. He hadn't spoken a word.

Several of her soldiers were with him. "He is alone Majesty," said one. "We've been all over it, there is no one else in the castle."

"Merci gentlemen, merci." Isabella sat down opposite him and tried to look into his face. He wouldn't respond.

~

Edward had been taken to Windsor and placed under house arrest.

DesPenser had disappeared, his estates confiscated by an Ordinance unanimously supported by the House, and a warrant had been issued for his arrest.

So why was Edward acting so superior?

Neither he nor DesPenser cared, soon all would be put right. And what delighted both was their wicked little secret. DesPenser was right under everyone's nose, and had been very busy working for his King. It wasn't that he was so loyal; it was that without Edward on top, he was reduced to nothing.

Somehow in the months following the raid on his castle he had managed to sneak into Windsor in the guise of one of Gloucester's soldiers reporting for night duty. Within days he was found duty Officer on the desk, and when asked by a superior the whereabouts of the assigned man, he replied, "I doesn't know Sir," he adopted the accent of the common soldier, "I come on this evenin' an' there weren't no one 'ere, so I tooks the post Sir in figurin' that's wot you'd want me to be doin' Sir."

The Officer, impressed by his initiative, seldom shown in the very lowest ranks, asked not another question and offered him the post on the spot.

It was the perfect setup. DesPenser had his days to drum up support for Edward, and his nights uninterrupted to report to him. And finally after months of intrigue and conspiracy, his plans were working. "Edward ... I have wonderful news," he said one night, "there are thousands more than ever I thought possible ... all wanting to put you back in your place ... it seems dear boy that I am not the only Englishman that dislikes the idea of a French whore on the Throne of the Lionheart."

Edward was pleased at the news but not committed to any action. "That's great to know Hughe, but what good does it do us. We cannot just attack her. The House and the Council have accepted her. My cousin will defend her to the death. ... We would have to attack our own country."

"We don't have to attack anyone ... that is the beauty of it. The support is all the victory we need.... All we have to do is rid ourselves of her, and the rest will fall into place."

DesPenser, convinced as always of his own brilliance, expected Edward's enthusiasm in response, but there was none.

Instead Edward stared blankly out of a window. "I can't know what you are planning."

DesPenser, taking this as insufficient, was not going to let Edward off the hook that easily. "I have selected the right men for the job. ... It will be blamed on the Scots, and I will use our supporters to rally for revenge with you as our leader. Who will deny your right to avenge the death of your wife?"

~

Isabella did not like the way the guards were becoming so deferential to Edward. One by one the originals were disappearing and new ones, by and large unfriendly, formal and aloof with her, took their places. And with Gloucester, now acting Head of State, he was often away and unavailable, and Mortimer had his own estates in Wales to manage and had been gone for several weeks. She was powerless to select replacements.

So when the chance came, she was all over Gloucester. "I am 'ere dear cousin because I fear that if 'e is kept at Windsor any longer I will be murdered in my sleep. One night I wake to catch 'im stand in my room, in the dark, just stare at me. 'E frighten me so much I scream, an' 'e run like a ghost. I think my 'eart would stop.

Constance, she say she 'ear men come to the castle late at night ... almost every night. Something is going on and I think it is not good pour moi."

"What about Mortimer, is he not there with you?"

"Non, 'e is in Wales. I don't know when 'e will be back." What she did-n't say was that she was pregnant and therefore better that he was away. In another month she would show, and it would be tough enough to explain. Rumor had it amongst the nobility, if not the whole country, that he shared her bed; only no one outside of Constance knew the truth. So for now no one could dispute its paternity.

"I will look into the Guard my dear, and see to it that he is not allowed out of his apartment at night; but as long as he is causing no harm and not meddling, I cannot easily make changes."

Isabella knew he spoke the truth. Edward was still the King of England with many of the nobility entrenched in the belief that it was a Divine right. And although he may be unfit to govern, he was not unfit to live - decently and with dignity.

And those same Barons harbored enough guilt over what they believed was their unholy participation in a civil coup; they would not be persuaded to go any further.

Besides, it would be sheer folly to go any further. As long as Edward stood for something, they were all protected; her son was protected, his birthright protected.

"I can move you just a few miles down the river to White Hall if you wish my dear. It is not as big and luxurious as Windsor, but some insist that it is the most comfortable palace in London."

"Will I have my baths?"

"You will lack for nothing, my Lady." Gloucester bowed formally, as he always did when she needed humoring.

Mortimer had shown up late one night only days after her move to White Hall. The first place she took him was to bed. Later in the wee hours they lay there talking.

Much had changed since her meeting with Gloucester. Defend her as he might, there was a tide of opinion that overnight had become quite vocal, that would put Edward back in office, officially, and send her back to the drawing room 'where every good wife of a King should be.'

The mood hadn't escaped Mortimer, even hundreds of miles away. No one in Wales would accept Edward back on the Throne. He had returned to London as fast as he could.

"Every one of the Welsh Barons are with you. They are ready and will move at your command."

"That is what we 'oped for and that is tres bien. But my darling, we need more. Gloucester tell me that DesPenser still 'ave friends and Edward 'ave many friends an' they are angry at the French whore on the Throne of England. They don't trust that I am not to give this country to my family. Maybe I should do it. The House even vote to withdraw the charge and give DesPenser back 'is title. Can you believe that – if 'e pay lots of money to the government for 'is pardon, 'e has no longer to hide any more.

"'E say that the Barons are 'appy now wis Gaveston dead and Edward showing interest.... even some want 'im to be King even if 'e 'as no power, ... they even say that if 'e, Gloucester, does not go along with it, then 'e is a traitor. ... I cannot see this 'appen. So I tell 'im I go to France to get 'elp from my brother.

Many will go along with Edward, which will force Gloucester to make a choice, an' if Gloucester is to challenge them, 'e must 'ave the support."

"Then I will go with you." Mortimer patted her slightly swollen little belly. "What is this," he grinned at her, "too much rich food?"

"More like too much rich meat," she joked. "It is you growing inside me 'ere."

CASTLE RISING

Chapter 9
1316 - 1327 AD

1

Six years of waiting.

Six years of arguing and cajoling with her father and then her brother. And five of those years away from her son.

Her father, God rest his soul, had been doting, loving, understanding; her brother, Philippe also, the fifth Philippe of France, was not so tolerant. But then, he didn't have the fist that their father had. She did, but he didn't. But she could never rule France. She could however, rule England, and it was that idea that kept her and her father going.

Philippe the Fifth saw things differently. He could have England any time he wanted. To hell with her son, to hell with Mortimer, to hell with her friends in England; right now he wanted more peace at home, and with her around he wasn't getting any.

Their father had put her up at Boulogne and for half a dozen years the two had waited for a sign, an opening, a weakness that would vault her back in control. Early on Gloucester had begged her not to bring the French army. In one dispatch he pleaded that if she was to attack, that everyone would have to oppose her; that she would end up friendless, win or lose. And a win would not necessarily put her on the Throne, much less the young Edward.

He had made sense. A loss would have her and the boy exiled forever; and a win would only put her brother in the seat. Either way she would end up a forgotten Royal idling her life away in some townhouse in Marseilles.

She hated it when her brother came to visit. Lately the conversations were always the same.

"Ma soeur, sister, I cannot 'ave you 'ere at zis palace any longer." He spoke English as well as he could so that Mortimer would understand his wishes. "Your children are old enough to travel and you either 'ave to go back to England or take one of our 'ouses on the Cote d'Azur; but either way you cannot stay 'ere prochaine, any longer. Now you are make problem for me wis all of my Ministre."

"Philippe I am just as eager a retournez en Angleterre, ... but I cannot go without your 'elp. I 'ave tell you this!"

"I will 'elp you ma cherie as much as I am able. Mais, I cannot order my army to follow you. I do not like your 'usband any more zan you do, but I do not make a declaration of war. You may 'ave all ze mercenary who wish to follow you, but zat is ze best I can do."

Over the years she had come to know and love her handsome brother, and as angry as she was at his miserly offer, she also understood all too well that he had inherited a difficult job and he was doing it to the best of his abilities. Without showing any adverse emotion, she curtsied to him and kissed his Royal hand.

He cupped her chin, raised her up, and looked at her lovingly. "Ma belle soeur, je t'adore, mais tu faites plus de probleme pour moi! ... you 'ave ze bastard children, everyone know it ... Mortimer, 'e is your lover while you claim to ze srone of England ... zis confuse mon Ministre, zey don't trust you cherie ... some ask if zis young Edward, ze Heir, is vraiment l'Angleterre Roiaume, of English Royal blood ... an' ze worst is zat Mortimer is live 'ere, in my palace, wis you, an' 'e is a condemned pirate under ze laws of France. His head should be on ze guillotine ... not on ze pillow wis you!"

As she listened to him, that moment, that day, she got an idea.

"Brother. ... si mon fils swear allegiance to you, are you not obliged to become 'is ally if 'e need you?"

"Oui."

"You know that 'e will do this."

"Why would 'e do it?"

" 'E will do it because I tell 'im 'e will do it."

//

A terrified, badly beaten little man now unable to move slumped in a chair while Hughe DesPenser and several others, thugs mostly, circled slowly around him.

In DesPenser's hand was a large belaying pin and with it he was jabbing it at the man's chest as he talked to him. "You will bring every message that Gloucester or anyone else gives you, directly to me ... do you understand?"

He didn't wait for the answer. DesPenser hit the man hard on his chin. In his agony the man could muster nothing more than a rasping yelp.

"Throw water on him," snarled DesPenser," wake him up."

The cold water had the desired effect. "Ahgggg ... yes sire, yes ... I will sire , I will .... Please , please no more!"

"You won't tell anyone of our arrangement ... and you will report everything you are given or that you learn ... do you understand!"

DesPenser raised the pin as if to hit him across the head this time. The man wildly nodded in agreement.

"Good, very good. ... Because if you do not, and I learn of it ... and I most assuredly will ... then your woman and your children will be hacked into little pieces of meat and thrown to the wild dogs that roam the streets."

///

Eager for a message, any message from England, Isabella met the priest at the gate herself. She was told that a man had arrived in Paris from England a few days ago and had asked the Bishop for her whereabouts. He had sent the man to her brother, and that was why he, the priest, had been sent to collect her.

"Discretion ma soeur, discretion. Who knows if zis man even tell ze truse, but we don't take any chance, oui."

If there was any doubt, she noted that her brother still saw fit to have his top ministers on hand.

She took pity on this frightened little man. What with her tall powerful brother looking down his cultured Prussian nose at him, and these other two powdered vultures ready to make a meal of anything he said, it was a wonder he could communicate with them. It took a lot of courage to be here at all.

"Isabella, ze time 'as come. You 'ave all ze men I can give you, and I cannot ask mon Ministre for any more time for Mortimer. ... but I sink you are about to make your fortune zis time anyway. Zis man 'ere as beg to see you from our Bishop 'ere in Paris. 'E 'as been 'ere now for two days, an' would not go away. When I 'ear of 'is persistence, I agree to see 'im. Je m'excuse monsieur, votre urgence is worthy."

"Oui m'sieur , que dites moi!"

The little man was wringing his cap. His moment had come. "T'ank you ... er ... yor Majesty," he struggled with an awkward bow, "Oi've come from his Lordship your Majesty with very urgent news." He looked about at the others, not sure he should say any more."

"It is safe m'sieur. You may speak."

If Gloucester hadn't specifically told him to do it, the question would have been impossible for him to ask. Here he was, in the same room with the most powerful King in the world.

"Majesty ... please forgive me Majesty, my Lord Gloucester wonders why you have not replied to any of 'is messages ... he 'as sent several Majesty?" He shrunk from the blow that surely would follow.

"I 'ave received none ... not one!"

"Pardon Majesty ... I do not wish to be disrespectful."

"You are not m'sieur ... do not be afraid. ... Please, dites moi, tell me everything from his Lordship."

More relaxed, he found it easier to talk. "Things are very bad Majesty. ... The King 'as appointed Lord DesPenser as manager of the Royal household and 'as given him two estates. Lord Gloucester said that it means that now Lord DesPenser 'as licence over the welfare accounts and some of the military payroll."

"Now brother, do you 'ear this ... now do you believe moi?"

"Oui monsoeur. J'ecoutez. ... Mais zis does not change mon position wis Mortimer ... 'e must go."

"But brother!"

"Attendez ... permit me to finish ... Mortimer must go ... but I will do honor to my nephew for his allegiance ... I will order tree sousand soldiers and ships to go wis you ..."

"Oh Philippe ... merci mon chere ... merci..."

"Now go ma petite ... and hurry ... anozzer few days and even I could not stay ze guillotine ..."

~

It was the second time in her life that she had sailed into Dover with all of England waiting on tender hooks.

What kind of reception would she get? Any second now she would find out. Her flotilla of French warships was rounding the headland and about to sail right into Dover harbor. Once they had safely made the English side of the channel, she had struck the French flags and hoisted her Royal insignia.

At once from her position on the master deck of the fleet leader she could see, as she once saw years ago, the huge wharf and harbor row. There were lots of people all right, but they were not brandishing weapons. They were waving flags and colorful banners and cheering so loud that she could hear them all the way out to sea.

There was no resistance, no military, no angry mob. The people on the shore were so happy to see her they were in a frenzy.

Was that Gloucester she saw? Yes it was, there was no forgetting that wonderful face, he was there to greet her. She became as excited as them to be on shore.

And she had chosen the perfect dress - of red and gold with gold lions rampant on her sleeves.

She hadn't laid eyes on her son for five years. He had been sent back to England, back to Gloucester for protection.

It had been the only way. The boy was the Heir, and any forced absence on her part would be taken as abdication.

He would be fourteen years old, the same age as she when her marriage to Edward took place. How that very night, coming to this very place, she had become a woman – in more ways than one. Would he be a man? Surely, at his age.

Would he have sided with the King, the man he believed to be his father; or with Gloucester? Would her son, the love child of her loins, now stand opposite her on the battlefield?

The march to London was a triumph. Gloucester used the analogy of Cleopatra's famous arrival in Rome. She couldn't have been more beautiful or more stunning than Isabella. Thousands flocked to join her on route.

She had chosen to ride sidesaddle on a huge white horse, not hidden in a carriage, but bigger than life, out in the open, wearing the red outfit, now surmounted by a huge red cape trimmed in white ermine, highly visible and symbolic of a coronation. The people's Queen. If a sniper's arrow found her heart, so be it. It was in God's hands now; England was in God's hands.

The boy, Edward, had not been in Dover to greet her, and Gloucester had hesitated to tell her why.

The camp was set up just outside of London. In fact she had chosen a hill to the southeast from the top of which she could see the city off in the distance, and virtually anything coming or going to and from her direction.

A number of Barons, most of whom she knew or recognized, had wasted no time in getting to the site, once they learned where and how close she was setting up.

Wearing the same dress, which was intended to be symbolic of her purpose, she agreed to an immediate conference with them. The formalities took little time; they were unnecessary. But instead of inviting them into her tent and out of the elements, she walked them to the highest knoll, and coincidentally the windiest, on this the highest hill in all of south east of England.

It was visibility she wanted. For miles the red and gold could be seen, a powerful image and an emotional reminder of their legendary Ruler.

The first Baron to speak was one that Gloucester told her was heavily indebted to DesPenser. "Majesty, we must know your intentions by tomorrow ... and you must know that our intentions are clear. This action can only be considered an invasion ... even though you say you do it for England, you come leading French soldiers. My Lady, this will be turned against you and you will be found guilty of treason."

"My good Lords, moi bonne Gentilehomme, I wish not to 'arm any honest Englishman ... nor do I wish to make war against my own armies ... but I am your Queen and I do intend to rid my nation of the evil of DesPenser and those who follow 'im."

She paused in her speech and looked about her large camp that seemed to be growing by the hour, moved by the overwhelming support of the people.

"'Ow must it 'ave been for m'sieur Wallace ... your great enemy m'Lord, ... for 'im to know that so many brave Scottish people were willing to die to rid themselves of your tyranny m'Lord – 'an we 'ave learn nothing ... 'an now so many English are willing to die to rid themselves of the same thing. ... A' demain m'sieur."

She curtsied low to the group, stood for a moment as if daring anyone else to speak and then walked on down the hill to her tent.

~

Edward, DesPenser and others were gathered in the Throne Room at Westminster. DesPenser was screaming for her arrest and immediate execution. Edward, afraid to stand up to his psychotic friend is boasting agreement.

"Why can't we go now, right now," screeched DesPenser, "and take the bitch and find every horny, sick fuck in England and throw her to them. The fucking whore is dead ... dead ... I want her burned Edward ... I want her staked out in front of all of London ... I want to hear her screams ... I want the people to know what a whoring, fucking, harlot witch they so love ...."

"Hughe ...Hughe, it is all but done my darling ... by tomorrow there will be ten thousand men in the field ... she cannot last but an hour or two ...and then she is yours ..."

DesPenser starts jabbing his finger at two Generals in the room. "You have heard your King gentlemen ... tomorrow ... and not a day later ... not one fucking day later."

~

As the same night wore on, Isabella, Gloucester and Mortimer sat in her tent discussing their options.

"Cousin, first I want to know of my son. Why you 'aven't brought 'im to me?

Gloucester looked from her to Mortimer and back to her again. How to be sensitive and direct at the same time? Clearing his throat he thought here goes, "My darling, it was my decision not to bring him …."

"Cousin, how could you, how could you be so cruel … it 'as been six years …"

He could see her eyes welling up, "it is not what you think my precious, I did it for his own good. Believe me, he wanted to come, but I'll tell you just as I told him. If he stood with you here, tomorrow, and you lose, he will lose also. He will never be King, because he would be branded a traitor. And, trust me, DesPenser would do everything in his power to see that happen. The boy would probably be executed."

"So he does what, stand with Edward …?"

"Absolutely not," interrupted Gloucester, anxious to finish the explanation lest the train of thought be broken, "to stand with him would be equal folly. If you win the day, your son will be included in Edward's defeat, and no longer qualified as the Prince of Wales. None of your best efforts could ever put him on the Throne …"

"Then who …?"

"That is why I have kept him out of this … independent so to speak … even if I go down he will not … he is the property of the people as it were, and stands a good chance of being the next King no matter the outcome of tomorrow. And all of this is about him, is it not?"

"Oui, oui, yes … but you didn't answer … who would be King if my son were to choose the wrong side …?"

"Do you really want to know my dear, does it really matter? All is well now, and pray the Lord it stays that way."

"Cousin, answer me, s'il vous plait!"

"Very well my dear," he sighed, "it would be me."

She stared at him for the longest time and the tears came freely. "You make the greatest sacrifice of all."

"No my Lady," he bowed his slightly to her, "I only hope I make things right with England."

"They want to say I make war. So be it. I send a messenger to my brother … I promise to deliver England … et voila! … it will be over so quickly … (she chuckles) 'e will demand that Edward kiss 'is boots in Westminster .. just before 'e chop his 'ead off ." She made a chopping motion with her hand. "Whoosh!"

"Unless we get some sleep, he may chop off all our heads, m'Lady." The goblet of wine Gloucester drank had gone to his tired body and he laughed heartily at his own joke.

She laughed with him and took his hand. "Non … non … mon cousin … just the one's I tell 'im to." She paused and looked softly at him. "Do not be worried mon chere … it is just an evil dream. A war with France is out of the question. … non? A war will invite every ambitious beast that wants a piece of this nation. … the Scots and yes, votre Welsh amis my darling, they will come an' kill for sport … an' mon frere will make an end to the Royal family" … at best my son will receive a pleasant Dutchy in Tours, non, non "War is out of the question."

"But if you surrender, they will execute you …"

"Then cousin, we will find another way, non?"

IV

Isabella would have one roll of the dice. It had better be a good one; she was outnumbered five to one.

She and Mortimer had emerged from their tent the next morning to be greeted to two awesome sights: a magnificent sunrise which promised a magnificent day; and a glittering, fulsome battle deployment of English military spread out for at least a mile wide and half a mile deep across the meadow below their post.

"Lord Jesus," said Mortimer, "will you look at that!"

She was looking.

Throughout the night Gloucester had filled them in with all the gory details of the last six years. England was bankrupt. Things were worse than they had been in almost two hundred years. While Edward's ancestors had been largely tyrants, they had at least been benevolent ones – they knew how to govern, to maintain a balance of domestic affairs, to keep putting back – this one knew, or rather, had learned nothing.

They were in the grip of an insidious, self-serving tyranny.

Gloucester had joined them and was looking as well. "Don't be overly impressed my dear, those poor bastards down there haven't seen a penny in months. One shake of the tree, and they'll turn on him in a heartbeat."

"Edward doesn't have absolute power," he told them, "but he doesn't need it. DesPenser figured that out for him. Ultimately the Crown owns all the land. Now new laws prevent arbitrary confiscation, but under certain emergencies, the Crown can oblige any landowner, Barons included, to turn over their properties for a fair price.

As goes the land goes the economy. From the land comes sustenance, from sustenance income, from income the taxes, from the taxes comes relief, welfare and the military.

As long as the House was able to bypass Edward, and keep him on an allowance, things went smoothly. But DesPenser showed him another way. Edward couldn't terrorize the more powerful of us, but he could get to the fringe. Those who had titles or the merchant class "Barons" with holdings and income, but no physical power, became their victims.

DesPenser went about demanding partnership, legal partnership, for himself and the King in their lands and businesses in return for "the King's" protection from what he called "the unfair practices of the government." Suddenly the King was in business for himself, and anyone who didn't join his little partnership soon found their businesses vandalized, their crops and livestock destroyed, wives and daughters abused and raped, young children mysteriously crippled or killed.

There are so many now that pay this exorbitant protection money, that Edward and his friend have bled the economy dry. What flowed has all but stopped. And those who support the House have become fewer and fewer in number. Even some of the more substantial Barons are becoming fearful.

And when any of them can't pay, DesPenser gets the land or the business. Where does the money go; into their pockets and no further. Where do they get their power? Simple – keep the brutes happy and terrorize the rest. The military rely on a rationing system dreamt up by DesPenser that keeps families at a minimum existence, in sub-human housing, so long as the man serves or is able to. The consequences are dire, don't serve, don't live.

"Do you know how many families I have living on my estate because the men can no longer serve the Crown? And that goes for all of us who still hold down the House. We have no money for anything else, never mind mounting a defense. These miserable creatures can't form an army any more. Most are so crippled, sick or badly wounded that they can hardly walk let alone fight.

Their women and children are wonderful, and do much of the work. I have no end of willing help, but they have to be fed and clothed and housed and it takes a lot of money and consumes a lot of what I grow.

That is why for the past two years or more I have been so desperate to reach you. I sent dozens of messages, but nothing came back - silence. I was giving up, I thought you just didn't care any more or worse, that maybe you were dead and your family was keeping it a big secret."

Then he told them about his messenger. About how DesPenser had had his woman and his daughters violently raped as an example of what would happen if the man informed. "He was to continue to keep my trust, while all along my messages to you went no further.

It wasn't until his woman, far more worldly than he fortunately, found out what he was being forced to do for her sake and the children's, and came to me. He then confessed everything and I moved them onto my estate. Why he didn't see that in the first place, I don't know."

Desperate men do desperate things. And while the tide could shift in their favor, Mortimer was not counting on it.

Isabella's army, pathetic in size now it appeared, was lining up. The French were cunning fighters, and so far putting on a good show. These men had been well paid to be there and doubtful wanted to cheat her; but the numbers were still obvious and their families would not starve to death if they retreated.

As for the camp followers, gratitude alone did not win battles. The peasant masses, who made their numbers look better, would be of little or no help when deadly swords were flashing.

She had to come up with an idea. Losing was not an option. Gloucester and some of the other Barons, who had declared their colors and joined with her, now rode along side of her, which meant that their lives and the lives of their families were now on the line as well.

Civil war had been declared. It may only last a few hours, but it was Civil War nevertheless.

Outfitted in the light leather gear that she preferred with her sword strapped down her back, head uncovered, astride an enormous stallion, she galloped to the center of the field.

Fearless, absolutely and totally without fear she must be. These thousands of starving, enslaved English soldiers that now faced her, must be convinced to drop their weapons; and an attack would not do it.

Isabella sat her horse boldly, alone staring across the hundred yards or so that separated her from her husband, staring directly at him, not taking her eyes away for a second.

He could see her doing it; he could feel her stare, and his bowels began to churn. "Hughe, what do we do? Turn everybody loose, charge the field, what?"

"No, no – not yet." DesPenser could see what she was doing. Most of these men with him had once adored her, and their memories could be long. Even though it had been only for a short while in the whole scheme of things, she was the harbinger of better days, happier days; and this incredible act of defiance may be all the confidence they need to rally to her.

An attack may never leave this side of the field. "Edward, you will ride out to meet her …"

"What! Are you mad?" his voice was almost a squeak. "No fucking way. Are you trying to get me murdered …?"

"Shut up you fucking idiot, shut … up. Look around you; this whole thing is about to blow up in your face. You're worried about getting murdered, well stay here and I'm pretty certain that's what you'll get…"

"No Hughe, no! You're out of your …"

"LISTEN! I will ride out with you but you are going. Even if you shit your pants you are going. Take a hard look around you - right now she has just turned every one of our men against us. If she makes another move they will join her. Now, no one less than yourself can go out there. You must show the same lack of fear if you are to remind these soldiers of ours of the consequences.

So here's what we do."

Spurred on by DesPenser, he and Edward imitated her show of brava-do and galloped pell-mell towards her. Edward's nerves were so diffused he was barely able to stay in his saddle.

They reined up just short of her, Edward bobbing about like a puppet tied to the seat, nearly ran past but his horse had the good sense to imi-tate DesPenser's.

She didn't flinch.

Edward was spent. That was all the show, as little as it was, that he had in him. He couldn't find his voice. It was up to DesPenser to deliver the ultimatum and do it so all could hear.

He demanded that she surrender the field; that she would be treated fairly by the Court, and that all her French soldiers would be allowed to return safely home. Otherwise her death and the deaths of any one who fought with her or supported her would be excused under an act of war.

Isabella sat calmly and listened, and when he was finished said not a word but stared intently for several minutes into his face. The stink emanating from Edward told her what was happening to him.

Then she rose up in her stirrups and in a voice surprisingly loud she made her declaration. "My Lord DesPenser you are a traitor and a murderer. I am the true Queen of England, divinely ordained by marriage under law and sanctioned by our Holy Mother the Church and it is my right and my duty to defend my Crown and my nation in any way I see fit."

A huge grin spread across Gloucester's face. He could see where she was going.

"Even if by opposition I advise my husband of the error of 'is ways, I do it with respect and loyalty to 'is office. And so m'sieur I come here before my husband and my King as a dutiful wife, to enlighten him to the error of his ways, and to accuse you. J'accuse you m'sieur, you are a usurper of the King's mind, body and fortune and I hereby demand your execution."

She paused and smiled wickedly at DesPenser; then resumed addressing the field, "my Lords ... your Majesty ... loyal sons of England. I am not here to make war ... I am your Queen and I am here to pay homage to my husband, our good King, ... and to die if I must ... to save our nation from a most evil cancer."

DesPenser broke in, "we waste time ... order the archers ... the sooner I cut off her tits the happier I'll be ..."

"M'sieur DesPenser ... you have something to say to your Queen ... or are you so afraid of a woman that you cower behind our King ..."

"You fucking bitch!"

Those were his last words. As he jabbed his heels into his horse's flanks in an attempt to ride away, her sword was in the air and in one clean slice, his head was removed neatly from his shoulders.

With the same slice, the tyranny was removed from England. A huge roar of approval went up from both sides of the field.

Isabella had done what no one else could do, and brought England back from the brink of extinction.

Hughe Despenser's head and body were taken back to London for a symbolic, public execution.

~

Edward sat frozen in his saddle and stared wild eyed at the headless corpse pouring blood on the ground around him. Isabella urged her horse along side his and took up his reins. Without touching his sword which remained in it's scabbard – he wouldn't use it – she lead him slowly off the field and to the care of Gloucester.

~

Edward the Second of England had slipped into a strange kind of dementia. He seemed not to know any one with whom he had any familiarity. Not Isabella, not the young Edward whom he always assumed was his son, and certainly not the other children who didn't really know him. Gloucester was a complete stranger but who seemed content to have it that way; and for his staff he had no recognition.

And yet he was content to read and delighted in writing letters, intelligible, insightful letters, some to Isabella, some to imaginary friends. The only demand he made, and which was granted, was that he receive a change of clothes, to consist of the latest fashions, at least three times a day; of which he insisted modeling for his staff.

In order to keep him safe from harm, prison of any kind was out of the question. Isabella had a large apartment set up for him in Berkeley Castle, not far from Windsor, with all his familiar belongings, and from where, if escorted, he could come and go when he pleased. But he chose to spend all his time in its smallest room atop a remote tower. It was as if he wanted to be as far away from life as he could get.

V

It was this way for over five years. Isabella once again resided at Windsor Castle and supervised its on-going growth. Her bid to act as Regent until her son became of age was rejected in favor of Gloucester. A bittersweet reward for her brilliant coup that saved the Empire.

Yes, the son she gave England would become its next King; but no, her desire to run things and make changes she felt were due, was thwarted.

From time to time she raged against it, but always she had her passionate Mortimer; and her revenge was to flaunt their unabated, uninhibited love affair all over London society. Still beautiful, still desirable, she was in demand everywhere, and didn't hesitate to regale and entertain her fashionable friends with erotic tales of Mortimer's prodigious male endowment and his unquenchable lust for her prolific body.

And Constance was just as bad, urging her behavior on, especially to throw huge and wild parties, which invariably wound up as great nude orgies in and around her bathing pools. It was nothing for couples to stumble over other couples in the dead of night fornicating in the gardens.

And it was the morning after one such bacchanal that she and Constance and some other women were recuperating in the garden when a servant came up to her and whispered in her ear.

Isabella turned and looked up to see her son, Gloucester and several other Barons gathered on a balcony not far away. Excusing herself, she got up, hurried across the lawn and up a wide flight of stairs to join them.

She addressed her son first. "My darling, 'ow are you?" He leaned towards her and gave her a polite kiss on the cheek. "What is zis ... no hug for your mother?"

"Mother I have bad news." He was stiff and formal.

She looked from Edward to Gloucester and the others and back to him. They all had grim expressions.

"Oui mon chere ... what is it?'

"Our father is dead ... he has been murdered."

She reached out and steadied herself on his arm.

"Murdered my lady,' added Gloucester, " ... in his rooms at Berkeley."

She stared into her son's eyes for several seconds. They registered no grief, but then neither did hers. Then she stepped back from him, curtsied very low and said quietly: "Long live the King."

~

The case would not go away. Six months had passed, there had been no clues, no evidence found, no witnesses, no one had heard anything; early on that one morning the nurse had come across the King's lifeless body, on the floor of his tiny favorite tower room, impaled through his rectum on what had been a red hot steel pike.

Isabella had been pressed from time to time for answers but always it was the same; Mortimer as well, but there was nothing that could pin it on either.

Until one mid-week afternoon, Edward made a special uncharacteristic trip to Windsor with a specific request to see his mother alone.

"Mother ... there will be no argument ...the opinion is overwhelming that you and Mortimer did have a hand in our father's death ... no longer can I protect you ...."

She couldn't let her son finish. For a split second she hated him. "Edward, surely you cannot suspect that I murder your father ... what kind of a person do you think I am? And if you say I had motive, I will slap your face off – King or no King!"

"It is out of my hands, mother. You are lucky that I am here and not the others ... others who were directed to tell you what I am about to say ... I demanded the right to do it instead. ... At this moment Mortimer is being arrested ... and you are to be taken from this room and transported to Norfolk to an estate on the coast called Castle Rising, which shall be yours, and where you shall remain until the end of your days."

Isabella felt a kind of pain that words or doctors can't describe. "Mon fils, you are the King of England because of me and only me, seulement. Whoever killed your father, and it was not me or Mortimer, pas rien, d'accord ma chere, his death is better for you, meilleur and only I know why."

She looked at him for a reaction.

He looked at her like she was raving. She never thought she could feel contempt for her own son, especially one conceived with such passion. "Go on, go away from my sight. I will move where you send me. And I hope m'sieur, that you have better luck with your little country."

It hurt more than she ever imagined to turn her back on him and walk away.

VI

For over a year she didn't set foot outside the forlorn pile of rock she called home. Clinging rapturously to a memory, for hours almost every day she would lay on her bed with her eyes closed imagining him making love to her.

She didn't care that they could hear her wailing; it got her through the long nights.

And if it hadn't been for Constance, who had chosen to accompany her into exile, she may have never survived. It was Constance who forced her to eat, to bathe, to take care of herself; it was Constance who lit the fires at night, and who shut out the bitter north sea winds; who decorated and made the hard, cold fortress a home.

Castle Rising sat high and alone on a bleak promontory of land that jutted out into the violence of the North Sea. There was hardly a day go by that the pounding of the ocean didn't make the little castle vibrate, and sometimes so constantly that things would work themselves right off shelves and smash into pieces on the stone floors.

Whenever it would happen she would cry with glee that it suited her, that it was England shaking in it's boots; that one day the whole castle would come crashing down around her.

Then gradually, slowly the pain subsided. She didn't even realize it until one unusually bright day, Constance suggested they go walking and she found that she very much liked the idea.

Maybe if she went outside she could put her problems behind her for a while. Bundled up against the wind, they set out and it felt so good that she got the notion that maybe if she walked she could walk away from them, so they walked all the way to the top of the cliffs overlooking the ocean.

There was warmth in the sun and underneath all the layers of clothing they were comfortable, and so for hours they stood and watched as the wild sea pounded relentlessly against the rocks below.

For how long had it done this? Since forever, and it never quit. Its mystery overwhelmed her. And as they made their way back to the castle, she saw it in a whole new light. How long had it been there? Not as long as the sea obviously, but a very long time. And how tough it must be, to sit here year in and year out, buffeted by these winds and storms, and never give an inch.

She laughed joyously, but this time for another reason. How it suited her. It was time.

Goodbye my darling Roger. The Gods will certainly have need for a man of your talents. And I daresay some of those pretty Goddesses as well. You and I both know we didn't do it, but then how do I prove to my son that a mother who lay moaning in the arms of her lover the night of his father's death, didn't have something to do with it.

As the Court had finally reasoned, love affairs were the number one motive for murder, and short of being caught with the weapon, who would have better reason for wanting him dead.

"Constance, how far is Scotland from here?"

~

The year was 1328. Isabella called Castle Rising her home for the next thirty years. She never again saw London but she left a Crown and country more united than ever in its history, giving rise to the expansion of the only empire that ever truly covered the globe.

And she brought a civility to the English-speaking world that has endured to this day.

Upon the death of her brother, the King of France, who left no Heir, Isabella's son Edward lay claim to the Throne reversing the fortunes of power in the world forever. For the next one hundred years war ravaged Europe and the British Isles, with only Britain rising supreme in it's Empire powerful enough to assert domain over the New World.

It is safe to say that she changed the course of history.

VII

On cold nights Isabella loved her bedroom.

And on this one she sat alone curled in a heavy robe enveloped by a huge overstuffed chair in front of a perfectly large fire that spread its warmth all over the room.

She was beside herself with excitement. The letter had been answered, and the day had arrived.

Constance had told her about an hour earlier that two riders could be seen through the spyglass several miles down the valley and that they were definitely on the road to the castle. The big one was easy to spot.

~

The voice hadn't changed, and when she stood to greet him fifteen years dropped away.

"So my beautiful wee princess .... Once again they send you to me ...it seems that I win."

She stood arms outstretched, glowing at the sight of him, just as beautiful as ever. And she could see in his eyes what he thought of her. In two strides he was across the room and had her wrapped around him.

A flood of memories poured over her, "It seems we 'ave to start all over again my darling."

End

ILLUSTRATED INDEX
of Characters & Principal Locations

EDWARD II

Born: Caernarfon, 1284
Ascended throne, 1307.
- Reigned 20 years (deposed)
Father: Edward I
Married to Isabella of France
Two sons, two daughters
Died: Berkeley Castle 1327
- (murdered), age 43.
Buried: Gloucester Cathedral.

Edward II was Edward I'st and England's greatest failure. Feeble and perverted, he did nothing to carry on his father's work of consolidation. Yet by default, his laziness and incompetence strengthened the influence of Parliament, and the bureaucracy was improved by various reforms.

Addicted to worthless favourites, first Piers Gaveston, and later the Despensers (father and son), the King spent most of his life fighting with the Nobles as well as his wife and Queen, Isabella, who ultimately deposed him. Edward was forced to abdicate and in 1327 was murdered in Berkeley Castle.

ISABELLA

A film Artist's conception

1292 – 1358
Queen to Edward II of England
Born: 1292 Paris, France
Died: 1358 Castle Rising,
Norfolk, England
Buried: Grey Friars Church,
London
Father: Philippe IV, King of
France Ruled – 1285 - 1314
Mother: Jeanne I, Queen of
Navarre

From childhood Isabella was known as "Isabella The Fair", and considered the most valuable Royal prize in all of Europe.

Later, as her reputation for her power and her hold over Edward spread, she earned another title, "The She Wolf of France", and even later, "The Harlot Queen".

Her intense beauty was legendary, and one scholar of the time claimed that she was the most beautiful woman in all the world.

Promised in marriage to Edward when she was only four years old and he fourteen, England was the logical choice for her; her aunt, Margeurite, was the Dowager Queen of England (married to Edward I).

CASTLE RISING

Norfolk, England

The keep at Castle Rising was built c1140 by William d'Albini II. Isabella, Queen of England (Wife of Edward II), for whom it was purchased in 1331, was its most famous resident.

The Castle entrance, as it looked then and now.

In 1331 she was accused of being an accomplice in her husband's murder along with her lover Mortimer and was exiled to Rising on the orders of her son, Edward III. However, she was not kept strictly as a prisoner, and led her life much like any dowager Queen with a £3000 a year income. Her household consisted of 180 people. There is some evidence that Edward III came to regret his decision to exile his mother and in later years from 1342 on visited her often. There is also evidence that so did The Bruce shortly after her arrival. It is reasonable to assume that she had some complicity in the Hundred Years War, after all she was out for revenge; but it is more likely that the visits from The Bruce were of a more romantic nature. She retained and rebuilt Castle Rising throughout the years until her death in 1358.

After her, Edward granted the Castle and Manor to his son, also an Edward, but historically famous for his nickname The Black Prince of Wales. The Black Prince added it to his vast possessions and retained it until his death in 1376. During his ownership, and after, much money and effort was spent strengthening the fortifications in case of an attack from the French. Two early canon found at Castle Rising date from this time and can now be seen at the Tower of London. By the end of the 14th Century, Castle Rising remained in excellent structural condition.

The Crown maintained it until 1544, but doing only minor repairs. It was then that Henry VIII swapped Rising, along with several other estates, to Thomas Howard, The Duke of Norfolk, for Walton, Falkenham and other Suffolk Lands.

The last efforts to revise it were attempted in 1572, when a surveyor described it to Queen, Elizabeth I, as : " Erected at the first but for the speare and shield, and for that force it may be maynteynde if it please her Majestie to be at the charge, 'This charge they estimate at £2000. 'And further, 'if the same castle should be taken downe and sold for benefitt, it is so greatlie declaired as the same will not yeald above one hundred markes" (£66-67p)

Fortunately the Castle was not pulled down, though increasingly in disrepair. It remained with the Howard family until 1968 when custody passed to the State. Much work has been done to restore what remained and Rising is now managed by Mr Greville Howard.

Castle Rising
FROM THE GATEHOUSE

Site Information. Popular tourist site. Open all year round. 1st April to 30th September 10am to 6pm; 1st October to 31st October 10am to 5pm. 1st November to 31st March - Wednesday to Sunday 10am to 4pm. Closed Christmas Eve, Christmas Day & Boxing Day.

Telephone: 01553-631330.

Rail Station: King's Lynn.

Castle Rising lies in the County of Norfolk, 5 miles to the northeast of King's Lynn, near the Norfolk coast of the Wash, just off the A149. Good parking facilities.

Thanks to mwcook@crusader-productions.com as a source of photos and information.

WILLIAM WALLACE

William Wallace is perhaps Scotland's greatest hero. Immortalized by the film Braveheart, other than the affair with the Queen of England, much of what you learned about him is true.

William Wallace was born around the year 1267, in Elderslie, Renfrewshire [now Strathclyde] Scotland, and was the second son born to Malcolm Wallace, a middle-class landowner, and a Knight of Elderslie in the service of the Earl Of Carrick (father of Robert The Bruce).

William was a highly educated man and spoke three languages.

Legend portrays him as tall, standing six foot six inches.

Later knighted himself, Sir William Wallace had but one passion … Freedom and Honour for Scotland!

KING ROBERT THE BRUCE

1274 – 1329 Robert the Bruce was probably born in Turnberry Castle in Ayrshire on 11 July 1274. However, there are alternative claims for the place of birth, notably Lochmaben Castle in Annandale, Dumfriesshire which was the seat of the Bruce family. (The illustration here is a drawing of Lochmaben on display at the now ruined castle).

Robert the Bruce lent support to William Wallace and became a Guardian of Scotland (with John Comyn) but when Edward offered a truce in 1302, Robert accepted and joined Edward's "Scottish Council". In 1304, on the death of his father, the Earl of Carrick, Robert was reputedly the richest man in England.

But in 1306, after a quarrel and murdering John Comyn, Robert declared himself King of Scotland. He was crowned at Scone in March 1306. He then began a guerilla war against the English. He captured a number of castles - chivalrously allowing the defenders to return to England.

Having heavily defeated the English army at the Battle of Bannockburn in 1314 and defeating Edward II's invasion in 1322 by a "scorched earth" policy, Edward III of England eventually agreed to the Treaty of Edinburgh in 1328 which recognised Scotland's independence, ending the 30 years of the Wars of Independence.

King Robert was gravely ill by this time and died at Cardross on 7 July 1329. His body was buried in Dunfermline Abbey. At his request, his heart was taken on a Crusade by James Douglas. In a fight against the Moors in Spain, Douglas was killed and the embalmed heart was returned to Scotland. It was buried in Melrose Abbey. Recently a new casket (pictured here) was created for the embalmed heart. A new stone and was placed over the spot where his heart is interred. It says, in Scots, "A noble hart may hae nae ease, gif freedom failye" - "A noble heart may have no ease if-freedom-fail".

EDWARD III

(1327-1377 AD)
Born: 13 November 1312 at Windsor Castle, Berkshire
Died: 21 June 1377 at Sheen Palace, Richmond, Surrey
Buried: Westminster Abbey, Middlesex
Parents: Edward II (Recorded) and Isabella of France
Siblings: John, Eleanor & Joan
Crowned: 1 February 1327 at Westminster Abbey, Middlesex
Married: 24 January 1328 at York Minster, Yorkshire

Although Edward was crowned at age fourteen after his father was deposed, his mother and her lover, Roger Mortimer acted as Regents and ruled for the next three years until he became of age.

War occupied the largest part of Edward's reign. Edward's claim to the disputed throne of France (through his mother, Isabella) led to the first phase of the Hundred Years' war.

EDWARD I

A fitting portrayal by Patrick McGoohan in Braveheart, shown here. In makeup the likeness was uncanny, and he played the powerful man to a tee, capturing his tremendous style and charisma

(1272-1307 AD)
Born: 17 June 1239 at the Palace of Westminster
Died: 7 July 1307 at Burgh-on-Sands Cumberland
Buried: Westminster Abbey, Middlesex
Parents: Henry III & Eleanor of Provence

Crowned: 19 August 1274 at Westminster Abbey, Middlesex.
Spouse: (1st) Eleanor daughter of Ferdinand III, King of of Castile & Leon; (2nd) Margaret daughter of Philip III, King of France).

Edward I, nicknamed "Longshanks" due to his great height and stature, was perhaps the most successful of the medieval Monarchs. His reign marked a high point of cooperation between Crown and community. In these years, Edward made great strides in reforming government, which included framing the first ever Constitutional Parliament, consolidating British territory and defining constructive foreign policy.

Photo compliments of Magic Dragon Multimedia

EDWARD & GAVESTON

Always the seducer and manipulator, Gaveston's selfish character brought about his own sudden and violent death. This rare painting is the only known visual record of the two.

Marcus Stone's remarkable painting of "Edward the second and his favourite Piers Gaveston".

Historians agree that Piers Gaveston almost single-handedly was responsible for the near collapse of the British Empire.

Born the son of Edward I's Man-At-Arms, Gaveston was given, at an early age, a prominent position at Court as companion to Edward II.

Little did Edward I know how disastrous his benevolent gesture would prove to be.

WINDSOR CASTLE

Windsor Castle is an official residence of Queen Elizabeth II, and the largest occupied castle in the world. A Royal Palace and fortress for over 900 years, the Castle remains a working palace today. Visitors can walk around the State Apartments which include extensive suites of rooms at the heart of the palace; and for part of the year they can also visit the Semi State Rooms, the splendid interiors of which capture the essence of the grandeur of the Royals throughout the ages. They are furnished with the treasures of a thousand years of rule including paintings by Holbein, Rubens, Van Dyke and Lawrence; fine tapestries and porcelains, sculptures and armour.

Within the Castle complex there are many other attractions. In the Drawings Gallery regular exhibitions of treasures from the Royal Library are mounted. Another popular feature is The Queen Mary's doll house, a miniature mansion built to perfection. The fourteenth century St. George's Chapel is the burial place of ten sovereigns, home of the Order Of The Garter, and setting for many Royal weddings. Nearby on the Windsor Estate is Frogmore House an attractive, period country residence once occupied at various times by three Queens – Queen Charlotte, Queen Victoria, Queen Mary.

TOWER OF LONDON

Official Palace of English Kings from 1066 - c1500's.
London England

A modern look at Isabella's first home upon arriving in England. From bride to prisoner in a single day. When Duke William of Normandy invaded England in 1066 his first action after landing was to build a castle. It's still in use today as government offices and home to the Crown Jewels.

After his coronation in Westminster Abbey on Christmas Day 1066, William ordered the construction of a castle in London for his triumphal entry.

The layout c.1100. Then it was referred to as The White Tower.

Initially the Tower had consisted of a modest enclosure built into the south-east corner of the Roman City walls, but by the late 1070s, with the initial completion of the White Tower, it had become the most fearsome of all. Nothing had been seen like it in England before. It was built by

Norman masons and English (Anglo-Saxon) labor drafted in from the countryside. It was intended to protect the river route from Danish attack, but also and more importantly to dominate the City physically and visually.

  The White Tower was protected to the east and south by the old Roman City walls (a full height fragment can be seen just by Tower Hill underground station), while the north and west sides were protected by ditches as much as 750m (25ft) wide and 3.40m (lift) deep and an earthwork with a wooden wall on top.

From very early on the enclosure contained a number of timber buildings for residential and service use. It is likely these included the Royal residence from the beginning. Certainly William the Conqueror's immediate successors made use of the White Tower itself. A dark, brooding, dismal place; it always had the atmosphere of a prison. A far cry from the Palaces which ultimately succeeded it – WhiteHall, Windsor, Hampstead, c1300's.

 It is important for us today to remember that the functions of the Tower from the 1070s until the late 19th century were established by its Norman founders. The Tower was never primarily intended to protect London from external invasion, although, of course, it could have done so if necessary.
Intended to be a temporary residence of Kings and Queens, though many did live there, its primary function was always to provide a base for royal power in the City of London and a stronghold to which the royal family could retreat in times of civil disorder.

Medieval Tower

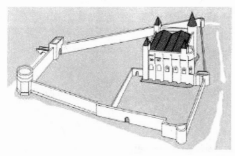

When Richard the Lionhearted (1189-99) came to the throne he departed on a crusade to the Holy Land leaving his Chancellor, William Longchamp, Bishop of Ely, in charge of the kingdom. Longchamp soon embarked on an enlargement and strengthening of the Tower of London, the first in a series of building campaigns which by about 1350 had created the basic form of the great fortress that we know today.

The reign of the next king John (1199-1216) saw little new building work at the Tower, but the King made good use of the accommodation there. John had to cope with frequent opposition throughout his reign. And the Tower earned its reputation, and rightfully so, as one of the most gruesome and fearsome prisons in the known world.

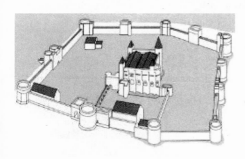

The Tower c.1270

In 1272 King Edward I (1272-1307) came to the throne determined to complete and extend the defensive works begun by his father. Between 1275 and 1285 the King created England's largest and strongest concentric castle. (a castle with one line of defenses within another).

The work included building the existing Beauchamp Tower, but the main effort was concentrated on filling in Henry III's moat and creating an additional curtain wall on all four sides and surrounding it by a new moat. This wall enclosed the existing curtain wall built by Henry III and was pierced by two new entrances, one from the land on the west, passing through the Middle and Byward towers, and another under St. Thomas's Tower, from the river. New royal lodgings were included in the upper part of St Thomas's Tower. Almost all these buildings survive in some form today.

As early as the reign of Henry III the castle had already been in regular use as a prison: Hubert de Burgh, Chief Justiciar of England was incarcerated in 1232 and the Welsh Prince Gruffydd was imprisoned there between 1241 and 1244, when he fell to his death in a bid to escape. The Tower also served as a treasury (the Crown jewels were moved from Westminster Abbey to the Tower in 1303.

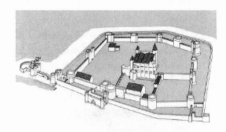

The Tower c.1300 When it became home to its most famous inmate, Isabella.

Richard II's reign brought to an end the peaceful interlude under Edward III. During the Peasants' Revolt of 1381 the 14-year old King and many of his family and household were forced to shelter in the Tower while over 10,000 rebels plundered and burnt the capital for two days. Just as Richard's reign had begun at the Tower of London, so did it end; on 1 October 1399 the King, condemned as a tyrant, renounced the crown in his chamber in the White Tower and Henry IV was proclaimed King the next day.

The Cradle Tower built by Edward III

During the reign of Henry VI (1422-61 and 1470-71) England entered the period of civil disorder and political instability known as the Wars of the Roses. Throughout this period the Tower of London was a key asset to those who held the throne or wished to.

The Byward Tower. Constructed during the time of Edward I

The part of the Tower where Isabella's apartments were most likely kept.

14TH CENTURY FRENCH ROYAL PALACE

By comparison, this modern photo reasonably describes the way in which French Royalty lived during this period (1297 – 1327) as opposed to Castle living in England. Imagine Isabella's surprise at being housed in the Tower Of London after living like this.

PHILLIPE IV OF FRANCE

Phillipe IV, the Fair (French Philippe le Bel) (1268 - November 29, 1314) was King of France from 1285 to 1314. A member of the Capetian Dynasty, he was born at the Royal Palace of Fontainebleau, Seine-et-Marne the son of King Philippe III and Isabelle d'Aragon. He was called Philippe the Fair because of his handsome appearance.

Phillipe married Jeanne of Navarre 1271 - 1305 on and fathered four children:

Louis X – (1289 -1316)
Isabella - (1292 - 1358)
Philippe V - (1293 - 1322)
Charles IV - (1294 - 1328)

A prolific and powerful Royal family, all three of their sons in succession, would become king of France; and their daughter Isabella Queen Of England (wife of Edward II).

But only Phillipe, the namesake, remained on the throne for any length of time, and played a large role in Isabella's masterful plan to take control of the English crown.

The young Phillipe was succeeded by his brother Charles who lasted only one year. Ironically Charles had no heir and Isabella's son Edward III claimed the Throne of France.

BERKELEY CASTLE

Although we are using a modern photo, Berkeley hasn't changed much in 700 years. The photo accurately represents the Castle as it looked in 1327.

Berkeley Castle, in Gloucestershire, England is a perfect specimen of Norman architecture. Noted in history as the scene of the murder of King Edward II.

Completed in 1153, this ancient castle has been preserved and gradually transformed from its roots as a savage Norman fortress into a truly stately home.

CARLISLE CASTLE

Carlisle Castle is one of the great Medieval fortresses in history. Located in north western England, it has been one of the unbreachable bastions of English Kings since the eleventh century.

The Castle was the major staging post for the English in their many battles with the Scots through the years 1270 – 1320, and is reputed to be the scene of Gaveston's grisly death.

STIRLING CASTLE

STIRLING CASTLE, Scotland, as it is today, and as it would have appeared to William Wallace on the battlefield that horrific day in 1297.

The battle was fought on the meadow in the foreground, and it would have been high above in the ramparts atop the cliff face that deCressingham was skinned alive.

SIR ROGER MORTIMER:
1293 — 1327

Nobleman, pirate, warlord: the lord of Wigmore, Radnor and Ludlow castles.

Self proclaimed King of Wales and devout enemy of King Edward II.

He held half the county of Meath and the castle and lordship of Trim in Ireland, and had twice been the governor of that country. He was one of the most experienced warriors in England's history having fought campaigns in England, Scotland, Wales and Ireland.

He was also Isabella's lover, and therefore likely the father of three of her four children.

Convicted in 1327 of the murder of Edward II, he too was murdered in his cell while awaiting execution.

This colorful character came into Isabella's life early and always seemed to be there when she needed a strong, handsome arm. Loyal and devoted to her, he was at her side throughout her campaign to overthrow her husband, and quite literally for about three years, from 1324 to 1327 he ruled the Empire.

THE EARL OF GLOUCESTER

Born Humphrey de Bohun VIII c1276.

The 4th Earl of Hereford and the 3rd Earl of Essex. He was also the Lord High Constable of England. He married November 14, 1302, at Westminster, Princess Elizabeth Plantaganet, widow of John, Count of Holland and Zealand, and daughter of King Edward I. of England and Eleanor of Castile, daughter of King Ferdinand III. of Leon and Castile in Spain.

THOMAS THE EARL OF LANCASTER
(c. 1277-1322)

Was the eldest son of Edmund, earl of Lancaster and titular king of Sicily, and a grandson of the English king, Henry III.; while he was related to the royal house of France both through his mother, Blanche, a granddaughter of Louis VIII., and his step-sister, Jeanne, queen of Navarre, the wife of Philip IV. A minor when Earl Edmund died in 1296, Thomas received his father's earldoms of Lancaster and Leicester in 1298, but did not become prominent, in English affairs until after the accession of his cousin, Edward II., in July 1307.

Having married Alice (d. 1348), daughter and heiress of Henry Lacy, earl of Lincoln and added the earldom of Derby to those which he already held, he was marked out both by his wealth and position as the leader of the barons in their resistance to the new king. With his associates he produced the banishment of the royal favourite Piers Gaveston, in 1308; compelled Edward in 1310 to surrender his power to a committee of " ordainers," among whom he himself was numbered; and took up arms when Gaveston returned to England in January 1312.

From then on he remained an outspoken opponent of Edward II, and nearly succeeded to the Throne. However The King's powerful friend Hughe DesPenser managed to have Lancaster murdered in 1322, which for a time put the power back in Edward's hands.

BARON DESPENSER
(1262 — 1326)

Father and son "favorites" of King Edward II, both of whom were executed in 1326. The younger by Isabella herself. Source: The Dictionary of National Biography "founded in 1882 by George Smith, edited by Sir Leslie Stephen and Sir Sidney Lee," published since 1917 by the Oxford University Press.

HUGHE LE DESPENSER - EARL OF WINCHESTER,

b 1262 - d 1326, Bristol, England

From 1294 to 1303 the elder served Edward I faithfully. At the coronation of Edward II the younger carried part of the royal insignia. When in 1308 the barons leagued themselves together against Gaveston, he stood alone in upholding the king's favourite. His conduct was put down to avarice, he was regarded as a deserter from the common cause, and the parliament which met at Northampton procured his dismissal from the council. His disgrace was not of long duration; he received the castles of Devizes and Marlborough, and became the chief adviser of the king.

On the death of Gaveston, Despenser became the chief man of the court party, and encouraged the king to form plans of revenge against the barons. He was bitterly hated by the Earl of Lancaster, and was excluded from the general pacification of 1313. He accompanied the king on his unfortunate expedition to Scotland in 1314, and when the defeat of Bannockburn placed Edward at the mercy of Lancaster, was forced to withdraw from the court and the council. In 1318 the king seemed on the point of making a vigorous effort to overthrow the power of Lancaster, and Despenser, with the other lords of the same party, attended the parliament at Northampton armed, and at the head of his retainers. A pacification followed, greatly to the king's disadvantage, »and he stood alone in refusing to bend to the earl's will.

About this time his son, Sir Hughe le Despenser, joined the king's side. The Despensers received many large grants from the crown; they were generally hated, and were accused of many acts of oppression and wrongful dealing. Although both, and especially the son, succeeded Gaveston in the royal favour, they had little in common with him. Unlike Gaveston, they were of noble family, and were connected with many great baronial houses. They held the most prominent place in the party opposed to the unscrupulous designs of Lancaster, and sought their own advancement through alliance with the crown, while the earl carried on an equally selfish policy by thwarting and limiting the royal power. Greedy and ambitious, they used the influence they gained over the king for their own aggrandisement. The wealth and honours he showered upon them strengthened the hatred in which they were held. In the case of Gaveston, the hatred of the barons was mixed with contempt for the upstart foreigner; in the case of the Despensers, it was near akin to fear.

The quarrel between the Despensers, Humphrey Bohun, earl of Hereford, and Isabella led to a league against the Despensers, which was joined by the great lords of the Welsh marches and many other powerful nobles, who in 1321 ravaged their lands and took their castles in Wales, and spoiled their manors and levelled the fences of their chaces in England. The king was anxious to interfere on their behalf; he was prevailed on to call a parliament, and pressed to consent to their banishment. He consented, and in July the charges against them were formally stated and considered in parliament.

They had estranged the king from his people, had usurped his authority, and had debarred the magnates of the realm from access to him. Sentence of banishment was pronounced against them both. The elder

Despenser went abroad. In the following December Edward obtained a condemnation of this sentence from the convocation of the clergy, and on 1 Jan. 1322 Archbishop Reynolds pronounced it illegal. Despenser returned, joined the king in his attack on his enemies, and after the battle of Boroughbridge took part in the death of Lancaster.

He was created earl of Winchester in the parliament held at York. They were now all powerful, and put no bounds to their greediness. Grants were made to them in extraordinary profusion. Isabella hated them, and gladly went to France on an embassy to her brother who became Charles IV. There was some talk of war between the two countries, and Edward spoke of leading an expedition in person. To this, however, Despenser would not consent, for he knew that if he was deprived of the support of the king's presence he would not be able to stand against his enemies, and Edward, who was now wholly under the dominion of the two favourites, gave up the idea.

When the Queen returned to England, a plot had been hatched in France to overthrow the DesPensers. Despenser's advice to the king was to outlaw her and his son, who agreed with her. The Queen landed in England with an armed force in September 1326, and put out a proclamation against the favourites. Edward retreated before her. The queen marched with Gloucester to Berkeley, where she restored the castle which had been seized by the Despensers to its rightful owner, Thomas, lord Berkeley. Thence in Bristol, with the townspeople on her side, DesPenser was unable to hold it against her and she killed him herself. The next day, 27 Oct., he was sentenced symbolically, and was forthwith 'officially' put to death as a traitor on a common gallows outside the town amidst the shouts of the Bristol people. His head was sent to Winchester.